ACCESS
ONE STEP

The Official History
of
The Joiners Arms

Compiled by
Oliver Gray

Sarsen Press
Winchester, UK

Design: David Eno and Oliver Gray

Cover design: Duncan Whitfield

Printed by: Sarsen Press, 22, Hyde Street,
Winchester, SO23 7DR, UK

Published by Sarsen Press

Join in the fun at: www.joinerslive.com

**One pound for every book sold over the bar at
The Joiners will go to Macmillan Cancer Relief.**

ISBN: 1 897609 28 0

Grammatical note:

Much heartache has been experienced deciding where, if anywhere, to put the apostrophe in the word Joiners. The full name of the pub is the Joiner's Arms (if it's the Arms of only one Joiner), or the Joiners' Arms (if it's the Arms of many Joiners). But for many years now, it has simply been known as the Joiners, so that's what we've gone for.

A similar issue occurs with the Fo'c's'le Folk Club. Yes, it should have three apostrophes but here you will find numerous versions. The days of the apostrophe are sadly numbered anyway.

More complicated is the problem of the street name. It is actually St Mary Street, but is often confused with St Mary's Road (which exists, but is a different street). This, in turn, is often mis-spelt as St Marys Road or Street (as, for example, on page 19, in Due South magazine).

Are we bothered?

Dedication: To Mint Burston
and the Spirit of Rock and Roll.

Scores of people have willingly contributed stories, information, photos and memorabilia.

Thanks to: Mint Burston, Dave Misselbrook, Les Haigh, Michael Chapman, Alan Downes, Pete Holden, Geoff Wall, Andrew Napier, Martin McNeely, Fred Eynon, Mike Perry, Jamie Summers, David Hamilton, Pat Muldowney, Ben Ward, James Baker, Bob Pearce, Chris Shakespeare, Brian Hooper, Jim Sykes, Paul Moody, Martyn Goodacre, Jez Gale, Glenn Lovell, Rob Ellis, John Otway, Christian Francis, Jane and Trevor Gilson, Keith Emery, Andy Graham, Andy Iles, John Elliott, Sally O'Shaughnessy, Rob Whatley, Pete Harvey, Greg Gilbert, Ian Binnington, Claire Davies, Louise Glyde, Paula Hambly, Graham Weaver, Crackout, Andy Burrows, Maria Croce, Paul Green, David Schaffer, Stephen Stafford, Alex Barinov, Ronnie Taylor, Paul Dominy, Phil Campbell, Cole Matheson, Steve Gladders, Mandy Garman, Kai Harris, Amy Brown, John Robb, Tony Hill and many, many others.

Thanks also to Due South, the Hampshire Chronicle, Sound Info, the Advertiser, the NME, Logo, and the Daily Echo for permission to reproduce articles and news items.

Foreword

by Andy Burrows (Razorlight)

I first went to the Joiners in 1995, to see the Bluetones. It was my local venue and my first experience of a proper, sweaty little gig. Prior to that, I'd only been to big stadium gigs to see people like Michael Jackson. I always remember being so excited just to be in the Joiners, and it became my dream to play there one day. It was the first time I'd seen a load of people all sitting on the floor expectantly waiting for the band to start. The gear was all on the stage and the stage lights were on. There were all those pictures on the walls of the famous bands that had played there.

The first band I actually played the Joiners with was User, which was my first "proper" band. I was only sixteen at the time. In a naive way, it felt like we'd finally got onto the gig ladder. After several Joiners gigs with User, I played there with Southampton band Blue Book Park, opening for the Jeevas. At the end of 2001, User played a show with the line-up of Pete Hobbs, John Hassall of the Libertines, and me. That was the show at which Johnny Borrell first saw me play, and he remembered that when I turned up to audition for Razorlight. Razorlight themselves played at the Joiners before I joined.

So all in all, the Joiners has been very important in my musical life. The place has got such charm and it means a great deal to me, so I'm very happy that its history has finally been written.

My Joiners

A personal preface by Oliver Gray

It's ironic that I should be embarking on researching the history of anything at all. My father was a historian, an archivist indeed, and he was endlessly disappointed when I turned out, at school, to be even more useless at history than at other subjects. I succeeded in failing O-level history three times, and each time, the grade was worse than the time before.

Still, when the history is of something you're more interested in than the Corn Laws or Rotten Boroughs, it's different. Some people get like that about their family trees; for me, it's music, bands and venues that do the trick. I've seen terrible bands at venues such as Hamburg's Kaiserkeller, New York's Bottom Line, Austin's Saxon Pub and San Francisco's Hotel Utah, merely in order to say I've been there. On any given night, half the audience at London's Borderline are similarly-minded music tourists. I have often been known to take a detour and stand in silence outside Winchester's Lido for five minutes, just because I know the Stones played there in 1964.

I have spent a considerable percentage of my adult life in the Joiners, because I love it. Why? Well, Mint Burston, the most important person in the Joiners' history, can explain it better than me: "There's rock music in every brick in the place – it's what holding it together!"

The history of the Joiners pub itself is a long one. Stephen Stafford, writing on the BBC Southampton website, makes it sound enticingly like something out of Treasure Island: "The Joiners Arms Public House itself dates from the 1850s when, in a bustling and rough part of town, sailors, dock workers and prostitutes would have piled through the doors – the precursors to the punks, heavy metallers, bluesmen, folkies, indie-kids, britpoppers and techno-heads when the Joiners eventually became an exclusively music venue. Back in the 1970s and 1980s, the Joiners was already the main pub gig venue in Southampton, a 'spit and sawdust' bar, with an infamously manky carpet and a back room that put on all kinds of music." I wanted more of this sort of thing and so approached the brewers Eldridge Pope, who had owned the pub throughout almost all of its period as a music venue. This was their reply:

Dear Mr Gray

Further to your fax dated 21ˢᵗ April regarding The Joiners, Southampton. Unfortunately EP has recently changed ownership and all previous records were destroyed.

We are sorry that we cannot help in this instance.

A brewery which has no knowledge of the history of its own pubs? What's that all about? It's almost as if they don't care, and judging by the comments of some licensees, yep, that's the case. They certainly never showed much interest in the glory reflected from the venue's music pedigree. Well, it was their loss.

Luckily, the Southampton Records Office was much more forthcoming, providing some interesting information about the pub's history:

> **"Standing on the corner of St Mary Street and Cumberland Street (its address then being 47, Lower St Mary Street), this pub dates back to the 1850s, when Tom Manning, who was also a shoemaker, was the landlord; the 1878 Drink Map shows a fully licensed house on this site. John Wentworth was the licensee between 1874 and 1878, and Eldridge Pope's Dorchester Brewery purchased it in November 1883. William Hansford was their first tenant, at a rent of £30 per annum. Subsequent landlords included Charles James (1886-1890), A.H. Lever (1899), George Delbridge (1907-1909) and William Martin (1909 to the early 1920s). H.P Collett took over from then and was there well into the 1950s, but little of note seems to have happened until the music commenced. The pub is listed in the 1970s as 'the centre of the Southampton jazz scene'.**

So the history of the Joiners is its musical history, and that began one fateful day in 1969. By forgetting the rollicking sailors and painted ladies of the early days, we are doing what all good rock biographies do, namely omitting the tedious schooldays and family details of the subject and jumping in when he/she forms his/her first punk band, which is when it gets interesting anyway. I once read a biography of James Taylor in which he still hadn't been born by page 120. It may all have been vaguely relevant to his development as an artist but it certainly wasn't rock and roll.

That Old Joiners Magic

So what is so special about the Joiners?

Well, it's a dump, of course. In the inverted pyramid of the music world, the venues where bands start out are invariably shabby and down-at-heel, black walled and sticky-floored. The Joiners has all these attributes, but it is competely lacking in the features that so many other "toilet" venues share: over-priced drinks, over-zealous security, crowd barriers and the obligatory surly bloke in a kiosk by the door saying "You're not on the list".

It's a paradox that bands absolutely rely on the "toilet circuit" (it's a term of affection, by the way) to get their careers started towards a possible goal of great riches. Yet places like the Joiners don't make any money. I've known generations of Joiners licensees and all of them have struggled. Of course, there are plenty of hard-nosed promoters around who screw down bands' fees and deny them facilities, but they are the ones whose venues have the unwelcoming features mentioned above. Places which are genuinely hospitable, are really in love with music and which treat their existence as a mission rather than a business, are the exception. The Joiners is such a place.

People have described the St Mary's area as "dodgy", but that's absolutely not my experience. Or, if there are "dodgy" bits, the Joiners isn't one of them. As a mild-mannered and easily intimidated adult, I have never once felt frightened, either in or around the venue – and that's in thirty years of Joiners gig-going. There are shops, take-aways, pubs, a college, a church, a market and student residences in the street, and it's recently been the subject of regeneration finance. So yes, it's been a deprived part of town in its fabric, but it isn't threatening in any way. It's not fanciful to imagine St Mary's as Southampton's Islington one day.

Much like Islington, too, the buildings, and especially the Joiners, are brick-built, traditional and solid. The Joiners itself has a very pleasing aspect, something you only notice if you step back and gain some perspective, which you are unlikely to do when pitching up for a gig. Inside the front door (which has recently moved from the right to the left of the building, fact fans), you will find an unassuming person (often Mint or Ian Binnington, both of them slight, bespectacled and diffident in manner), who will take your money or ticket. Currently, the

licensee Pat Muldowney will greet you in the street. At first glance, he might appear to be the traditional meathead bouncer (he's big), but within seconds you realize he's the man for whom the term "gentle giant" was invented. He's there to welcome you, not to intimidate, and he just loves to chew the fat about music, of which he has encyclopaedic knowledge. It's a mystery that he knows everything about every Joiners performance, even though he seems to spend the whole of every evening outside.

Over the years, several systems have existed for gaining admission to the music. For most of the Joiners' history, the pub has been free to enter, while the back room, as the place of entertainment, has required a fee. During the golden "Mint Years", the only concession to security was a felt-tip cross on your wrist as you entered. It would have been simple to forge this at home before setting out, or indeed, not to wash and thus to gain admission to several gigs in a row, but that would have been so contrary to the "spirit of the Joiners" that no one would have done it.

Nowadays, as detailed above, the whole pub is the venue and you pay as you enter the building. You get your beer and chat in the front bar (it's unmistakably a pub and has never attempted to assume any pretensions). Here you can look at the posters of past shows and the murals which adorn the walls and have conversations along the lines of "surely the So-and-Sos didn't REALLY play here?" You'll be served by the invariably cool, friendly and unflappable bar staff, who normally sport unfeasible amounts of tattoos and piercings.

The music room at the back is where the real magic begins. At various times, the stage has been against all four walls of the room; currently, it's at the back, where it logically belongs. Similarly, the "back bar" has been on three different sides, but now it doesn't exist at all, replaced by a sound desk and merchandising area. You enter what is effectively a lobby, part of the main room but with poor sound quality and sight lines. Here is where people can socialise without disturbing the fans crammed into the main, square room. As the stage takes up a good half of the room, the feeling of intimacy is complete. For the best view, nip round to the left, past the toilets, and enter via the other door. If the night isn't wildly busy, this will give you the best view and the best sound. Also, you are most likely to rub shoulders with stars of the future as they push past you on the way to the stage.

Yes, no band can get to the Joiners' stage without walking – or often shoving – through the audience. The mysterious cellar dressing room (which is just as you'd expect it to be, dingy, sweaty, smelly and graffiti-covered), is positioned at the back of the lobby, near the entrance. It's down to the whim of the band which route they take to get to the stage. Sometimes, half will go one way and half the other. Occasionally, they will have a minder with a torch to lead the way. The very coolest bands

"Surely they didn't REALLY play here?"

Murals by Alex Barinov.

(Stereolab spring to mind) will simply drift incognito towards the stage and languidly set up their own gear.

My personal memories include being mildly burned by a joss stick wielded by Crispian Mills of Kula Shaker, and noticing that Pete

Doherty had bad breath as I became aware that he was tapping me on the shoulder and saying "S'cuse me, mate". I tried to take a snap and now have a revealing close-up of a pork pie hat and nothing else.

In other words, it is impossible for any band playing the Joiners to give themselves airs and graces. A few have tried, invariably with disastrous results. These you will find in the body of the book. Step forward, for example, Birdland, An Emotional Fish and – oh God – The Cranberries.

So the magic of the Joiners lies in its relaxed, friendly nature and its natural function as a "great leveller", where band and audience are as one. "Welcome to our front room", said Big Dipper, and everyone looked at each other in shared pleasure. Of course, if you wanted to, you could come every night of every week, because who knows who you might be seeing who might turn out to be a megastar of the future? If you'd seen Corky or Idoru in one of their many appearances, you'd now be boasting of experiencing the Delays when they were knee high to a grasshopper (they still are, actually). And in due course, you can go along and see the bands again when they are on the skids and return on one of their many comeback tours. The listings regularly trumpet the "Such and Suches (ex-So and Sos)". Myriad members of the Wonder Stuff, Carter USM, Inspiral Carpets, Boo Radleys and their ilk still pass through the Joiners to this day in normally doomed attempts to buck the whims of the industry.

In 2006, The Research introduced themselves with one of the most astute and realistic comments ever heard from the Joiners' stage: "Welcome to the Joiners, famous for being the place where bands play twice: once on the way up and once on the way down. It's nice to see you again!"

Pre-Joiners Music in Southampton

It's incorrect to suggest that the Joiners is Southampton's only music venue. There's Lennons (which used to be the Onslow), the Talking Heads (a nice roots venue) and of course The Brook, a fantastic venue which is wasted on an almost exclusive diet of (very popular) tribute acts. It's also certainly not true to suggest that there was no live music scene in pre-Joiners days. Legend has it (truthfully) that the Fleming Arms pub, just under the railway bridge in Swaythling, was a Joiners-style venue in the early Seventies. The pub was a stage coach stop on the Portsmouth to Southampton route, and the old coach house building at the back was converted into a club called, guess what, the Coach House Club. Bands which played there included Sharks (with Chris Spedding and Andy Fraser from Free), Camel, Ducks Deluxe, the Sensational Alex Harvey Band and, on their first UK tour, Bob Marley and The Wailers.

In the Sixties, Southampton was, indeed, home to one of the UK's finest tour venues outside London, namely the Concorde Club, which occupied a function room attached to the Bassett Hotel (recently demolished). Nowadays, the Concorde (still run by the same person, Cole Matheson) is located near Eastleigh and is a smart night club and hotel, but in the sixties, it was a sweaty back room ranking alongside cool London venues such as the Crawdaddy and Ricky-Tick Clubs. Virtually anyone who was anyone played there, including Joe Cocker and the Grease Band, Free (several times), Steampacket (with Rod Stewart), Bluesology (with Elton John), and Eric Clapton, with both John Mayall's Bluesbreakers and Cream. So the Joiners certainly had antecedents in the business of presenting breaking bands.

Prior to the Joiners assuming its current pre-eminent position, there was a flourishing music scene featuring musicians whose names will crop up again and again throughout this book. Sadly, little in the way of fame or fortune beckoned for most of them, but local names like the Brook Brothers (who released seventeen records in the 1960s), Fleur-de-Lys (a very cool band signed to Immediate in 1965), contemporaries The Meddyevils (signed to Pye in the same year) and Brownhill Stamp Duty (who released four singles in the 1960s and 1970s) are all fondly remembered.

Further details of many other early Southampton rockers can be found in the various band profiles of Joiners "stalwarts" later in the book.

Strike up the music
(just for a while)

Southampton's music lovers owe a huge debt to Les Haigh, who certainly had no idea what he was initiating. What is interesting about it is that the band he booked was exactly the sort of act the Joiners is renowned for attracting today, namely a cool, newly-signed "buzz" band from out of town.

Les Haigh: "I was the guy who started the music at the Joiners way back in the Spring of 1969. I was 22 years of age and moved with my stepfather Ted Steer and mother Vera from the Royal George pub in Salisbury for them to take over The Joiners as landlords in 1969. As we moved in, the pub was freshly decorated and the back bar renovated into a large new lounge area. I was music mad and had been an avid collector of US soul music imports since 1965 and therefore had a huge record collection of rare music. To bring new young people to the pub (which at that time had an awful reputation as a 'rough' dive), I christened the new lounge the Aztec Bar and advertised in the Echo its opening that Spring of 1969 as a music venue.

The Aztec was an immediate hit and throughout that year, a mixture of genuine soul disco and the first live acts (mainly Salisbury guitarists and folk singers I knew) were booked to create music intervals and give interest to certain week nights.

In the late summer of that year, I went to the first Isle of Wight Festival, which re-awakened my taste for a wider range of music from Richie Havens and Bob Dylan through to the new 'progressive rock'. By the Spring of 1970, with a group of friends, we had built and lit a stage in the Aztec and decided to book our first 'big name' act. Through agents we secured and advertised with flyers etc., a Yorkshire band called "Jan Dukes de Grey", who had just cut their first album (LP and cover which I still have). The gig went well (really too loud for the size of the Aztec) and brought a new 'progressive rock' crowd into The Joiners. Unfortunately, the gig was not packed enough to make money and so Ted and Vera were rather financially hurt from my attempt at becoming a big-time promoter. Nonetheless, we went on to intersperse our regular crowd-pulling soul weekends with several other bands, so as you can see, that was the birth of The Joiners (Aztec Bar) as a music venue.

It was great for me to be a part of that birth and when Ted and Vera decided to leave The Joiners to get a bar in Spain in 1971, I was accepted for the job as the House DJ at the then new Bird's Nest discotheque at the Bargate (the rear of the Bargate Hotel pub, which is now the Burger King), where I stayed until 1974. At the time I started the Aztec Bar I had no idea just what an important band venue it would become in the years to follow. Unfortunately, when I went to the Bird's Nest, I lost all contact with The Joiners, oddly only going back for the first time last year because a close friend's son from Winchester is now in a band and they played The Joiners."

Jan Dukes de Grey

Following on from that auspicious beginning, music at the Joiners was sporadic until the arrival, in the mid seventies, of a landlord called Sam Costa (not to be confused with the BBC radio DJ of the same name). Bearing a startling similarity to Roger Moore (for which he was frequently lampooned by bands), Sam, with his wife Julia, was the licensee who really established regular music at the Joiners. Sam it was who was in charge in 1978, when our proper listings begin.

Listings

Don't you just love them? No? Well, apparently, you're in the minority. Look at any issue of the monthly music magazines and you're guaranteed to find a major "listing" feature. The hundred Best Prog/ Ska/Trance/ Metal Albums Of All Time, as voted by our readers? Check. But in this book, you'll find real flesh and blood listings and you might even find them interesting. Here's a task to start you off: It is said that both Nirvana and Green Day have played at the Joiners. One did, the other didn't. To find out the truth, you'll have to read all the listings, heh heh.

Or maybe your band, or your friend's band, or your dad's band played at the Joiners one time. Acting on the same principle as local newspapers (which print as many names as possible in the hope that the owners of those names will buy the paper because they are in it), we've included loads and loads and loads of gigs. The idea is the same: We want to sell lots of books because it's in a good cause. But one thing we had to adopt as policy (to avoid the book being bigger than the Encyclopaedia Britannia) was not to include every name on multiple-band bills. In recent years, promoters with names such as Oomph, Bitch and Fangfur have regularly put on showcases featuring four, five or even six bands in one evening, on the time-honoured small venue principle that if each band brings twenty mates, the hall will be full. In practice, each group of mates normally only stays for its own particular band. This does mean, however, that if your band Egyptian Mummy played third on the bill to Heart Failure and Scarlet Strumpet on June 27th 1992 (I made them up, by the way), you probably haven't got a mention. Similarly, the listings are based on bona fide research of advertised shows, but if your particular gig was cancelled or postponed, it might possibly be listed even if it didn't take place. If that's the case, tell us! Who knows, there might even be a second edition.

Finally, and most heartbreakingly, there are gaps. Certain licensees simply disappeared, taking all documentation with them. The Daily Echo's Joiners coverage over the years has been sporadic and entirely dependent on whether or not they happened to have a music-interested rookie reporter on board. Sound Info, Due South and Logo have been fantastically helpful sources of data but each of them only lasted a limited length of time. So again, if you can help to fill any of the gaps (they become pretty apparent but the most obvious ones are 1982-3 and 1998-9), please contact us.

• LISTINGS 1978 - 1979 •

1978

During 1978 and 1979, there was a Sunday jazz residency featuring Timepeace. Rock was only on Thursday nights.

8 June: Devereux Drive
22 June: Gold Rush
   Not to be confused with the Oxford indie band of the 2000s.
29 June: Idol Threat
6 July: Last Orders
   A cool "new wave" band from the Portsmouth area.
13 July: RPM
20 July: Barricade
27 July: Vtol
3 August: Last Orders
10 August: Paradox
17 August: The Take
24 August: RPM
31 August: Juggler
7 September: Loaded Dice
14 September: Schedule D
21 September: Double Xposure
28 September: Stray Dogs
   A Winchester punk band.
5 October: Xperts
12 October: Alchemist
19 October: Stray Dogs
26 October: Ptarmigan
   This prog-rock outfit hailed from the Chichester area.
2 November: Attic
9 November: Staa Marx
   A great new wave quartet from Bognor Regis.
16 November: Trader
23 November: Fountain

30 November: Catch 22
   Southampton punks.
7 December: Confusion
14 December: Thieves Like Us
   Winchester theatrical new-wavers.
21 December: Fool Moon
28 December: Yggdrasil

1979

4 January: KGB
11 January: Gus
18 January: Last Orders
25 January: Refugee
   Stalwart Southampton heavy rockers.
1 February: Night Ride
8 February: Debut
15 February: Deep Freeze
22 February: Willpower
1 March: Double Xposure
8 March: Cedar Vale
15 March: Debut
22 March: KGB
29 March: Last Orders
5 April: Interference
   This Poole-based band later became the Jags.
12 April: Loaded Dice
19 April: The Dials
26 April: Dirty Pictures
3 May: Paradox
10 May: Night Rider
24 May: Airport
31 May: The Executives
7 June: King Rock
   Dave Legg led this eccentric Southampton outfit.
14 June: Identity Crisis
21 June: Road's End

Jazz at the Joiners

Andy Iles, chair of the Southampton Jazz Society, 1997 – 2001:

"In 1975, the Society moved to the Joiners Arms Music Bar from the Bridge Tavern on Six Dials. Chairman Gary 'Skip' Conway and his dedicated committee set about a long-term programme of jazz, in a very hospitable and lively atmosphere. Jazz at the Joiners lasted until 1988, before moving to the Nuffield Theatre.

Skip and his team put the Joiners on the international jazz map. I greatly enjoyed working with landlord Sam Costa, who liked to remind us of his days as a Roger Moore stuntman. He moved to Ferndown in the late 80s. The membership in those days was over 200, which shows the popularity of the venue.

We offered an eclectic and extensive programme. One year, we ran all through the summer, offering a full 52 weeks for our enthusiasts. A superb range of jazzers played at the Joiners, including elite trumpeters Kenny Baker, Ken Colyer, Humphrey Littleton, Alex Welsh, Cuff Billett, Bunny Austin and a younger Guy Barker with Clark Tracey on drums. My own favourite night was in the summer of 1981, when we booked the all-American Harlem Jazz and Blues Band, classic jazz veterans with a collective age of over 400 years. Their energy, experience and enthusiasm pulled in an audience of over 250, which spilled out into the lane at the side of the pub. That was probably a record Joiners attendance for any genre of music.

A commanding figure on our old piano was Ram Ramirez, who co-wrote the Billie Holliday classic 'Lover Man'. The pianist and the band swung like the clappers, and the warm summer evening soon had the audience and the walls sweating profusely, it was unforgettable. Guest stars performing at the Joiners included Al Cohn (of the Woody Herman Four Brothers fame), Benny Waters, Jean Toussaint, Al Casey, Pepper Adams. Conrad Herwig and vocalist Kim Parker (step-daughter of the legendary Charlie Parker).

The beauty of those days was being able to book the visiting

Americans to play with our superb local musicians Monty Warlock, Ray Ember, Ian Anderson and the ever-present Ray D'Inverno. Ray did so much as a player, band leader and chairperson, and also played a major part in the Southampton Musicians' Co-operative, which participated in major events at the Joiners. Ray was also there for the superb Sunday sessions which helped shape Andy Sheppard into the richly-deserved international stature he now holds. Great times indeed!

Among the galaxy of great British jazzers doing sessions for us were Alan Skidmore, Bobby Wellings, Jim Mullen, Peter King, Bruce Turner, Lol Coxhill, Tommy Whittle, Ronnie Ross, Stan Sulzmann, Mike Carr, Pete Jacobson and Don Weller. In other words, a who's-who of everyone who was anyone on the UK jazz scene, much like the venue later became in the rock field. Plus there were our outstanding local musicians like Sid Carter, Colin Brinton, Bill Pritchard, Paul Stiles, Mike Herridge, Lee Goodall, Dave Good and Pat Bond.

There were often humorous scenes at the door, where there was always the need for someone to look after the entrance to the L-shaped room. Pam Cotton got short shrift when asking Al Cohn for some entrance money: 'What are you talking about. Don't you know who I am?!' The remarkable jazz impressario Cole Matheson of the Concorde Club has always had my highest regard, so I squirmed quietly when treasurer Jill Nixon insisted on charging him for admission.

I will forever be grateful to the Joiners for all those fantastic years of great music."

Bruce Turner, Alan Jackson, Lol Coxhill, Dave Green

Guitarist goes unheard

WHERE have all the guitarists gone? That was the plaintive cry at Southampton Jazz Society's Joiners Arms headquarters in St. Mary's Street last night.

For not only was there a sad absence of fans to hear Terry Smith, arguably one of the top six jazz guitar players in Britain — there was not a solitary guitar player there either.

"Usually the guitarists flock here whenever a guitar player is the star," said society committeeman Alan Greening.

"All the jazz buffs must be taking in the Herb Miller band at the Mayflower," said gig arranger Skip Conway in a closing announcement.

Whatever the explanation, the 20-or-so audience sat back and enjoyed a guitar evening — bending an ear not only to the guru himself but two other guitarists also.

Terry Smith, an exciting player whose style ranges from the ultra-cool to funky blues, was backed by a trio led by "stick" bass player Dave Good from Southampton. Bill Pritchard on guitar and John Baker, drums.

Daily Echo

Wild and cool jazz master

LIGHTNING fingerwork and a dazzling creative ability generated the highlight — a rapid-fire blues sequence — of the terrific tenor playing rangy Jean Toussaint at Southampton last night.

Toussaint (30), main support of famed American Art Farmer's Jazz Messengers from 1982 until last year, blew both wild and cool, thoughtful and exotic during another National Jazz Month session down at the Joiners, St. Mary Street.

A four-month tutorial stint at the Guildhall School of Music is the reason this rangy black New Yorker was able to play at Southampton Jazz Society's well-worn HQ.

He was staunchly supported by a trio led by one of the Jazz South organisation chiefs, Adrian Kendon. Effective bass-player Kendon, nimble-fingered Brian Wait on piano and rocksteady Ron Parry on drums.

Good sound standards like All the Things You Are and Misty proved more than adequate vehicles for the swinging Coltrane and Pres-influenced tenor saxman.

Derek Eates

21

SOUTHAMPTON
JAZZ SOCIETY
event **88**
FOR

Art Project
supported by
SOUTHAMPTON CITY

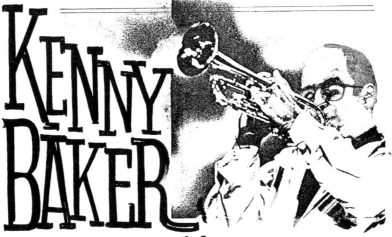

KENNY BAKER

with

THE CHRIS WALKER BAND

Make it a date.

STARTS **8** PM

TUESDAY *FEBRUARY 2ND.*

MEMBERS £   NON MEMBERS £

THE JOINERS ARMS · ST. MARY'S STREET · SOUTHAMPTON · HANTS

• LISTINGS 1979 - 1980 •

19 July: Thieves Like Us
26 July: King Rock
 2 August: KGB
 9 August: Lip Moves
 The first sighting of the band
 later to become Stitch.
16 August: Adam West and his
 Gotham City Rockers
23 August: Lip Moves
28 August: Thieves Like Us
30 August: King Rock
 6 September: Lynx
13 September: Last Orders
20 August: Dials
27 August: Trader
 4 September: King Rock
11 September: King Rock
18 September: Voltz
25 October: Crickmay
 1 November: KGB
15 November: La Plage
22 November: Mean Streak
29 November: King Rock
 6 December: Refugee
13 December: Full Marx
20 November: King Rock
27 December: Blazers

1980

From 1980 to 1983, Sundays
were reserved for a residency
by the highly accomplished
modern jazz outfit Sphere.
Mainstay of this Salisbury
based band was the
saxophonist Andy Sheppard,
later to become renowned
as one of the UK's top jazz
musicians. Wednesdays
featured rock jams. Fridays

were reserved for blues.
The venue was frequently also
hired out for bands to put
on their own shows on other
nights. This was a period
of great variety, with
everything from heavy metal
to indie rock turning up at the
Joiners.

17 January: China Doll
 One of the loudest and
 heaviest regular bands.
24 January: Bitter Lemmings
 A very popular and seminal
 Southampton indie outfit.
31 January: Blazers
 New wave band featuring
 established Southampton
 musos.
 7 February: King Rock
14 February: Bitter Lemmings
21 February: Lone Wolf
28 February: Ricky and the
 Cufflinks
 6 March: King Rock
13 March: Bitter Lemmings
20 March: Lone Wolf
22 March: King Rock
27 March: Sly Scandal
29 March: Blazers
 3 April: Last Orders
10 April: Lone Wolf
12 April: Ricky and the
 Cufflinks
17 April: The Dials
24 April: Crickmay
26 April: Lights
31 April: The Kitchens
 8 May: Warbeck
10 May: Vertical Motion
15 May: Blitz
22 May: KGB

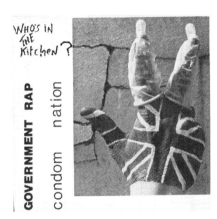

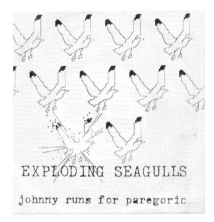

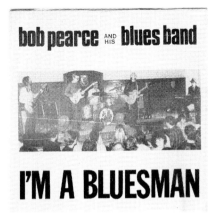

• LISTINGS 1980 - 1981 •

24 May: Lone Wolf
29 May: Blazers
31 May: Exploding Seagulls
This band featured Nick Jacobs, shortly to co-found the Blue Aeroplanes.
14 June: Bitter Lemmings
19 June: King Rock
26 June: Blazers
28 June: Lone Wolf
10 July: Blazers
12 July: Steamers
17 July: Exploding Seagulls
24 July: Lip Moves
31 July: Fury
7 August: Exploding Seagulls
9 August: King Rock
11 August: TVs
21 August: Z-Cars
23 August: Exploding Seagulls
28 August: Blazers
30 August: Program
4 September: Exploding Seagulls
11 September: TVs
13 September: Blazers
25 September: Metraque
27 September: The Ds
2 October: The TVs
9 October: Paradox
11 October: Lip Moves
30 October: Exploding Seagulls
6 November: Steamers
8 November: Exploding Seagulls
11 November: Grown-Ups
12 November: Perfect Strangers
13 November: Lifebuoys
15 November: Manhattan Slide
20 November: Exploding Seagulls

22 November: X-Band
25 November: Truffle
26 November: Talon
Both the above bands were leather-clad hard rockers.
27 November: Steamers
29 November: Skavengers
Police-like three-piece from Bournemouth.
3 December: The Lens
Prog-rockers from the Southampton area, later to become IQ.
4 December: Convertibles
10 December: The Britz
Not to be confused with Blitz, this lot came from Salisbury.
11 December: Exploding Seagulls
13 December: Temple
17 December: Duballup
18 November: Truffle
20 December: Export
22 December: Duballup
23 December: Exploding Seagulls
24 December: Blazers
26 December: Lone Wolf
27 December: Skavengers

1981

Sphere's Sunday residency continued throughout 1981.
1 January: Overkill
3 January: Young Solicitors
7 January: Z-Cars
8 January: Polecats
10 January: Truffle
17 January: Exploding Seagulls
21 January: The Artecs
22 January: Philip The Cat

St. Marys Street
A Complete Shopping Experience ?
Mandy Garman puts her mouth where her money is.

I can predict that in the 1990s the general public will tire of 'complete shopping experiences.' Mauled by malls, recovering from covered concepts,we will return to the streets. Who needs clowning on the mezzanine level or piped music or precincts ? We don't. There is St. Marys Street.

St. Marys Street is Southampton's heart, and if it has one, its soul. There isn't a Next in sight, you don't need a car, you can buy anything from a synth to a salami, and the prices can rarely be beaten.

Have your hair cut at one of the excellent hairdressers - I suggest The Nuthouse or The Syndicate which has just branched out into selling furniture, china and objets to make a house into a home . Decades sells classic clothing and accessories from the 1900s to the 1960s and students get 10% off. Kingsland Market is always worth a browse, and when you've worked up an appetite there are dozens of cafes to choose from.

Marie and Fabrizio's Caffee Lecco is reccommended. Home made pasta and pizza are specialities but full English breakfasts,lunch, afternoon teas, and a take-away service at competitive prices are available too. Caffee Lecco is open between 8am & 5pm, Monday to Saturday. St. Marys Street is a musician's paradise with The Joiners Pub, Future Music, The Classical Guitar Centre, Underground records and much more. Future Music sells all imaginable equipment. Prices sometimes have to be whispered, they are too low. The Classical

Guitar Centre has provided guitar tuition at all levels since 1973. The teaching staff includes Adrian Neville, a well known concert guitarist, who has a large and varied repertoire including including classical, flamenco and contemporary styles. The centre also stocks Spanish guitars chosen by the teachers, music, strings and accessories. Underground Records sells more than discs; they are an agent for for concert tickets with travel included. Thanks to them,Due South readers have the chance of winning Magnum tickets - just answer the simple question.

Competition

Due South in association with the Concert Travel Club are able to offer two free tickets to see Magnum at Poole Arts Centre on 30th May. Prize included free return coach travel from Southampton or Eastleigh if required. Simply answer the question and send the coupon below to us. Winners will be the first correct entry pulled out of a hat.
Q Magnum are from
1. Birmingham? 2. St. Mary's Street? 3. Timbuktu?
Answers and name and address to Due South, 37 Mountpleasant Road, Southampton SO2 OEG

Those were the days: Due South, February 1990

John Clare's Memories Of The Joiners

John Clare was the manager of the famous Henry's Records in St Mary Street. From his home in Australia, he looks back:

"I spent half my life in the Joiners from 1980 until about 1984, when I married Henry's niece, Linda, gained an instant stepdaughter and my life changed forever.

I used to live in the flat above Hurrell's The Jewellers, next door to Henry's Records in St Mary St, so the Joiners was practically my local. The landlord and landlady for most of this time were Sam and Julia Costa. Sam was a gregarious, very jovial and cordial sort of guy with a million tall stories and a laugh like Tommy Cooper's. Julia was a full-figured, matronly type lady. She had a rather dominant, outgoing personality and you wouldn't want to get on the wrong side of her, but she also had a heart of gold.

Roxoff (see Joiners Stalwarts section) would have the place jumping every Friday night with extended versions of 'Walking the Dog' and 'I Don't Need No Doctor'. It may sound old hat now, but the place was packed every week. Then there was A Band Called John. They played jazz rock music in the style of the instrumental Jeff Beck albums and used to have free open rehearsal sessions in the Joiners every Saturday lunchtime. I would nip out of Henry's to have my lunch there, accompanied by a couple of pints of Royal Oak.

Sphere, the well known jazz fusion quartet from Salisbury, which featured the now famous Andy Sheppard, had a regular Sunday night residency at the Joiners when they weren't on tour. Doris and the Dots played an amazing gig one night with something like a fifteen-piece line up, augmented by Big Brother's horn section and girl singers and the percussionists from Ebony Rockers (who featured Craig David's dad). The two front men vocalists/toasters, Tony Eccles and Earl, were trying to out-perform each other all night and there was a particularly amazing version of 'Big 'Ead' which went on for half the night.

The debut gig by Five (although there were actually six of them) featured guitarists Arnie Cottrell and Gerry Aubrey and the drummer, Tim Fitzgerald, plus ex-Exploding Seagulls Fred and Sue Bolton and a rather strange vocalist in the David Byrne ilk called Steve Marchment-Bennett from Cardiff. They sounded like Talking Heads meets Can meets Devo meets Suicide. A lot of noise, in other words, but really good noise."

Stick It In Your Ear

Stick It In Your Ear was a successful indie cassette label based in Southampton. Alongside it ran the fanzine Ear To The Ground. Mastermind behind both these was Geoff Wall.

Geoff Wall:

"Over the years, I have spent a large percentage of my life in the Joiners' smoky back room, enjoying live music. The pub had previously been the venue for various itinerant Folk Clubs and the Southampton Jazz Society, but it really hit its musical heyday during the eighties.

Looking back, the thing that impressed me most about the Joiners was that under the stewardship of Sam and Julia Costa, I was exposed to the absolute best in local music. Realising the audience potential, the couple actively supported local bands, knowing that live music would bring crowds into the pub and help the bar takings. They encouraged bands to book their back room, allowed them to keep all of the door takings, and only took the bar takings for their trouble. Never once did they ask for a door percentage.

Surprisingly, although the venue was frequented by Hippies, Goths, Skins, Punks, Rastas and almost every kind of warring, sectarian youth culture, I never saw any friction between the disparate factions. The Joiners was a tranquil oasis to these tribes, but I suspect that this had much to do with the size and nature of the landlord. Sam was Roger Moore's stand-in on a number of James Bond films and always claimed that he got the job because Moore couldn't run, and thus looked funny on camera. Not the action-man image Moore wanted to present to the public!

Many of the greatest gigs that I have ever witnessed have been at the Joiners. And this is from someone who saw The Beatles at Southampton Gaumont [1963] and Bob Marley and the Wailers in The Coach House Club [1973], a small outbuilding behind Swaythling's Fleming Arms! Nothing beats the small club experience of seeing bands at close quarters.

I started the 'Stick It In Your Ear!' fanzine in January 1981 and exposure to Southampton's numerous, wide-ranging musical genres at the Joiners led directly to 'SIYE Tapes', a cassette-only record label that was dedicated to presenting local music in all its aspects and glory. Throughout the early eighties, we released some forty albums, EPs and singles, all of which reflected the diversity of local music that was on offer.

Local music within Southampton always seemed to me to be split down the centre. On the one hand, you had the older-aged bands such as Roxoff, Bob Pearce, etc., the Blues/R&B/Jazz end of the musical spectrum, whose peer group audience had more of a disposable income. For many a year, Roxoff held the Friday night and Saturday lunchtime residency at the venue, and it was always sold out. The flip-side of the coin were the younger, more experimental bands such as Bitter Lemmings, Exploding Seagulls, Games To Avoid, Five and Laughter In The Garden. I recall Julia once telling me that although she loved The Lens, (a progressive rock band which evolved into the successful IQ), she wished that their audience would buy more beer! It appeared that, whilst the older audience members watched their favourite bands whilst swilling down gallons of beer, the younger audience tended to make one pint last all night, a landlord's nightmare.

Iguana, a superb local band, had been adopted lock, stock and barrel by Jess Roden, and become the Jess Roden Band, but record company pressure for Roden to go solo, combined with the financial logistics of keeping such a large band on the road, saw them disband and return home to Southampton. At the instigation of bassist Joss Jones, the nucleus of Bruce Roberts, Pete Hunt and Ronnie Taylor formed Roxoff, who successfully returned to the semi-pro local circuit, and two Joiners residencies.

During this time, SIIYE were organising local showcase gigs at the Solent Suite, and Roger Kennedy and I decided to promote our own, lower-key version, centred around The Convertibles and Ex Band. Once a month, we booked the Joiners' back room for a Saturday night, and the gigs became very successful, leading Roger and me to undertake a second series of monthly Joiners' gigs with the Poor Batchelors as headliners. One notable gig was the 'Twang & Croak' event, a sort of pre-'Unplugged' show, where Nick Petford (Exploding Seagulls), Dave Smales (Bitter Lemmings), Simon Vincent (Games To Avoid/Stitched-Back Foot Airman), Paul Blatchford (Bitter Lemmings/Poor Batchelors), Nigel Gordon (The Convertibles) and Fred Bolton (Five), each performed an acoustic set.

This was highly unusual, as all were electric guitarists but collectively, they rose to the occasion. I've still got a tape of it somewhere, along with most of the other gigs that I attended during this time in the company of my trusty Sony Walkman.

Scattered throughout this showcase of local musical talent, the Joiners shoe-horned in such national acts as Michael Chapman, Kevin Coyne, Arthur Brown, Kevin Ayers and the Wizards of Twiddly, Mike Heron and the Incredible Acoustic Band, and the one that still stands out in my mind as one of my greatest musical moments, the Jaki Whitren Band.

Looking through back-issues of 'Ear To The Ground' SIIYE's freebie monthly music magazine, I am astonished to see the diversity of musical genres ever present at the Joiners. Once Sam and Julia departed for the quieter life of a pub in Bournemouth, never again did the venue serve up such a diverse musical feast of local talent."

STICK IT IN YOUR EAR'S

 **"TWANG & CROAK**

featuring

 GIG"

DAVE SMALES
(EX - BITTER LEMMING)

SIMON VINCENT
(EX - GAMES TO AVOID)

plus **SPECIAL GUESTS**

THE **POOR BATCHELOR**
(EX - BITTER LEMMING)

NICK PETFORD
(EX - STRATE JACKET)

at the
JOINERS
SATURDAY
7th JULY
8·30 START

admission £1.00

• LISTINGS 1981 •

24 January: Talon
27 January: Trader
28 January: Latecomers
29 January: Games To Avoid
  This great band had evolved
  out of Lip Moves.
31 January: Skavengers
 7 February: Duballup
10 February: Overkill
11 February: Tomorrow
14 February: The Captains
18 February: The Lens
19 February: The Talkies
  A band from Bournemouth
  featuring future top record
  producer Richard Mazda.
21 February: Zena Xerox
24 February: Prime Suspect
26 February: Moulin Rouge
28 February: The Lens
 4 March: Program
 5 March: Truffle
 7 March: Duballup
11 March: Instants
12 March: Temple
14 March: Captains
18 March: The Lens
19 March: The Talkies
21 March: The Time
24 March: Vertical Motion
25 March: Spirit Level
28 March: The Blazers
 1 April: Strider
 4 April: Games To Avoid
 7 April: Missing Ear
 8 April: Dream Sequence
 9 April: Driving Sideways
15 April: The Gestalt
18 April: The New Brendas
  Another offshoot from Lip
  Moves.

25 April: The Press
28 April: Headless Horsemen
  A three-piece led by John
  Parish, future PJ Harvey
  collaborator.
29 April: KGB
30 April: The Elite
 2 May: Exploding Seagulls
 5 May: Zena Xerox
 7 May: Five
  The reason that Exploding
  Seagulls disappear and Five
  appear at this stage is that
  Five was formed by ex ES
  members.
 9 May: Duballup
13 May: Inferior Complex
14 May: Outsiders
16 May: Games To Avoid
20 May: Jet Set
21 May: Dodgers
23 May: Motifs
27 May: The Secret
30 May: Skavengers
 3 June: Young Solicitors
 4 June: The Press
 6 June: Prime Suspect
11 June: Zip Code*Stylish new*
  wave band from Winchester.
13 June: Roxoff
  This is an early appearance
  by a band destined for
  many Joiners shows.
  Their residency continued
  throughout the year.
19 June: Teenage Kicks party
  with Artex, Young Solicitors
  Teenage Kicks was a
  successful fanzine of the
  time.
25 June: Auto da Fe

• LISTINGS 1981 •

27 June: The Boosters
29 June: Marrakesh
1 July: Burlesque
2 July: The Press
3 July: Roxoff
4 July: Games To Avoid
6 July: Zip Code
9 July: Fatal Dose
10 July: Roxoff
11 July: Microdisney
*Yes, this is indeed the cult
Irish band. DJ Hammy: I
confirm that Microdisney
definitely did play and it
was at the height of the riots
of 81. This was their first
gig over here and my niece's
partner helped arrange it,
as one of the band was a
relative from Cork.*
15 July: Teenage Kicks
16 July: Boosters
18 July: Five
20 July: Strollers
22 July: Prime Suspect
23 July: Motherfolkers
24 July: Roxoff
25 July: New Brendas
29 July: The Secret
1 August: Pancho
3 August: Convertibles
5 August: X-Band
6 August: Games To Avoid
7 August: Roxoff
8 August: Zip Code
10 August: Zena Xerox
13 August: Jack In Irons
19 August: V-Necks
20 August: Scratch Band
26 August: Zip Code
27 August: Marrakesh

29 August: Motifs
3 September: The Mets
9 September: The Press
12 September: Fugitive
14 September: Teenage Kicks
16 September: Convertibles
17 September: Lovers and
Other Strangers
23 September: Export
24 September: Five
26 September: Exploding
Seagulls
29 September: No Exit
30 September: Rocking
Burne-Jones and the Pre-
Raphaelites
*Became the Remarkable
Family and featured future
music journalist Howard
Male.*
1 October: Cosmetics
*Richard Mazda's post-
Talkies band was seriously
funky.*
3 October: Night School
7 October: Strider
8 October: Auto da Fe
10 October: The New Brendas
12 October: Hickory Wind
13 October: X-Band
14 October: Caught In The Act
15 October Rhythm Method
16 October: Scratch Band
17 October: Zip Code
22 October: The Time
*This great new wave band
from Gosport featured future
TV comedian Kevin Eldon on
vocals.*
24 October: Doris and the Dots
26 October: Refugee

33

From the Underdogs to Stitch

The early eighties was a particularly fertile period for Southampton music, as Pete Holden recalls:

Pete Holden: "John Peel had just begun to play "Uptown Top Ranking", regularly and enthusiastically, when Andrew "Stass" Stacey and I were first introduced at lunch break in the canteen of the Royal Naval Stores at Weston, Southampton. Our mutual enthusiasm for all things Peel was our first conversation. It was my first day in the job and fourth day living in Southampton.

Stass had graduated from Southampton University earlier that year. He lived with a bunch of other long-haired, lefty, beery and dopey grads in "Hollywood", a scruffy house on the then main drag between Portsmouth and Southampton, Bursledon Road in Bitterne.

One of Stass's house mates and all round best buddies was Andy Wallace, a cheery and enthusiastic type who could not only play guitar and sing but also wrote songs and fancied himself as the front man in a band. Stass was just at the preliminary stages of becoming a bass player and they had been practising together at Hollywood. I visualised myself as a rock writer and did have some tenuous connections with Sounds and NME. I became their manager and on March 4th the next year, we auditioned for a drummer.

The only applicant was Dave Atkin, also new in Southampton, having just arrived from Nottingham. His sister was working on the production of one of the Enid Blyton kids' TV programmes always being filmed in the New Forest and Dave had a job with them as a driver. Dave had some experience of gigging on the Nottingham indie scene and was, I think, like me, anxious to impress his new pals. Dave is tall and in those days carried quite a few extra pounds topped off with a blonde mop and big, shaded glasses with strong lenses. He had a quite ballsy confidence and was indisputably and obviously an excellent drummer. His arrival certainly injected an energy and gave a sense of possibility to everything. We now had a band and they were called The Underdogs. With the benefit of hindsight I have to say that choosing names for the various bands and labels we were all involved in was not a strong point.

The Underdogs sound was punky r&b with a few covers ('Down At The Doctors', 'We Gotta Get Outta This Place', 'I Saw Her Standing There') mixed with some of Andy's naturally jaunty power poppy songs.

34

Excited by punk music, but unable to be punks, we were much more at home with the dawn of 'new wave'.

Rock Against Racism rallies were being organised nationwide at that time in response to the prominence the NF had gained, partly by linking themselves to punk and ska. One of the organisers of a Rock Against Racism Carnival being planned for Hoglands Park was Paul Blatchford, a.k.a Rancid Disco, notorious for providing bizarrely spaced out and eclectic DJ services to student parties. Chelsea were set to headline the main stage in the park, whilst we landed the 'on the back of the truck' slot that was set to accompany the march through town preceding the gig.

There was a bit of a hoo-ha as we crawled down Above Bar with a couple of local skins jeering and throwing things at the band. It was no big deal, but it was enough to get a good mention and the biggest photo in the Echo's Page 3 report.

For the first gig proper, we ambitiously booked The Solent Suite, the council-owned low-ceilinged bunker decorated with all the pizazz of the lounge on a cross-channel ferry. As a mix of ex-Uni and out of towners, we had had barely any contact with other local bands. We knew the names (Stratejacket and Catch 22 were most prominent) but weren't in any way part of a scene.

Guitarist Dick's replacement Simon Vincent was a first year at Southampton University. Captain Beefheart, early Talking Heads and The Cure were primary influences and he came ready armed with loads of ready-to-play songs full of elliptic literary, political and musical references. He was clearly

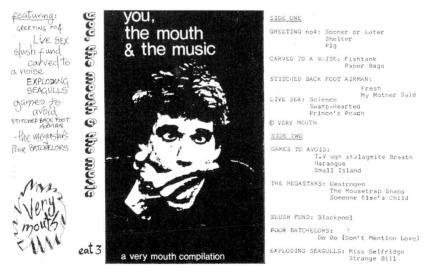

featuring:
GREETING no4
LIVE SEX
slush fund
carved to a noise
EXPLODING SEAGULLS
games to avoid
STITCHED BACK FOOT AIRMAN
the megastars
POOR BATCHELORS

Very mouth

eat 3

you, the mouth & the music

a very mouth compilation

SIDE ONE

GREETING no4: Sooner or Later
                Shelter
                Pig

CARVED TO A NOISE: Fishtank
                    Paper Bags

STITCHED BACK FOOT AIRMAN:
                    Fresh
                    My Mother Said
LIVE SEX: Science
          Swamp-Hearted
          Prince's Peach

© VERY MOUTH

SIDE TWO

GAMES TO AVOID:
            T.V ugh stalagmite Breath
            Harangue
            Small Island

THE MEGASTARS: Oestrogen
            The Mousetrap Snaps
            Someone Else's Child

SLUSH FUND: Blackpool

POOR BATCHELORS: '
            Do Do (Don't Mention Love)

EXPLODING SEAGULLS: Miss Selfridge
                    Strange Bill

superior musically, could sing and was notably cooler and more attractive to women than the other members, so he was in.

Simon's arrival changed the whole emphasis and direction of the band. First to go was the name, quickly exchanged for 'Lip Moves'. It was taken from 'Half Machine Lip Moves', the title of an obscure LP by Chrome. The band's last gasp as an Andy Wallace-led unit was the recording of their first single 'Guest (on the DHSS)', released on their own newly-formed label 'Ticonderoga Records'. The single got a few reviews, mentions, plays and gigs but no great attention. Soon after this, Simon's unarguable claims to be the front man of the band were too much for Andy and he left. As a three-piece, Lip Moves got very tight and at times quite impressively powerful. Dave and Stass were always solid and Simon's guitar skills and effects pedals gave them a range of sounds. I think we were all a bit surprised at just how well it worked and, for the first time, we all felt a little bit cool. We were also pals with the quite extraordinary Exploding Seagulls and the marvellous Bitter Lemmings.

We played a fair bit in Bristol, Bournemouth, Weymouth, Swanage and Dorset, and in Southampton we would play at The Joiners, of course, and up at the University.

Other bands around and friendly were The Point Fives, The V-Necks and the all-girl Mega Stars, some of whom featured on The City Walls compilation album. I became very matey with Catch 22, a connection that paid dividends when they landed the support to The Clash in Portsmouth and Poole on the London Calling tour.

Looking back, what the local scene was short of was energetic and imaginative promoters. Mint held it together through his early days at The Joiners but most gigs were organised and promoted by the bands themselves and few bands from beyond the South Coast played in town. The Stick It In Your Ear guys were fantastic at reviewing and covering local bands and their tapes were a joy, but there was little or no press advertising of local gigs.

Lip Moves gradually evolved through endless nights of druggy jamming in Hollywood. The sound was looser and less frenetic and another name change was necessary. Games to Avoid were born and we tried to get the Very Mouth label off the ground. We were all quite pleased with the Games to Avoid cassette and the compilation 'You, the Mouth and the Music'. It won glowing praise from a very young Andy Kershaw, who was just starting out on Radio Aire in Leeds.

Meanwhile, Andy Wallace was getting busy with his own band 'Laughter in the Garden'. For a while, they were touted locally as 'most likely to', but the perceived hype caused some sneering amongst others on the scene. They suffered from seemingly having to try a little too hard. No matter what he did, Andy could never really look or act like a pop or rock star. His efforts and his clowning could be quite entertaining on stage but something was always missing.

Gradually, another band developed around Simon and his brother Robin. Named after a headline in the Southern Evening Echo after a local air crash, Stitched-Back Foot Airman had a memorable live debut one classic night at The Kingsland Hall. Swapping instruments and lead vocals throughout the gig, SBFA were a revelation and years ahead of their time. It signified the end of the Southampton era for us, as we all gradually migrated to London.

As Stitch, they went on to release a few more singles, before signing to Manchester's In Tape label in the mid eighties. Probably one of their most significant achievements was being the first ever band to appear at the Joiners under the Next Big Thing banner.

After Laughter in the Garden, Andy Wallace moved with his partner and child to Andalucia, where they bought some land and a derelict collection of bricks. Against the odds, they made a go of it and are still there and surviving. Stass emigrated to Barcelona where he married and has had a happy time ever since. Dave Atkin lives in York and manages Phat Planet, an online mail order music service specialising in global music. And I work as an agent in the same musical field."

Sam's off his rockers

THE UNTHINKABLE has happened. The Joiners Arms — once Southampton's premier live venue — is semi-closing its doors on rock.

And it seems some of the blame must be laid at the bands' doors.

Sam Costa, the pub's landlord, said that falling attendances, and bands letting him down, had forced him to turn to the more prosperous evenings of folk, jazz and blues.

"I called a lot of bands asking them to confirm their gigs within 24 hours or they would be called off. Most of them did not call back . . ."

He also laid the blame on the opening up of many smaller venues in the city.

"It could be just a temporary thing," he said, "but it is up to the bands to change their attitude."

The move is a shame, really, because the Joiners is one of the few pubs to give new bands a chance when other pubs might say: "Come back when you are more well-known in Southampton."

In the meantime the Joiners will be keeping to the big names Sam knows can attract audiences.

Daily Echo, 9 / 4 / 81

Making merry at St. Mary's

CHRISTMAS EVE at the Joiners Arms, St. Mary Street, this year will be a raucous affair without doubt, writes Bridget Hamilton.

And if the atmosphere becomes a little blue on occasions, it must be remembered that the panto hosted by landlord Sam Costa and his wife Julie is strictly for adults only.

Stage stars for the evening are musicians from Rox-off, Southampton's popular rhythm and blues band, plus supporters who have twisted the traditional concept of the seasonal show to meet their own devious ideas.

The result is a humorous send-up with a laugh-a-minute script and many naughty-but-nice characters — such as A-Lad-In-Leather and a Widow Twankey with a difference.

The title is unrepeatable, a take-off of Alice in Wonderland, sufficiently bawdy to bear little if any resemblance to the original story but enough to make Alice Liddell turn in her Lyndhurst grave. It would probably be fairer to say that this performance will combine a pick 'n mix jumble of characters from every conceivable plot.

Mrs. Julie Costa wasn't in a position to give away much of the game last week, but she was confident the show would meet the 150-person limitation.

"The boys have had this idea up their collective sleeve for some time now," she said, adding dubiously, "and I'm sure there's some secret I'm not supposed to find out about."

Rox-Off, who usually pack the Joiners Arms, will be playing a pre-panto gig on December 18.

The Joiners also hosts another Christmas party on December 22 when the Southampton Jazz Society celebrate festive cheer with the Mission Hall Jazz Band.

Daily Echo

• LISTINGS 1981 - 1984 •

27 October: Communiqué
28 October: Vertical Motion
29 October: Loaded Dice
31 October: Midnight Rockers
2 November: Air Conditioning
3 November: Convertibles
4 November: New Brendas
5 November: Scratch Band
*This was the start of a
lengthy Thursday residency.*
7 November: Four People I
Have Known
A new name for Zip Code.
9 November: Look Back In
Anger
*A briefly successful Goth
band beloved of Sounds
magazine.*
11 November: Lovers and
Other Strangers
14 November: The Time*
17 November: Communiqué
18 November: Five
19 November: Zena Xerox
23 November: The Press
25 November: IQ
*Previously The Lens, these
prog rockers went on to
become internationally
successful and remain so
today.*
28 November: Games To Avoid
5 December: Dancette
9 December: Look Back In
Anger
10 December: IQ
12 December: New Brendas
17 December: Motifs
19 December: Exploding
Seagulls
23 December: Gestalt

1982
10 February: Laughter In The
Garden

1983
*Yes, we have failed. No amount
of Googling and begging for
info has filled this, the first
Joiners "black hole". Sorry!*

1984
28 September: Two Times
Twice
29 September: First Light
2 October: Spirit Level
3 October: Steppin' Out
*This blues band played
scores of times in the
Eighties.*
4 October: Focus On Sanity
16 October: The Ya-Yas
17 October: Stag Brothers
20 October: The Choice
21 October: Rib Joints
10 November: Strange
Locomotion
14 November: Stepping Out
15 November: The Flagg
Brothers
16 November: Banny Waters
and Al Casey
17 November: Florida
19 November: Vatican Dance
Band
20 November: Focus On Sanity
22 November: The Ya-Yas
9 December: Vanishing Point
11 December: Dave Green's
Fingers
12 December: Micky's Rock
and Soul Band

The Battle of St Mary's Street

Paul Dominy, manager of The Time:

"Big in Bognor! Not the kind of achievement most self-respecting bands would want included in their resumé and something that The Time did their best to keep out of theirs but with which they were nonetheless saddled. As a result of many gigs at the seaside resort's Sussex Hotel, The Time developed quite a substantial following of Bognor music lovers. Unfortunately, a number of these were also football lovers of the genus Hooliganismus and, with Brighton and Portsmouth being almost equidistant, these particular Neanderthals had chosen to adopt the latter as the Promised Land for which they were willing to fight and die.

Over several months, The Time's hardcore Bognor fan-base grew in number to the extent that they could fill a 50-seater coach, and they became sufficiently organized to occasionally arrange one to transport them to a Time gig outside of Bognor. One such excursion was to the Joiner's Arms on 14 November, 1981. So, let me describe the scene.

A coach load of drunks from Bognor Regis have descended on a small Southampton venue. Among this band of travellers are the aforementioned supporters of Portsmouth F.C. (bitter rivals, of course, of Southampton F.C.). Soon after their arrival, our visitors have rapidly begun to diminish the alcohol supply and with it their level of responsibility which, frankly, had started out pretty low anyway.

Nobody can quite remember exactly what sparked events, but my recollection is that the flashpoint occurred before the band started playing. One particular Bognor boot boy was tampering with, and eventually broke, a beer tap fitting. The barman was understandably miffed about this, so he asked the fellow to cease the destruction. The Bognor chap's alcohol-assisted interpretation of this simple request was that it was some kind of personal insult and so an angry verbal exchange ensued, resulting in him being asked to leave the premises and then being assisted in doing so. He saw this as an invitation to hurl obscene insults at the 'Scummers' (the delightful nickname with which Portsmouth supporters refer to their south coast neighbours) inside and then outside the pub and also to hurl any object he could find to begin the destruction of his surroundings.

I don't think anyone in the band room really noticed anything was happening until the males with shaved heads and connected eyebrows began disappearing as word reached them from the frontline that hostilities had commenced. Very soon the cacophony of a riot could be heard. As luck would have it, as the Sussex Freedom Fighters arrived in the street, the people already there included a number of Southampton F.C. faithful, who were not averse to an unsporting engagement with a bunch of Pompey supporters. As both groups gleefully joined the fracas, in a very short time it morphed into a football related conflict and so the Battle of St Mary's Street began.

As was our modus operandi in such situations, the band members, roadie and I armed ourselves with mic stands and prepared to repel attackers. I ventured briefly out to the street to witness two angry groups facing off and indulging in an occasional scuffle. However, I quickly withdrew as the situation escalated into a mixture of hand-to-hand combat and the launching of improvised projectiles along the street. Periodically popping my head out of the side door to look down the alley to the street, I remember watching volleys of bottles, rocks and various other items flying through the air as combatants ran at each other with feet and fists flailing.

I don't know how long it went on (it seemed like a long time), but eventually the forces of law and order arrived to quell the uprising, but not before the pub had suffered some damage, the street was strewn with debris and The Time's reputation at The Joiners was in tatters. I actually don't remember if the gig finished but I don't think the band ever played at The Joiners again. Not surprising, really.

The Time, with Kevin Eldon on vocals.

• LISTINGS 1984 - 1985 •

15 December: Strange Locomotion
20 December: Idid Idid
24 December: Blood Sisters
26 December: Slagg Brothers
27 December: The Press
28 December: Mickey's Rock and Soul Band
31 December: Grown Up Wrong

1985

During 1985, the jazz sessions at the Joiners expanded to three nights a week.

2 January: Artistic Egg
3 January: Stepping Out
4 January: Kipper Family
5 January: Roxoff
9 January: The Ya Yas
10 January: Aquila
12 January: Vatican Dance Band
13 January: Vanishing Point
17 January: Crimes of Passion
19 January: Stepping Out
20 January: Vanishing Point
24 January: Abandon City
26 January: Micky's Rock and Soul Band
27 January: Laughter In The Garden
Andy Wallace, from Lip Moves and the New Brendas (not the Nirvana producer) fronted this commercial indie band.
28 January: Stepping Out
31 January: Crimes of Passion
2 February: Roxoff

3 February: Vanishing Point
4 February: Act of God
6 February: Colony Earth
7 February: Laughter In The Garden
9 February: Rufus Stone
16 February: Touch
19 February: The Feds
21 February: Aquila
22 February: Birds Of A Feather
23 February: The Choice
27 February: Vatican Dance Band
28 February: Rufus Stone
2 March: Roxoff
3 March: Vanishing Point
7 March: Abandon City
9 March: Stepping Out
14 March: Recluse
16 March: Rufus Stone
18 March: That Certain Feeling
21 March: Slagg Brothers
30 March: The Choice
23 March: Touch
30 March: The Choice
4 April: Stepping Out
6 April: Aquila
7 April: Nomad
11 April: I Am Seven
This Winchester band featured Richard Williams, later of Trip.
13 April: Abandon City
20 April: Recluse
25 April: Blues Busters
27 April: Roxoff
28 April: Paragon
2 May: The Quiltz
5 May: Timepeace
7 May: Dumb Waiters
8 May: Lip Service

• LISTINGS 1985 •

9 May: Idid Idid
11 May: Doris and the Dots
12 May: Timepeace
14 May: Vatican Dance Band
15 May: Hearts and Minds
16 May: Recluse
22 May: Cement Garden
23 May: Big Chief
29 May: Watch That Man
30 May: I Am Seven
1 June: Seeing Red
5 June: Big Chief
6 June: The Choice
8 June: TV Slaves
12 June: Idid Idid
13 June: Owl Service
15 June: Aquila
20 June: Abandon City
27 June: Wolfsbane
28 June: Micky's Rock and Soul
  Band
29 June: Doris and the Dots
30 June: That Certain Feeling
1 July: I Am Seven
3 July: Lip Service
4 July: Slagg Brothers
5 July: Rufus Stone
6 July: The Press
8 July: Rhythm Method
10 July: Vatican Dance Band
11 July: JAB
12 July: Abandon City
13 July: CIA
16 July: Up Balloon Up
  *First appearance of Pete
  Harvey, also later of Trip.*
18 July: Against The Wall
20 July: Aquila
21 July: Boss

24 July: Flik Spatula
  *One of Southampton's best
  ever post-punk bands.*
25 July: B4
26 July: Doris and the Dots
27 July: Big Brother
31 July: Up Balloon Up
1 August: Cement Garden
2 August: Rufus Stone
3 August: The Choice
7 August: The Citizens
8 August: JAB
9 August: Abandon City
14 August: Crimes Of Passion
15 August: Slagg Brothers
16 August: Rufus Stone
21 August: Cement Garden
22 August: Suburbia
23 August: The Choice
24 August: Aquila
28 August: Blood Wedding
29 August: Jinks
31 August: Doris and the Dots
4 September: Slagg Brothers
5 September: Sentinel
8 September: Hearts and
  Minds
12 September: Big Bear Little
  Bear
14 September: Abandon City
18 September: I Am Seven
19 September: Up Balloon Up
21 September: Partners In
  Crime
22 September: Timepeace
25 September: Ipso Facto
26 September: The Dilberrys
28 September: Playhouse
30 September: Cement Garden
2 October: Camrada
6 October: Paragon

Folk at the Joiners

Brian Hooper: "The Fo'c'sle Folk Club first moved to the Joiners in 1975, at a time when the pub wasn't in regular use as a music venue. The back room was an awkward L-shape, with a long bar that didn't quite divide the room in two. There was a tiny stage, about a foot high (much higher and you'd be touching the false ceiling), in the far right corner as you went in – but if you wanted it somewhere else, you could move it easily enough, because there was no sound system or stage lighting at all. It was a pretty basic pub room, but it worked for the Fo'c'sle. There was a bit of a noise problem, because people near the door couldn't hear the music properly and tended to chatter, to the annoyance of people in the main bit of the room trying to listen to the music – often a single unaccompanied voice. At some time a partition wall was put in, which helpfully reduced the noise problem but unhelpfully also cut the audience capacity.

For the next six years, we routinely packed the place out every Friday, and the guest list included virtually anyone who was anyone on the folk scene at the time. The legendary Nic Jones, arguably the finest English-style guitar player ever, was one of our first guests, on 3 October 1975, returning several times over the years. Later that season (the Fo'c'sle season runs from September to June/July) Shirley Collins, a pivotal figure in folk music for the past 40 years, graced us with her extraordinarily pure, unaffected voice. She, too, was to return many times. Highlight of the 1976/77 season was a visit by two giants of the folk scene, Ewan McColl and Peggy Seeger. Ewan almost single-handedly masterminded the British folk revival of the early 1960s, gave the world his daughter Kirsty, gave Roberta Flack a big hit with his song 'The First Time Ever I Saw Your Face', and often gave folk club organisers a hard time and audiences a great time. Peggy, sister of the godfather of American folk music Pete Seeger, was steeped in traditional music from an early age and between them they communicated a huge repertoire and a quiet passion for the music that was just awesome. On another visit to the Joiners, in December 1988, they broke new ground by insisting there be no smoking – up to then there had been many a time you could hardly see across the room for the smoke.

Other highlights included Scottish star Dick Gaughan (4 November 1977), Martin Carthy (13 October 1978), the last working shantyman on British ships, and author of the definitive "Shanties From The Seven Seas", Stan

Hugill (29 February 1980), and several visits by superb Irish ballad singer Sean Cannon before he was recruited by the Dubliners to replace Ronnie Drew.

The club left the Joiners in 1981 after some now long-forgotten tension with the landlord, but in 1984 new landlord Mike Gulliver invited us back and we stayed for eight very successful years. The big names kept on appearing, such as Cyril Tawney (composer of 'Sally Free And Easy' among many other fine nautical songs), and wonderful singers such as Devon's Tony Rose and Sussex-born Martyn Wyndham-Read. On 22 November 1985, the father of British folk-rock, Ashley Hutchings, founder of both Fairport Convention and Steeleye Span among other bands, appeared in a one-man show about the great Victorian folk-song collector Cecil Sharp, coming on stage in costume and pushing a bicycle. Folk-rockers The Oyster Band helped the club celebrate its 23rd birthday on 9 May 1986, and the quirky Jake Thackray made the first of several Fo'c'sle appearances later that year – on Hallowe'en, to be precise.

1988 was the club's Silver Jubilee year and a whole host of big names came to the Joiners – mind-boggling guitarist Martin Simpson, Sussex's legendary Copper Family, the 'young tin whistle pest' Vin Garbutt, squeezebox supremo John Kirkpatrick, Martin Carthy again, luminaries of north-eastern traditional music Alastair Anderson and Kathryn Tickell, songwriter Leon Rosselson, guitarist John Renbourn, and the aforementioned smoke-free McColl and Seeger, among a wealth of lesser-known stars.

Folk music folk are a relatively conservative lot (not politically, though!) and with the front bar populated by 80s glammies, Goths, New Romantics and others, the visual clash of cultures was always entertaining. Some of the drunks who rolled in were entertaining too, and I occasionally had to switch from being MC to being bouncer, escorting people off the premises. My favourite drunk was the one who asked the price of 'Folk On Tap', the regional music magazine, which was then 50p, but he only had a pound so he bought two copies.

In the cold months at the start of 1992, alterations began to the back room. The suspended ceiling came out, doubling the height of the room, a high stage went in and took up what seemed like half the floor area, and the place no longer had the intimacy that folk music needs. So the Fo'c'sle moved again, to a fairly disastrous venue that nearly killed the club. At the time of writing, over fourteen years later, it's still going strong at the Duke Of Wellington, but those of us who remember the Joiners years do so with great affection."

• LISTINGS 1985 - 1986 •

9 October: Cement Garden
10 October: Grown Up Wrong
12 October: The Choice
15 October: Blue Murder
17 October: The Act
30 October: Panama
31 October: Carte Blanche
2 November: The Choice
6 November: Kuba
7 November: TV By Tears
13 November: Inner Vision
14 November: Peter Pod and
the Peas
16 November: Kuba
21 November: Slagg Bros
22 November: Ashley
Hutchings
23 November: Don't Feed The
Animals
24 November: Timepeace
27 November: Grown Up
Wrong
28 November: The Bushmen
4 December: Suburbia
7 December: Duballup
9 December: Vatican Dance
Band
12 December: Blazers
14 December: The Choice
18 December: Blue Murder
19 December: Big Brother
21 December: Doris and the
Dots
22 December: Timepeace
24 December: Blood Sisters
26 December: Slagg Brothers
27 December: The Press
28 December: Micky's Rock
and Soul Band
31 December: Grown Up
Wrong

1986

Throughout 1986 and 1987, Monday nights featured Big Band music. Bob Pearce and his Blues Band appeared every Sunday.

2 January: Artistic Egg
3 January: Upmarket
4 January: Rufus Stone
8 January: Freedom
Foundation
9 January: Long At The Fair
11 January: Duballup
14 January: Kafka Hag
16 January: Roadrunner
23 January: Bazooka Joe
25 January: The Choice
30 January: The Act
31 January: Pig's Ear
1 January: Duballup
5 February: Haze
7 February: Blades
8 February: Rufus Stone
11 February: Forget The Rest
12 February: The Farkle Family
13 February: Roadrunner
15 February: Doris and the
Dots
19 February: Attica
20 February: Mad Thatchers
21 February: Kipper Family
22 February: Kuba
24 February: Ulterior Motive
27 February: A Motion Industry
1 March: The Choice
4 March: Vatican
5 March: Slagg Bros
7 March: Cairo
8 March: John Kirkpatrick
9 March: Rufus Stone

• LISTINGS 1986 •

12 March: Doris and the Dots
13 March: Causeway
15 March: Make Like A Train
18 March: Angel Park
19 March: Big Bear, Little Bear
21 March: Duballup
24 March: Resound
27 March: Slagg Bros
28 March: Kuba
20 March: Doris and the Dots
1 April: Celeste
2 April: Grown Up Wrong
3 April: Haze
5 April: The Choice
12 April: White Lies
15 April: Don't Ask
16 April: Big Bear Little Bear
17 April: Backline Blues Band
23 April: Grown Up Wrong
24 April: Slagg Bros
26 April: Kuba
30 April: Suburbia
1 May: Cement Garden
2 May: Oyster Band
3 May: Doris and the Dots
6 May: Stan Tracey Quartet
8 May: Convertibles
10 May: Attica
14 May: Grown Up Wrong
17 May: The Choice
24 May: Kuba
27 May: Sneak Preview
31 May: Big Brother
4 June: Sneak Preview
5 June: John Otway
The Great Man appeared at least ten times at the Joiners.
7 June: Rufus Stone
11 June: Obsession
12 June: The Convertibles
14 June: The Choice

19 June: Grown Up Wrong
20 June: Blitz
21 June: Kuba
24 June: The Cherry Orchard
25 June: Haze
27 June: Big Brother
28 June: Partners In Crime
2 July: The Myth
5 July: Duballup
8 July: Malvinas Bros
11 July: White Lies
12 July: Rufus Stone
15 July: Radical Dance
23 July: The Act
24 July: Blood Wedding
25 July: Purely Medicinal
29 July: Timepeace
30 July: Riff Raff
31 July: The Jinks
2 August: The Choice
6 August: Overdrive
8 August: Bold Over
9 August: Duballup
12 August: Egg On Legs
16 August: Big Brother
21 August: Vox Humana
22 August: White Lies
23 August: Partners In Crime
27 August: Panacea
29 August: Kuba
30 August: Partners In Crime
3 September: Overdrive
4 September: John Otway
6 September: Rufus Stone
11 September: Carey Bell
17 September: Union
20 September: Duballup
24 September: The Caravans
25 September: Don't Ask
27 September: Kuba
1 October: Haze

47

IF YOU are an up-and-coming band in Southampton looking for your first live gig, the man to turn to is Mike Gulliver, landlord of the Joiners Arms for the past 18 months.

Mike has become an expert at booking bands and likes to give new groups a chance to play live.

"I ask for a tape but I also pay attention to their reputation as well," said Mike. "If a new band comes along I'll give them a go."

As well as the regular Fos'c'le folk club every week and jazz society gigs there are big multi-band events.

One of the most recent was the Doris and the Dots reunion gig, when all the musicians who had played with the band got together.

Before Mike took over the pub in St. Mary Street, he worked for P&O for 12 years. "My wife Jan and myself decided we would love to own our own pub so when this one came along we snapped at the idea."

Mike always has a smile for his customers but he won't stand any rowdiness or nonsense, and he believes the key to his success is treating everyone as an equal.

"You just have to treat everyone the same, customers, bands, staff. I like to keep an informal atmosphere without trouble."

Daily Echo,
4 /1 /86

• LISTINGS 1986 - 1987 •

4 October: The Choice
6 October: Future
7 October: Tridecema
8 October: Leap In The Dark
10 October: The Morrigan
11 October: Partners In Crime
16 October: A Motion Industry
22 October: Gloria Thing
23 October: Bang
27 October: Carl Sonny Leyland
31 October: Jake Thackray
1 November: Doris and the Dots
5 November: Blood Wedding
6 November: Timepeace
11 November: Egg On Legs
13 November: The Caravans
15 November: The Choice
18 November: Wild Willy Barrett
22 November: Rufus Stone
27 November: Blitz
29 November: New St George
1 December: Flick
4 December: Angel Park
6 December: Partners In Crime
13 December: The Choice
17 December: Haze
18 December: Blue Notes
19 December: Whippersnapper
20 December: Rufus Stone
23 December: Purely Medicinal
27 December: Doris and the Dots
31 December: The Choice

1987

This was a very settled period for the Joiners, with a selection of about a dozen acts filling nearly all the slots. These ranged from reggae (Doris and the Dots) through soul (Rufus Stone) and of course blues (the ubiquitous Bob Pearce). On Mondays there were Big Band sessions, Tuesdays were jazz and the Foc's'le folk club met every Friday, both of the latter often featuring big names in their field. Although it was arguably an unexciting period, it was at least providing regular work for local bands, not unlike it does today.

1 January: Colony Earth
3 January: Duballup
7 January: Eddie Kirkland
  First of a US blues series.
8 January: Wildheart
10 January: Rufus Stone
13 January: Tohu Bohu
15 January: First Men In Space
17 January: White Lies
22 January: Mad Thatchers
23 January: Kipper Family
24 January: The Choice
27 January: Purely Medicinal
28 January: Flik Spatula
4 February: Gloria Thing
5 February: Total Joe
6 February: Kathryn Tickell
7 February: Wildheart
10 February: Time Crisis
11 February: So What
12 February: Enigma
14 February: Rufus Stone

Blues at the Joiners

Another false piece of Joiners folklore is that it wasn't until the Next Big Thing era that the Joiners functioned as a "Little venue for big names". In fact, some great and renowned US blues artists played at the Joiners in the Eighties, largely thanks to Southampton's most famous blues practitioner, Bob Pearce.

Bob Pearce: "Blues nights at the Joiners started in late 1985. They were generally on a Sunday night, because that's when I had a residency there (two years – kind of a break between the 18 year Onslow residency!). The late Mike Gulliver was landlord at the time and was all for bringing in the U.S blues guys – subject to price of course – so we promoted Eddie Kirkland, Carey Bell, Louisiana Red and Phil Guy. All but the Eddie Kirkland date were sell-outs. I think because Eddie was known to only the die-hard blues fans, a few 'casual' punters gave it a miss – a shame, it was a blinding gig! It was the first date of his first ever U.K. tour.

One memory I have of the Joiners was the back room carpet – if you stood in one place too long, you'd stick to it and find it difficult to move! I used to finish most shows with a Chuck Berry song (or one that was written by me, but sounded like a Chuck Berry song). At the end of one of the regular weekly gigs at the Joiners, we'd gotten into the number, the band was cooking, it was time for the guitarist (Andy Graham) to play the solo and time for me to get onto the bar and do the famous Chuck Berry duck-walk along it. Waiting at the other end with an incentive for me (a double bourbon) was landlord Mike Gulliver. However, on this occasion, I'd decided to jump down into the serving area and take the drink earlier than planned – plus, I thought it would look quite spectacular, you know, leaping into the air over the bar staff as they ducked out of the way of me and my guitar! It was spectacular all right – I landed on a floor which was covered in beer spillage – my feet just slid away in front of me and I landed on my back. It hurt bad too, but hey, you're a 'pro', you gotta keep smiling and complete the gig, so, up on my feet, I downed the drink in one, made my way back to the mic and finished the song. But I never did jump down off a bar after that."

Prior to Bob Pearce's "Blue Sunday" jams, there had been regular Sunday blues jam sessions in the late Seventies and early Eighties, run by Keith Emery.

Keith Emery: "People would turn up with their instruments and I put them on where I could. Some nights you would have six bass players, eight guitar players and four drummers. My job was to group these people together so that each player had about three or four numbers. So, for example, you would get four people jamming three numbers, then we would swap a bass player or drummer but leave the main guitarist. This format allowed novices to play with semi-pros and thus it was a good learning curve. Many a student cut his or her teeth at these jams and then went on to form groups.

The problem with all those evenings was that after a while, the number of musicians who turned up exceeded the time allocation, so some people didn't get to play, were offended and therefore didn't come back. I can remember one night when we had loads of bassists and drummers but no guitarist."

51

Blue Sunday

Andy Graham: "I joined the Bob Pearce Blues Band in 1985, almost simultaneously with Bob's residency moving from the Onslow to the Joiners. We went from a packed standing room only bar that was The Onslow to a more 'jazz-like' atmosphere at the Joiners, with tables and chairs. Bob appeared to be going through a transition and wanted a less raunchy and quieter sound. This caused a bit of friction within the band. Bob would often sit down to play and this was not popular with many of the punters or Mike Gulliver, the landlord, who on at least one occasion hid the chair. I think Bob found another one though!

Matters came to a head after a gig elsewhere. A discussion about Bob's approach had taken place and when it was down to just Bob and bassist Pete Plascott, Pete said that he was unhappy with Bob's laid-back playing, and that furthermore, the rest of the band thought likewise. Bob replied that if that was the way everyone felt, then he would sack us all. When Pete picked me up for the following night's gig at the Joiners, he said something like 'I got us all sacked last night and this is our last gig!' We assumed that Bob would continue at The Joiners with a new band but instead, Mike Gulliver asked us if we could carry on.

As no one in the band could sing, the idea was that we would ask four different people to front the band. We chose Carl Sonny Leyland, Bob Still, John Wands and Pete Harris. It was an incredible amount of fun and brought so much variety to our performances. So we decided to continue on this basis. Mike Gulliver came up with the name 'Blue Sunday', simply because we were a blues outfit playing on a Sunday. Other artists that fronted the band were Arnie Cottrell, Mo Thomas, Bob Pearce (friendships remained intact), Sonny Black (Bill Boazman), Mick Williams, Rick Webb, Papa John Livermore and Bruce Roberts.

Blue Sunday started in Spring 1988 and lasted until early 1990. Paid musicians were part of the scene but people were regularly invited from the audience to sit in, often respected local musicians but sometimes merchant seamen stopping in Southampton or punters who felt bold and ready enough to give it a try. Each week, there was a raffle with some really naff prizes, i.e. the cheapest plonk or chocolates we could lay our hands on. We used to charge about £1 on the door and get between 80 and 150 people in each week. There was some wheeling and dealing going on between our soundman Harry Frith and Mike Gulliver's replacement and we all took home a standard fee of £20. At the end of the year, Harry would present the year's figures. He would then share out the surplus, which I think was about £200 each."

• LISTINGS 1987 •

18 February: John Otway
19 February: Egg On Legs
23 February: Fat City
24 February: Black October
25 February: Geno Washington
*The soul giant evidently
loved the Joiners, as he
returned several times.*
28 February: White Lies
4 March: Egg on Legs
5 March: Sole Survivor
7 March: The Choice
10 March: Refugee
18 March: Zeebra
19 March: Assassin
24 March: Purely Medicinal
25 March: Haze
26 March: Flik Spatula
28 March: Duballup
2 April: Bedlam Boys
4 April: Rufus Stone
7 April: The Jinks
8 April: Johnny Panic
11 April: Grown Up wrong
15 April: Zeebra
16 April: First Men In Space
18 April: The Choice
21 April: Timepeace
22 April: Nightmare
23 April: Dirt Road Blues Band
25 April: Sole Survivor
28 April: Up Balloon Up
29 April: Louisiana Red
30 April: Hair 200
4 May: Gloria Thing
5 May: Jinks
6 May: Colony Earth
7 May: Geno Washington
8 May: Strawhead
9 May: Flik Spatula
13 May: Galahad

14 May: Paragon
16 May: Rufus Stone
18 May: Zeitgeist
19 May: Cement Garden
20 May: Egg On Legs
23 May: White Lies
27 May: Haze
28 May: Colony Earth
30 May: The Choice
1 June: Flik Spatula
2 June: Jinks
4 June: Zeebra
10 June: Radical Dance
11 June: Refugee
17 June: Colony Earth
18 June: Leap In The Dark
19 June: Jadis
*This popular prog rock band
returned frequently. They
still exist today.*
20 June: Duballup
24 June: Drive
25 June: Dirt Road Blues Band
26 June: Wildheart
27 June: Sole Survivor
1 July: Fester and the Vomits
2 July: Progression
3 July: The Choice
8 July: Timepeace
10 July: Galahad
11 July: White Lies
13 July: Malvinas Bros
14 July: Mike Carr / Jim Mullen
15 July: First Men In Space
17 July: Zeebra
18 July: Rufus Stone
20 July: Assassin
22 July: Cement Garden
23 July: The Morrigan
24 July: Doris and the Dots

• LISTINGS 1987 •

27 July: Mild-Mannered
Janitors
*A Byrds-like underground
band from the Portsmouth
area.*
29 July: Nightmare
30 July: Progression
31 July: Fat City
 1 August: Duballup
 5 August: Fester
10 August: Skin Deep
12 August: Timepeace
13 August: First Men In Space
15 August: The Convertibles
19 August: Nightmare
20 August: 4 Play
21 August: Progression
22 August: White Lies
25 August: Space Craft 2
26 August: Zeebra
28 August: Jinks
29 August: Rufus Stone
 1 September: Henry Lowther
 3 September: Sole Survivor
10 September: Colony Earth
12 September: Jadis
16 September: The Key
17 September: Hybrid
19 September: Doris and the
Dots
30 September: Gloria Thing
 1 October: Zeebra
 3 October: Hybrid
 8 October: Phil Guy
10 October: Refugee
15 October: Blues Bunch
19 October: Trademark
20 October: Powerhouse
21 October: Haze
24 October: Rufus Stone

27 October: Oyster Band
29 October: Armageddon
31 October: Doris and the Dots
 2 November: Stitched-Back
Foot Airman
*This was the first appearance
by an early version of Stitch,
a significant band for the
Joiners later on. The next
day's band was yet another
one to feature Andy Wallace.*
 4 November: McCallisters
 7 November: Duballup
11 November: Drive
12 November: Colony Earth
14 November: Bedlam Boys
16 November: Trademark
18 November: Salad From
Atlantis
19 November: Tennessee no 7
21 November: Rufus Stone
24 November: The Morrigan
25 November: Skin Deep
26 November: Green Blues
Band
 2 December: Sonny Black
 3 December: Hybrid
 5 December: Duballup
10 December: John Otway
12 December: White Lies
14 December: Malvinas Bros
16 December: Haze
19 December: Rufus Stone
22 December: Skin Deep
23 December: Who's In The
Kitchen
23 December: First Men In
Space
31 December: Rufus Stone

NBT – The Next Big Thing

The 26th of January 1988 was a day of enormous significance for the Joiners, although on a cold and dingy Tuesday, not many people were probably aware of it. A quiet, diffident but enormously gifted promoter called David Burston (known even then simply as "Mint") had moved down from Birmingham, where he was already experienced in promoting shows at venues such as The Fighting Cocks in Moseley, a pub remarkably similar in size, character and outlook to the Joiners. Mint decided that his mission in life was to bring good music to Southampton, and that the Joiners was the place to do it. Christening his shows, with remarkable perspicacity, as "Next Big Thing", Mint was to spend fifteen years finding bands to play at the Joiners, just as they were on the cusp of the big time. It transformed the image and ambitions of the venue and made it a "cool" place to go. Mint is the reason why, from now on, you'll find listings that make you gasp, "Surely THEY didn't play there!"

Mint would later become a co-licensee of the Joiners and usher in one of its most fruitful eras, but for the time being, he had to fit in with the pattern of certain types of music being restricted to specific nights. The NBT night was designated as alternate Tuesdays, although occasionally we find other evenings being usurped, as the NBT shows became more and more popular. It would be many years, however, before the Joiners became simply a "rock venue".

One myth which can be dispelled is the notion that everyone who played a NBT show was destined for stardom. Most of the names have been forgotten over the years; however, the quality never wavered, and Mint's good taste and antennae for great bands never erred. Many of those who never became the Next Big Thing certainly deserved to. Similarly, many bands' reigns as "Big" didn't last much beyond a couple of albums and a NME front page (Birdland, Fabulous, Adorable, Kingmaker, etc., etc.) This still applies today, with many of the currently cool bands being destined for obscurity before too long.

Mint himself could be described as "owlish", or, as Ged Babey affectionately preferred, a pixie. Skinny, pale and bespectacled, he speaks so quietly, while blinking in a mildly startled way, that you have to strain to hear him. His only vice is the occasional "Mint Special", which is a Bushmills with lemonade, and I've never seen him be rude or short with anybody. His hair has ranged in the past from spectacular dreadlocks, through a brilliant waist-length pigtail, to the current feather cut, all of them carried with complete aplomb. You'll seldom see him wearing anything other than black combat or leather trousers with a long-sleeved sweatshirt tucked into them. As regards his ability to book the right bands at the right moment, I've used the word "genius" to describe him before, and I'm happy to do so again.

Mint: "At the Fighting Cocks in Birmingham, I arranged on average two or three gigs a week for three and a half years. The most famous show was The Smiths, who played to sixty people. It was a non-profit thing, as I was unemployed. When it fell apart, I started putting on gigs myself, about a dozen shows, while I was living in a tumbledown farmhouse. When I had to leave there, I chose Southampton, because I had had friends there since 1977. They had told me there wasn't much going on, so I thought I'd look into it. I arrived in August 1987 and the first gig was in early 1988. I worked with Phil Nelson, who managed The Levellers and had a label called Hag. Fran Beckerling from Hag was involved as well. Roger Francis was part of the set-up too, he was the singer of First Men In Space. I was the one who thought of the Next Big Thing name. It was meant ironically at first, but it turned out to be true.

I had some contacts when I got to Southampton and Phil Nelson's influence was very helpful. Through him I met Charlie Myatt, who over the years has had Manic Street Preachers, Supergrass, Skunk Anansie and others. Once you get the confidence of an agent, things get easier. I'd literally just ring

people or approach them. One person I approached and asked if he wanted a gig was Kurt Cobain, when Nirvana were third on the bill at Portsmouth Poly. Unfortunately, it never happened, although lots of people think it did.

The Joiners was already a proper music venue. We approached the landlord Mike Gulliver, who was a bit wary at first, but offered us every second Tuesday. At this stage, we were hiring in the PA from Arc Electronics in Portswood for each gig. We couldn't get into the pub until opening time at 7 o'clock, which gave us an hour to set up before the doors opened at 8. We used the back room, people walked through the pub and paid to get into the music room. There was never any security, just me and my felt-tip pen!

Right from the start, I did all the bookings. From 1988 to 1993, NBT was effectively me, until I teamed up with Dave Misselbrook, a guy named Ian Mackenzie and Woody, and together we formed a company called Darklead. By that time, I had my own PA and an office in the Joiners, and I realized we had a business which could no longer be run on the back of an envelope.

Between Mike and Dave there were several other landlords, including Tony Eccles, who was in Doris and the Dots. I'd known Dave Misselbrook for years, as he was a regular at the shows and we had a mutual interest in music. Initially, we were still hiring the room. The idea actually was to get a bigger venue, a venture that got quite a long way. Then Eldridge Pope approached me and asked if I was interested in hiring the building. All the previous landlords had been employed by the brewery. I consulted Dave and we agreed to give it a go as joint licensees. We went on a week-long training course and just got thrown in. Neither of us had any background in the licensed trade. We took over in March 1995.

We naively thought that with the gigs and the bar, we'd make a profit, but the terms were so bad that we always ran at a loss, with short-term leases. We probably turned over half a million in the first two years, but it all went straight out again. I had to pull out because I was living on the premises and putting on gigs six nights a week and it was just exhausting. If the gigs hit a bad patch, I'd find myself thousands of pounds in debt. At that stage, Dave took over as sole licensee.

In the meantime, I'd met Ian Binnington and we'd started co-promoting shows. He knew the nu-metal scene, with which I wasn't familiar, and gradually his influence expanded, but the PA was in such a state that eventually Ian and Dave fell out over it, and I became quite seriously ill and had to wait 18 months for an operation. Dave tried to carry on promoting shows but he didn't have the industry contacts I had built up, although his weekend dance nights were always successful. After Dave left, a lady called Alison Pennicott took over for a brief period, but the bar take dwindled and Eldridge Pope brought in Fred Eynon, who also ran the Railway in Winchester. Eventually, when I recovered from the operation, I started putting on gigs again, but now just as Ian's assistant and without the responsibility.

I have many memories, although the shows were probably more memorable to the people who came to them than to me. They're pretty much a blur now! Primal Scream were getting to be a big band by the time we put them on in and were big enough to demand a rider. Friends of mine had a vegetarian restaurant and produced a lovely spread for them. Primal Scream took one look at it and demanded to go to Macdonalds, so I gave them a fiver each and off they went.

The Manics did definitely sign a contract of some kind in the cellar, but I don't know what sort of contract. That was some evening. They all arrived separately. The drummer and bassist were difficult to deal with but the other two were fine. That was the night when several record company Rolls Royces were parked outside in St Mary Street!

The Cranberries arrived and set up. The manager and Dolores the singer had been arguing and he had gone off in a huff. When he came back, he announced that the PA wasn't good enough. I said, 'It sounds fine, don't worry'. He said, 'But what if someone fom the NME turns up? We're not playing!' So all I could do was shrug my shoulders and the show went ahead with just the support bands.

The highlights for me over the years may not be what people would expect. One of the earliest shows we did was a big risk on a German band called FSK, who were fantastic fun. Giant Sand were wonderful, Howe Gelb spent most of the night playing the battered old upright piano. The Charlatans I booked from a demo, and by the time they played, it was mental. We didn't do advance tickets and half the audience had followed them from up north. Allegedly, our show was the first one they'd actually been paid for, and they went off and bought themselves a curry.

Oasis was another crazy, packed night. Noel and Liam turned up after the rest of the band. Before the show, Liam was mouthing off to my assistant Anya about Oasis being bigger than the Beatles. When she raised her eyebrows, he tried to pick a fight with her! The bassist said, 'Take no notice of him, he's a twat!'

For a while, I persuaded the brewery to give me fifty quid a week to put on free gigs on Mondays. Sleeper did it and were great, but One Dove refused to play when they discovered it was free, it was beneath their dignity. The next time Dot Allison came back, she was working with Pete Doherty!

I was also able to indulge myself by putting on artists who certainly weren't Next Big Things, but who meant a great deal to me. Examples are Daevid Allen, Arthur Brown, Kevin Ayres, Kevin Coyne, David Thomas and Jimmy Carl Black. Kevin Coyne almost walked off when the stool he was sitting on collapsed underneath him, leaving him spreadeagled on the floor. We also started Techno dance nights on Saturdays. It was a scene which wasn't being catered for in Southampton, and the nights were always packed and the atmosphere was always great.

NEXT BIG THING has organised a charity gig with a difference next Tuesday night at the Joiners to raise cash to help Aids research and sufferers.

The cream of local talent will be appearing to pay homage to Sweden's classic pop band Abba.

Ranging from folk bands to jazz, rock and cajun each artist will deliver their distinctive version of one of the Swedish quartet's classic top tunes.

Those who are set to give their unique rendering include Flik Spatula, Blue Oranges, Watkins Ale, the Malvinas Brothers and the Flatville Aces.

Doors open at 8pm and it costs just £1.50 to hear this magnificent concoction of pop memories.

I bet Bjorn and Benny never thought it would come to this when they first wowed the world with Waterloo on the Eurovision Song Contest.

Daily Echo. This was the first in a series of SCUM charity gigs.

My knack of booking bands at the vital moment is often praised, but it's only a knack. For every Manic Street Preachers there have been several Sofaheads. My criterion was always whether something was innovative, whether it was Oasis or Terminal Cheesecake! You keep your ear to the ground, listen to customers and agents and keep your eye on the press.

The charm of the Joiners lies in keeping the balance between professional and up-and-coming bands, and keeping it as friendly and informal as possible. The band having to walk through the audience is part of it, there's no 'them and us'. My motivation was to give the bands an opportunity and for the audience to have a good time too. That's what gives me the buzz. That was part of the reason for stopping, because it would be no fun to put on a band you don't like, just in order to make money.

When people ask me to sum up the secret of the Joiners, I say the fabric of the place is held together by sweat, nicotine, alcohol and the spirit of rock and roll."

A New Year boost for sounds with a difference

SOUTHAMPTON gig-goers and local bands will be given a New Year boost with the news that the Joiners Arms is to start a regular gig night for alternative groups.

The night will help to fill a huge void in the city for venues which cater for bands who play less commercial music.

It is to start on January 12 and will be called The Next Big Thing.

The NBT is to be run by three promoters — Fran Beckerleg (HAG Records' Southampton representative) in partnership with Rodger Francis (singer with First Men in Space and Dave Burston). Dave recently moved to the city after involvement in promoting gigs in the Midlands.

Pub manager Mike Gulliver is keen to promote a diverse range of musical styles at his St Mary Street pub.

The promoters aim to bring in well-known bands from outside the city. They will be supported by local groups.

Alternative Tuesdays have been set aside for the promoters to put on whatever bands they like.

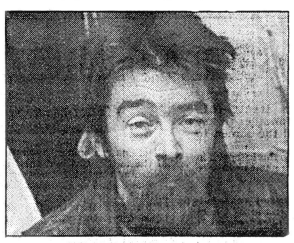

HELPING ALTERNATIVE GROUPS: Dave Burston

Daily Echo, 12 / 12 / 87

1988

^8 January: Martin Simpson
^9 January: White Lies
12 January: Bedlam Boys
16 January: Backline Blues Band
21 January: Wild Willy Barrett
22 January: The Copper Family
23 January: Duballup
26 January: Stitched-Back Foot Airman (NBT)*
29 January: Vin Garbutt
^4 February: Red Jasper
^5 February: Orion
^6 February: Duballup
^9 February: Blurt (NBT)
10 February: Carey Bell
13 February: Doris and the Dots
20 February: Backline Blues Band
23 February: Flik Spatula (NBT)
26 February: John Kirkpatrick
3 March: Malvinas Bros
6 March: Duballup
7 March: Enigma
8 March: Twelve 88 Cartel (NBT)
This was significant, because this band was on the Bite Back label, run by Ian Binnington, later to be a very important Joiners promoter.
11 March: Martin Carthy
12 March: Scum (NBT)
17 March: John Otway
19 March: White Lies
22 March: The Shrubs (NBT)
24 March: Bedlam Blues Band
26 March: Rufus Stone

31 March: Skin Deep
1 April: Fluke
3 April: Carl Sonny Leyland
5 April: I Am Seven (NBT)
6 April: The Immortals
7 April: Jinx
9 April: White Lies
Notice how the "old guard" were still mixing it with the new NBT acts. There was a sort of battle for supremacy going on.
13 April: Grown Up Wrong
14 April: Bedlam Boys
15 April: Machine Without Horses
16 April: Colony Earth
19 April: FSK (NBT)
A Bavarian band, much beloved by John Peel.
20 April: Enigma
21 April: Rolling Drunks
22 April: Sileas
27 April: S. E. Rogie (NBT)
29 April: Martin Wyndham-Read
30 April: Rufus Stone
1 May: Carl Sonny Leyland
2 May: The McAllisters (NBT)
4 May: The Simpleton Family
7 May: Kathryn Tickell
11 May: Malvinas Bros
12 May: Perfectly Frank
14 May: Doris and the Dots
17 May: Rough Ruff and Ready (NBT)
18 May: Writing Degree Zero
19 May: Jinks
20 May: Derek Brimstone
25 May: Stage Fright
28 May: Rufus Stone

• LISTINGS 1988 •

31 May: The Trudy (NBT)
1 June: John Otway
2 June: Up Balloon Up
4 June: Duballup
8 June: Blues and Trouble
9 June: Assassin
10 June: Dr Burke's Remedy
11 June: White Lies
13 June: Chainsaw Etiquette
14 June: Hook and Pull Gang (NBT)
16 June: Malvinas Bros
17 June: John Renbourne's Ship Of Fools
20 June: Daevid Allen and Friends (NBT)
22 June: Stan Webb's Chicken Shack
23 June: Writing Degree Zero
24 June: Assassin
25 June: Rufus Stone
28 June: Pig Bros (NBT)
29 June: Dana Gillespie
1 July: Stage Fright
2 July: Doris and the Dots
5 July: Zeebra
6 July: Pete Harris Blues Band
7 July: Jinx
8 July: Galahad
9 July: Rufus Stone
12 July: Bam Bam and the Calling (NBT)
13 July: Immaculate
14 July: Perfectly Frank
15 July: The Choice
16 July: Backline Blues Band
18 July: Malvinas Brothers
20 July: Jailbreak
21 July: Grown Up Wrong
22 July: Assassin
23 July: Ujamaa

26 July: First Men In Space (NBT)
27 July: Jim Mullen
28 July: Red Jasper
29 July: Flat Out
30 July: Rufus Stone
1 August: The Watchmen
3 August: Pete Ham's Blues Band
4 August: Immaculate
5 August: Stage Fright
6 August: White Lies
9 August: VEE VV (NBT)
10 August: Strange Fruit
11 August: Monolith
12 August: Malvinas Brothers
13 August: Backline Blues Band
17 August: Caiphas
18 August: Finger Stetson
19 August: Assassin
20 August: Doris and the Dots
22 August: Jadis
23 August: Scum Abba benefit gig (NBT)*
24 August: Stepping Out
25 August: Blind Lemon Davis and Whistling Willy Smith
26 August: Galahad
27 August: Rufus Stone
31 August: Whisky Love
2 September: Flat Out
5 September: Pump House Gang
6 September: The Levellers (NBT)

The Levellers were faithful performers at the Joiners for several years.

8 September: Perfectly Frank
10 September: White Lies
13 September: Power House

MOVING ON: Janet and Mike Gulliver.

Gullivers on their travels

THE GULLIVERS are off on their travels again.

Mike and Janet, of the Joiners' Arms, Southampton, have been described as a dream landlord and landlady for bands from rock and pop to folk and jazz.

But they fancy a change from the licensed trade and are taking over a newsagents' and tobacconists' shop at Milton Green, New Milton, next week.

So instead of keeping late hours clearing up after the gigs, they will be rising at 6am to get the papers sorted out.

They do not think they will miss the job they have had for the past four years. In any case the proximity of the seaside will be nice for their children Matthew (9) and Helen (7).

The Gullivers' decision to move rang alarm bells on the Southampton music scene. But Mike, who brought in bigger touring bands to the pub and got the 25-year-old Fo'c'sle Folk Music Club back on Friday nights, doesn't think anything will change. Incoming Alan and Sheila Harris have promoted music at their last pub, the Red Lion in Portswood.

• LISTINGS 1988 - 1989 •

14 September: Immaculate
17 September: Backline Blues
  Band
20 September: Jab (NBT)
21 September: Par-Equinox
22 September: Fatal Attraction
27 September: Juwon Trio
  (NBT)
28 September: Stepping Out
29 September: Galahad
 1 October: Rufus Stone
 4 October: Who's In The
  Kitchen (NBT)
  Excellent Southampton
  political pop band, later to
  become La Cucina.
 6 October: Power House
 8 October: White Lies
11 October: MDMA (NBT)
12 October: After Hours
13 October: White Spirit
18 October: Attacco Decente
  (NBT)
20 October: Mild Mannered
  Janitors
22 October: Ujamma
27 October: Flat Out
29 October: Rufus Stone
 1 November: Wishing Stones
  (NBT)
 3 November: Gamute
 5 November: White Lies
 6 November: Rhythm Sisters
  (NBT)
 7 November: 'Ere We Go
 8 November: Flatville Aces
  (NBT)
 9 November: The Void
10 November: The Rolling
  Drunks
15 November: Electric Sofa

16 November: Tom Beat
17 November: Immaculate
18 November: Pig's Ear
21 November: Personally Frank
22 November: Stitch (NBT)
23 November: Caiphas
24 November: Enigma
25 November: The McAlmans
26 November: Rufus Stone
28 November: Entre Nous
29 November: Blurt (NBT)
30 November: Steamkings
 1 December: Galahad
 2 December: Kashmir
 3 December: Backline Blues
  Band
 6 December: The Trudy (NBT)
 8 December: Flat Out
 9 December: Ewan McColl
  and Peggy Seeger
10 December: White Lies
13 December: The Cranes
  (NBT)
17 December: Duballup
20 December: SCUM do Sound
  Of Music (NBT)
21 December: Enigma
22 December: Jadis
29 December: Whisky Love
  Hunt
31 December: White Lies

1989

 7 January: Rufus Stone
10 January: Treason
11 January: The Daughters of
  the Late Colonel
12 January: The Wolfhounds
  (NBT)
13 January: The Kipper Family

65

• LISTINGS 1989 •

14 January: Red Jasper
18 January: Black Cat Bone
19 January: Wazz (NBT)
21 January: Hybrid
23 January: Kingmaker (NBT)
25 January: Blow Up
27 January: Beggar's Velvet
28 January: Mild Mannered
   Janitors
 1 February: Metropolis
 3 February: King John Mice
 4 February: Rufus Stone
 7 February: Watkins Ale
 9 February: The Levellers /
   Blyth Power (NBT)
11 February: Piggy Zoink
16 February: Attacco Decente
   (NBT)
17 February: Voice of Reason
22 February: Downtown Boys
23 February: Clea and McLeod
   (NBT)
25 February: Blues Bunch
28 February: Dr Brown
 1 March: Lost In Space
 2 March: Electric Sofa (NBT)
 7 March: Hair Of The Dog
 8 March: VHF
 9 March: Who's In The
   Kitchen? (NBT)
11 March: Rufus Stone
14 March: Big Boy's Blues Band
15 March: Sweet Addiction
16 March: Rough, Ruff and
   Ready (NBT)
18 March: Backline Blues Band
22 March: Private Lives
23 March: Strange Fruit (NBT)
25 March: Watch You Drown
28 March: The Apostles

29 March: Treason
30 March: Rory McLeod (NBT)
 1 April: The Wild Bunch
 4 April: The Embrace
 5 April: Persia
 6 April: Flatville Aces (NBT)
 8 April: Captivation
11 April: Hair Of The Dog
12 April: Mind's Eye
13 April: Marshall Law (NBT)
15 April: Rufus Stone
18 April: Gypsy Moth
19 April: Generic
20 April: The Waltones (NBT)
27 April: Flik Spatula (NBT)
26 April: The Untouchables
28 April: Floating Crowbar
29 April: Red Jasper
 2 May: Daughters of the Late
   Colonel
 3 May: Sweet Revenge
 4 May: Scumball (NBT)
 5 May: Jake Thackeray
 6 May: The Blues Bunch
 9 May: Black and Blue
10 May: Piggy Zoink
11 May: Underneath What
   (NBT)
13 May: Wild Bunch
16 May: VHF
17 May: Downtown Boys
18 May: Pressgang (NBT)
23 May: Big Dipper (NBT)
   *One of the earliest American
   bands to play. They were not
   unlike REM.*
24 May: Crafty Jack
25 May: Clea and McLeod
   (NBT)

Joiners Stalwarts

Every venue has its stalwart regular "local" bands which are its day-to-day lifeblood. This was particularly true of the Joiners in the Seventies and Eighties, when the gigs were largely the responsibility of the bands themselves.

Chris Shakespeare is a larger-than-life white soul singer who bangs out the Stax classics with Cockeresque gusto and a permanent huge grin. Research shows that Chris, arguably one of the most important figures on the Southampton music scene over the years (he is now the landlord of the Dolphin in St Denys), has a musical history so long that he would merit a book of his own. A brief summary takes us initially to the Globe Show (Shakespeare's Globe, geddit?), described in "Southern Roots" as "Southampton's mod band, specializing in Motown/Atlantic/Stax music". Other prominent Southampton musicians in the Globe Show included Bruce Roberts, John Cartwright and Ronnie Taylor. With Chris in the band, they recorded "Obladi-Oblada" for the Page One label, home of the Troggs, before Shakespeare left to form Combustion. Next came Happy Tobacco, a band which developed into Honky. Unfortunately, the restless Shakespeare had already quit Honky by the time they had a top ten hit on the Creole label in 1977.

The Globe Show bands listed in this book classified themselves by year (Globe Show 79, Globe Show 80, etc.) and played the Joiners so often, it's hard to imagine that they ever went home. The tiny stage would creak under the weight of the band's sizeable brass section and numerous guests. In 1980, the Globe Show morphed into Big Brother, a similar band which was briefly signed and tended to play more original songs. Big Brother also had a lengthy Joiners residency.

Certainly, the longest Joiners residency was that of Roxoff, largely a vehicle for Southampton guitarist Bruce Roberts and his sax-playing cohort Ronnie Taylor. These two had been in The Quik and various

67

Shakespeare bands before forming Iguana, a serious band which rehearsed for weeks in a New Forest farmhouse. The commitment paid off when they were signed to Polydor in 1974, recording one album. The story goes that Iguana also sent their tapes to Island Records, who turned them down but left the tapes lying round the office. Jess Roden found the tapes and asked to work with the band, resulting in arguably Southampton's greatest success story prior to Craig David. Unfortunately, the Jess Roden Band didn't sell enough records to keep Island happy, and told Jess that he could stay but the band (expensive to keep on the road) would have to go. Roberts was reportedly extremely upset and it took some time before he re-emerged with Roxoff.

Roxoff played a Joiners residency throughout the early Eighties, and continued after that as the Bruce Roberts Band. Their funky blues was loud, rocking and highly accomplished. The sweaty Roxoff nights always featured guests and had their own quirks, as described by John Elliott of the Lesser Known Tunisians:

"They always used to finish with an extraordinary extended version of the Eagles' Desperado. It was almost their trademark. I did a live recording of the band onto my reel-to-reel in my transit parked outside. Imagining it was the Stones mobile, I had a carpet and armchair set up with a mixer. There was a direct lead from their PA and I had extra mikes on the stage, which I then balanced as I went. Unfortunately, the keyboards got lost, since they were only going through the PA and too quietly. They had a great relationship with the landlord Sam Costa, who looked exactly like Roger Moore, and Roxoff would burst into the James Bond theme every time he entered the room."

Such was the sway held over the Joiners by Roxoff that a large mural featuring the band adorned the wall of the back room for many years. This artefact can now be found in the Bent Brief pub in Portswood.

Equal staying power was displayed by Rufus Stone, a hard-working Stax-soul covers band from Southampton, fronted by the diminutive Malcolm Eyes. Since forming in 1984, they played so many Joiners shows that we gave up listing them (which, by the way, also applies to the Globe Show, Roxoff, Duballup, Doris and the Dots and White Lies, stalwarts all).

Even today, the venue couldn't possibly function without good local bands with solid followings, playing regularly and reliably. Nowadays, they tend to perform original material rather than covers, but their function is similar. Step forward, then, The Flying Alexanders, Beautiful Life, Toupe, The Alaskan Pipeline, Fleeing New York, Stu Dent and the Wankers, Plastic Toys, Rival Joustas, Stout, Harsh, Accrington Stanley … the list is endless, but they deserve our thanks, since without them there would be no Joiners.

• LISTINGS 1989 •

26 May: The Morrigan
*This local folk-rock band
in the Fairport Convention
mould were frequent Joiners
visitors.*
27 May: Backline Blues Band
30 May: Perfectly Frank
1 June: The Pop Guns (NBT)
3 June: Piggy Zoink
6 June: The Nobbers From
Hell
7 June: Strange Brew
8 June: Basti (NBT)
10 June: Riff Raff
12 June: Underneath What
(NBT)
13 June: 3 Minute Warning
14 June: Judacutters
15 June: Bushmen
17 June: Backline Blues Band
20 June: The Innocents
21 June: Private Lives
22 June: The Angel Gang (NBT)
24 June: Rufus Stone
27 June: The Sprawl
28 June: Marins Jenson
29 June: Strange The Butcher
(NBT)
*Good, heavy punkers from
Southampton.*
4 July: Prime Time
6 July: The Perfect Disaster /
Carter USM (NBT)
*Support bands have
only been listed where
particularly significant.*
7 July: Roxoff*
11 July: Small Talk
13 July: The Levellers (NBT)
14 July: Dr Brown
15 July: Backline Blues Band

18 July: Fool's Gold
19 July: Hybrid
20 July: Hook & Pull Gang
(NBT)
21 July: The Wild Bunch
22 July: Rufus Stone
25 July: Baelrath
26 July: Poppycock
27 July: Who's In The Kitchen
(NBT)
28 July: Watch You Drown
29 July: Crafty Jack
1 August: Pumphouse Gang
2 August: Dark Summer
3 August: Flatville Aces (NBT)
4 August: Roxoff
5 August: Judacutters
8 August: Big Sky
10 August: The Family Cat
(NBT)
*They loved to play the
Joiners.*
15 August: 70 Policemen In My
Kitchen
16 August: Steel Mast
17 August: The Spoons (NBT)
18 August: Stitch (NBT)
22 August: Carolina Shout
23 August: Ear Ditch
24 August: Underneath What
(NBT)
25 August: The Wild Bunch
26 August: Rufus Stone
29 August: M10
31 August: Wazz
1 September: Primal Scream
(NBT)*
2 September: Caravan
5 September: Rich Rags

Primal Scream, 1 September 1989. Photo by Dik.

Ged Babey: "It was debatable at one point if Bobby Gillespie's huge(ly inflated) ego and Primal Scream's massive(ly filled) leather-trousered reputation would fit into the small but intimate confines of the Joiners' back room. But they did, along with 150-odd bright-eyed, bushy-tailed punters, and a night of Primal (almost Punk) rock ensued. Snarling Les Pauls, Marshall stacks, Iggy and Pistols re-writes and covers, people on the stage, beer on the floor, sweat on the ceiling, mass pogo / idiot dancing, bemused indie kids, goths going mental! Gillespie wanted to pull the gig on seeing how small the venue was … but at the end, he said it was their best gig ever. I bet he always says that though."

UPDATE

My, how they've changed! This gig was obviously well before Loaded was remixed and released. Actually, only about a month before. Gillespie, in my opinion, was always an opportunist, a totally conceited, arrogant little bastard with a huge over-fed ego. (Un)fortunately, he makes some wonderful records (occasionally). I remember that he wanted to pull the Joiners gig on seeing how small the venue was....but at the end he said it was their best gig <u>ever</u>. I bet he always sez that. Another major triumph for Mint though and a brilliant gig. Jane Pow are now based in Brighton and continue to trade in Mod-ish pop.

Comment by Ged Babey

• LISTINGS 1989 •

6 September: Cantel

7 September: Claytown Troupe (NBT)

9 September: Flik Spatula (NBT)

13 September: Up Ballon Up

14 September: Snapdragons (NBT)

16 September: Rufus Stone

19 September: Elisha

20 September: Accrington Stanley

21 September: The Lurkers (NBT)

22 September: Steve Turner

23 September: The Morrigan

27 September: Orange Street Mission

28 September: The Levellers (NBT)

29 September: Steve Tilston

30 September: Baelrath

3 October: The Sea

4 October: I Am Ted Bovis

5 October: The Jazz Butcher (NBT)

7 October: Joyce McKinney Experience

11 October: Red Jasper

12 October: Parachute Men (NBT)

13 October: Kathryn Tickell

14 October: Spin (NBT)

17 October: Quaser

18 October: Bedsit Poets

19 October: Blyth Power (NBT)

21 October: Rufus Stone

24 October: Les Voyeurs

25 October: Orange Street Mission

26 October: Family Cat / M

Walking On The Water (NBT)

M Walking On The Water were another eccentric but good German band.

28 October: Piggy Zoink

31 October: Baelrath

1 November: I Am Ted Bovis

2 November: The Popguns (NBT)

4 November: The Untouchables

8 November: Dark Summer

9 November: Bomb Party (NBT)

14 November: Sprawl

15 November: Colorblind James Experience (NBT)

16 November: AC Temple (NBT)

18 November: Rufus Stone

21 November: Red

23 November: The Telescopes / Ride (NBT)

25 November: Watch You Drown

28 November: Lush (NBT)

This was another early sign that the Joiners was becoming established as an important venue on the national circuit.

29 November: All In The Mind

30 November: The Wolfhounds (NBT)

2 December: Desantos

5 December: Firework Party

6 December: Flat Out

7 December: Badgeman (NBT)

9 December: Looking Glass

• LISTINGS 1989 - 1990 •

12 December: The Buttons
13 December: Mr Fusion
14 December: The Driscolls (NBT)
15 December: Third Degree Burns
16 December: Rufus Stone
19 December: Three Men In A Nightie
20 December: The Morrigan
21 December: Flik Spatula (NBT)
22 December: Jane Pow (NBT)
23 December: Judacutters

1990

Every Monday featured Jam sessions, Thursdays were Next Big Thing, every Friday the Fo'csle Folk Club, and every Sunday Blues.

4 January: Mild Mannered Janitors (NBT)
6 January: The Morrigan
10 January: Big Sky
11 January: Automatic Dlamini
See Joiners Madness section.
13 January: Piggy Zoink
17 January: Marshall Law
18 January: Ride / Carter USM (NBT)
20 January: Rufus Stone
23 January: Eat (NBT)
24 January: Read Them And Weep
25 January: Justice League Of America (NBT)
27 January: Jasmine Minks (NBT)

1 February: God's Little Monkeys (NBT)
3 February: White Lies
7 February: Sprats
8 February: The Charlatans (NBT)*
10 February: Rufus Stone
15 February: Giant Sand (NBT)
Mint was a particular fan of Howe Gelb's Tucson outfit.
17 February: The Wild Bunch
20 February: Finitribe (NBT)
21 February: Templemeads
22 February: Motorcycle Boy (NBT)
27 February: John Otway
See Joiners Madness section.
28 February: The Final Act
1 March: Blyth Power (NBT)
3 March: Baelrath
6 March: We Are Going To Eat You (NBT)
7 March: All In The Mind
8 March: The Wood Children (NBT)
10 March: Rufus Stone
13 March: The Seers (NBT)
14 March: Motion
15 March: The Spoons (NBT)
17 March: White Lies
21 March: Flat Out
22 March: AC Temple (NBT)
24 March: Looking Glass
27 March: The Brilliant Corners (NBT)
28 March: Corporate Grave
29 March: Carter USM (NBT)
31 March: Watch You Drown
3 April: After Hours
4 April: Red Jasper
5 April: The Family Cat (NBT)

The Charlatans. 8 February 1990. Photo by Dik.

Ged Babey: "This was the busiest NBT gig ever! Baggymania and chart success followed shortly. A superb bootleg of this gig exists. This was probably the best example of Mint's timing (or luck, maybe!). When he booked them, they were unknown, but by the time the gig took place, they were all over the music papers and on the Chart Show the day before and Top Of The Pops the week after. A hundred people or more were turned away (to make room for A & R men from several different record companies). Bar takings were an all-time high, the T-shirts went like hot cakes and dancing was compulsory."

Next Big Thing

THE STONE ROSES FAVOURITE GROUP....

THE charlatans

—a mix of Roses/Inspirals with a great loping organ sound and dreamy moods.

another contender in the Bands of the '90s stakes.

THURS 8 FEB

+ the hoverchairs

The Hoverchairs play the ultimate in tuneful indie pop. A David Gedge loo-kalike on vocals, thankfully not a soun-dalike, he leads the Hovers with a quickstep and into the brisk domain of jaunty, ohso jangly three minute pop songs.

They weren't soft or weak for all their jangling, but they won't change the world, though they may comfort-ingly remind you that its not really that bad. "Some people take things far too seriously..."   (James).

£2.50 — at the **JOINERS** — ST. MARY ST SOTON 225612

(ACCESS ONE STEP) — Doors open 8.30

• LISTINGS 1990 •

7 April: Rufus Stone
10 April: Press To Play
11 April: The Untouchables
14 April: White Lies
17 April: 70 Policemen In My
  Kitchen
18 April: Nous Sommes
19 April: Silverfish (NBT)
21 April: Target of Demand
24 April: Mad Thatchers
26 April: Finitribe (NBT)
29 April: Flatville Aces
1 May: Motion
2 May: Cowboy Killers
3 May: Beef (NBT)
5 May: Rufus Stone
8 May: Leatherface
9 May: John Otway
10 May: Five Thirty (NBT)
11 May: Julie Felix
12 May: White Lies
15 May: Final Act
16 May: Sharlot
17 May: Bob / Trip (NBT)
19 May: Decadence Within
24 May: The Walking Seeds
  (NBT)
26 May: Looking Glass
29 May: Sundowners
30 May: Pleasure Victims
31 May: Judacutters (NBT)
2 June: White Lies
5 June: All In The Mind
6 June: The Heartthrobs
7 June: The Levellers (NBT)
9 June: Rufus Stone
12 June: Pogrom
13 June: September Dean
14 June: Safe (NBT)
20 June: Colony Earth
21 June: Love's Young

Nightmare (NBT)
22 June: Riff Raff23 June:
  Baelrath
26 June: The Final Act
27 June: Blind Man's Rainbow
28 June: Hook and Pull Gang
  (NBT)
29 June: Read 'Em and Weep
4 July: UX Driver
5 July: The Trudy (NBT)
6 July: Judacutters
7 July: Looking Glass
10 July: Jane Pow
11 July: Maggot Slayer
  Overdrive
12 July: Anna Palm (NBT)
13 July: Final Act
14 July: Rufus Stone
17 July: Sprawl
18 July: Colony Earth
19 July: Senseless Things (NBT)
20 July: The Morrigan
21 July: White Lies
24 July: Press To Play
26 July: Sea Urchins (NBT)
27 July: Outback (NBT)
28 July: Watch You Drown
31 July: Rick Foot 5
1 August: Crafty Jack
2 August: Thrilled Skinny
3 August: The Keatons (NBT)
7 August: Jane Pow
8 August: Final Act
9 August: Stitch (NBT)
10 August: Gooba Patrol
15 August: Pagan Fringe
16 August: Blyth Power (NBT)
17 August: Godzilla Breadvan
18 August: Rufus Stone
21 August: 10.5
22 August: Inside Out

• LISTINGS 1990 •

23 August: Walt Disney But
SCUM Does (NBT)

25 August: Baelrath

28 August: An Emotional Fish
See Joiners Madness section.

30 August: Swervedriver /
Chapterhouse (NBT)
Shoegazing hits the Joiners.

31 August: Colony Earth

1 September: The
Untouchables

4 September: Press To Play

5 September: The Final Act

6 September: The Darkside
(NBT)

11 September: 32/20

13 September: Perfect Disaster
(NBT)

15 September: White Lies

18 September: Strange Brew

19 September: The Chosen

20 September: Ted
Chippington (NBT)

23 September: Heavenly

26 September: Maytrix

27 September: Flik Spatula
(NBT)

29 September: Sink

2 October: All In The Mind

3 October: Final Act

4 October: God's Little
Monkeys (NBT)

6 October: Judacutters

9 October: Older Than Dirt

10 October: Route 66

11 October: The Beyond (NBT)

13 October: White Lies

16 October: Beatnik Filmstars
(NBT)

17 October: Jadis

18 October: The Boo Radleys
(NBT)

19 October: Bread And Roses

20 October: Jesse Garon and
the Desperadoes

23 October: Press To Play

24 October: Pogrom (NBT)

25 October: Milltown Brothers
(NBT)

27 October: Rufus Stone

31 October: The Brilliant
Corners (NBT)

1 November: Th' Faith Healers
(NBT)

3 November: Looking Glass

6 November: All

7 November: The Bitter End

8 November: The Lurkers
(NBT)

10 November: Jasmine Minks

13 November: The Nuthins

14 November: The Chairs

15 November: The Becketts
(NBT)

17 November: White Lies

20 November: Doom

21 November: Edgar
Broughton Band (NBT)

22 November: The Charlottes

27 November: The Levellers
(NBT)

28 November: Strange The
Butcher

29 November: Beautiful
Happiness (NBT)

1 December: Rufus Stone

2 December: Bill Boazman

4 December: Press To Play

5 December: Paul Young 4
*A Southampton saxophonist,
not the pop star.*

Gig of the Year-so-far had to be the MANIC STREET PREACHERS. Twice rescheduled, it was a sell-out and yes they are as good as they are reputed to be.

Phenomenal in fact, full of energy, aggression and condensed power. Yes, they have re-invented Punk Rock'n'Roll, only its sharper, sexier and more pissed-off than before.

And no they don't just rip off the Clash (they rip off the Jam, Adverts, and Johnny Thunders as well). I could go on for several pages about why the Manic Street Preachers are probably the best band In the world, but let's just say that any band who display such total arrogance by starting their set with a two and a half minute blitzkrieg called *You Love Us* - and mean it, include the classic line "*I laughed when Lennon got shot*" in one of their songs (*Motown Junk*), punch holes in the ceiling with their guitars and leave the stage to the strains of Public Enemy's "*Dont Believe The Hype*" have got to be a bit special. They came, they saw, they converted....me at least.

MANIC STREET PREACHERS

+

STRANGE THE BUTCHER

£3.50
IN ADVANCE

THURS 2 ! MARCH
THE JOINERS ARMS

ST MARY ST SOUTHAMPTON. 225612. ACCESS 1 STEP DOORS OPEN 8.30

UPDATE: Opinion is still very much divided about the Manics. A lot of people HATE them but I stand by the Welsh windbags because they were simply what they said they were; Small town boys with big ambitions. Things have maybe got out of hand now (with the Stipe business) but the Manics revitalized Punk Rock'n'Roll and brought glamour back into style. Their gig at the Joiners made me feel 16 again.

Review by Ged Babey.

Supporting the Manics

Craig McEwan: "The first I heard I heard about the gig was in late 1990, when Mint approached my band, Strange the Butcher, and asked us, along with fellow local punkers UX Diver, to be the support acts. None of us had ever heard of this headline band with the weird name, the Manic Street Preachers, but what the hell, a gig's a gig right?

Well, that first gig never occurred; The Manic Street Preachers couldn't play that night (because one of them needed some kind of eye surgery, as far as I recall). Instead of being cancelled however, the gig was re-scheduled for a later date, with the line-up unchanged. As the rescheduled date approached, the band were beginning to draw the attention of the music press. Their first single 'Motown Junk' had been released to critical acclaim, and the Manics called 'most important rock band since The Pistols' by the NME. Once again, however, the gig had to be postponed.

By this time, it was becoming clear that the Manics were indeed the 'Next Big Thing' and that The Joiners would be sold out. A sell-out crowd, combined with the tiny stage, made getting three bands on in one evening a logistical nightmare; someone had to go, and when the date was re-re-scheduled for March 1991, UX Diver found themselves rudely dropped from the bill.

I had finally seen the Manics on TV a couple of days previously on some late-night indie programme; they looked incredible! There was a palpable air of excitement around The Joiners that evening, as many arrived early to try and catch a glimpse of these new rock stars. Strange the Butcher, meanwhile, were struggling to get our equipment on stage.

The Manics refused to share any of their gear, or even allow it to be moved to make room for ours. This meant that our drum kit had to placed in front of theirs, leaving no room for Joe, our singer. I think in the end he alternated between balancing precariously in front of the drum kits, and jumping around in the crowd.

By the time we started our set, the place was rammed. A room full of sweaty, expectant kids looking forward to an evening of fast, loud, hook-laden punk, which was exactly what we provided. I remember this as the best gig that Strange The Butcher ever played. Others were less impressed. Ged Babey recorded the event for posterity through a microphone pinned to his lapel. As well as both bands' sets, he unwittingly recorded a conversation between Tony and Martin, the singer and guitarist from ousted support act UX Diver, who were roundly slagging off our performance.

After our set, I was jubilant. The Manics set remains largely a blur, but I do remember their storming rendition of 'Motown Junk' at the end, and I can confirm that the crowd was ecstatic, and left howling for more. 'Good gig', I said to Nicky Wire as he left the stage.

As to the rumours that a major record contract was signed at The Joiners that night, I just don't know. Joe is certain he remembers seeing a signing take place in the dressing room; Mint has said that there were Rolls Royces and record company executives in the area. I just remember a fantastic night of rock 'n' roll, which is good enough for me."

Babycham?????!!

HEREINAFTER REFERRED TO AS THE ARTISTE: MANIC STREET PREACHERS

1. The Management agrees to provide ONE clean lockable heated dressing room for the sole use of the Artiste (to include a shower, full length mirror and sink with hot and cold water).

2. The Management agrees to provide two humpers at the Get-In time to assist with equipment. The same humpers to be available at Load-Out time.

3. The Management agrees to provide a hot meal for EIGHT (8) people at no cost to the Artiste. (2 MEALS TO BE VEGETARIAN).

4. The Management agrees to provide at its sole expense:

Unlimited Tea and Filter Coffee, Sandwiches (some Vegetarian). Biscuits, Nuts, Crisps and Chocolate to be made ready on bands arrival.

5 x PACK OF 20 MARLBORO CIGARETTES
24 CANS OF GOOD QUALITY LAGER
12 BOTTLES OF SWEET BABYCHAM
1 X HALF A BOTTLE OF WHISKEY
1 X HALF A BOTTLE OF VODKA
2 X LITRES OF FRESH UNSWEETENED ORANGE JUICE
2 X LITRES OF COCA-COLA
2 X LITRES OF LUCOZADE
2 X LITRES OF MINERAL WATER
6 X UNITS OF PURDYS OR AQUA LIBRA

5. It is agreed and understood that no part of the performance may be taped, filmed, photographed or otherwise recorded without prior consent of the Artiste.

Due South was undoubtedly Southampton's best-ever listings magazine. It was founded by Mark Ovenden in 1982. Mark is now a radio presenter in the North of England. In 1984, the famously unspellable Sally O'Shaughnessy bought the rights to Due South, reputedly using up all her savings in the process. The magazine continued until 1989, working in frantic and uncomfortable conditions in a succession of seedy offices, but providing a great service for the city, lucidly covering all aspects of the arts. In the process, Due South acted as a launchpad for many successful careers. Deputy Editor Rebecca Brown is now the novelist Rebecca Smith. Film critic Jason Best went on to write for the Radio Times and feature writer Giles Stanley is now Managing Director of Universal Music Management. Most significantly for this book, two music writers, who often frequented the Joiners, went on to very successful journalistic careers. John Aizlewood wrote for numerous music magazines, including Q, and now is a prominent music critic for the Evening Standard. Fanzine editor Mark Sutherland applied for freelance work with Due South on 5th October 1990 ("I have recently started studying journalism in Portsmouth and have discovered your magazine and would very much like to contribute to it"). Such enterprise paid dividends, and the ambitious Sutherland went on to write for the NME, and eventually to edit Melody Maker. He then became a presenter on BBC 6 Music.

Mint eventually became Due South's music editor and gave a break to Ged Babey, whose writings appear throughout this book. The Joiners advertised in every issue of Due South (which appeared sometimes monthly and sometimes fortnightly), thus providing much helpful information for this book.

Punk Throwback

Ged Babey: "In 1977, I fell in love with Punk Rock, thanks to Radio Luxembourg and John Peel. My first gig was the 1979 Rock Against Racism Festival in Hoglands Park. I moved to Southampton in 1983 and formed a fun but crap goth-punk band called Judas Hour, later joining UX Diver as singer for a while.

A negative review by one Adam Green in Due South magazine of Judas Hour, a chance meeting with him in a pub and a heated discussion about his lack of journalistic skill lead to the challenge: 'Well, if you can do any better, feel free to send in your efforts at reviews', which I did. They were published and my brilliant career/hobby began.

Mint took over as Rock Editor and continued to publish my reviews, inviting me to his Joiners gigs. I knew the pub because of its then-legendary jukebox, pool table and the fact that punks couldn't get a drink in many of the other pubs in town.

My attendance at the Joiners became more regular in tandem with Mint's NBT gigs. Free admission was the only bonus that came with being (one of) the Joiners' in-house journalists. I was never paid a penny by Due South or the later Sound Info magazine, for which I wrote literally hundreds of reviews and previews. Not that I minded, though. I became a Barfly and was deluged with demo tapes for review. Mint would loan me promo tapes, records and later CDs, which I had to religiously tape off and give back.

I had some of the best nights of my life at the Joiners and met some brilliant, wonderful people (that's both audience and band members). It was a homespun, 'family' affair back then in the '85-'89 years, with grumpy landlords and Hells Angels to contend with, not the slick business operation it is now. Mint had this Doctor Who like quality of always having a glamorous female assistant doing the door (Anya, Karen, even my wife Julie helped out on occasion). Its a shame the back room didn't have Tardis-like dimensions.

After the birth of my son Jack in 1996, I stopped going to the Joiners so much but started my own retro-punk-zine Punk Throwback – which inadvertently led to my becoming a regular contributor to monthly glossy Record Collector, specialising in my beloved punk and post-punk era. I've still got my boring day job, and am more of a fan than a proper critic. As I once wrote about Mark Sutherland (former zine writer turned Melody Maker editor): 'He's a businessman, I'm an art lover. He wants to sort out the money making pearls from the swine, whereas I just wanna tell people how brilliant I think this or that band is, and hope they love them as much as I do'.

I miss the Joiners days when it was a cliquey but friendly amateur operation, run on a shoestring production. When it ceased to be a pub as well as a venue, it lost much of its charm for me."

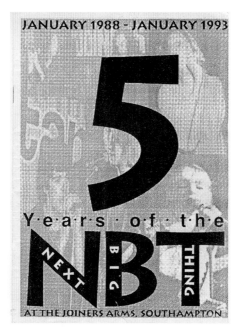

Ged Babey's fanzine celebrating five years of NBT.

Ged's Stories

"The front bar at the Joiners in the early Eighties had a couple of fixtures which I remember fondly. The jukebox contained all manner of punk rock delights, with Pistols and Dead Kennedys songs being favourites. The pool-table was popular. There was barely any room to play, so your game involved making every effort to stay at the bar end of the table, where there was more elbow-room, and avoid the other, more cramped, end. For the whole of the Eighties, there was an older, greying, bespectacled bloke, with his own cue and case, who took up residence at the pool table. It was an unspoken rule that 'the winner-stayed-on'. You would put down your five pence and wait for Perennial Cigarette-Smoking Pool-Playing Guy to thrash whichever punky reprobate dared to challenge him. And then it was your turn to face a crushing defeat. It was a real achievement if you beat the guy. He was really good, but somehow you always felt, what is this old dude doing here? This is a cool music fans' pub. But looking back (now we're greying and over forty), he had a perfect right to be there. He was probably a blues or folk fan who'd been using the pub for decades, when we had safety pins in our nappies.

Mike Gulliver, the landlord for much of the Eighties, was known, behind his back, as Smiley Mike, as he was seemingly always smiling. He had a lovely, voluptuous wife who seemed to be a few years younger than him. She was chief barmaid and quite probably the power behind Mike's throne and the reason for his ever-present smile. One of the post-punk crowd, known as 'Little Stuie The Bootlegger', fell in love with Mike's wife. Stuie was short, with a terrible temper and a fondness for getting off his head, but a loveable bloke underneath. He was a massive Joy Division and New Order fan, who followed them everywhere, bootlegging their gigs with his ever-present recording Walkman. He had a dog-eared notepad listing all of the hundreds of gigs he had taped, everyone who was anyone from 1979 onwards. Stuie looked more a fighter than a lover and was a lads' lad, and didn't have the luck with the ladies that his compadres did. Consequently, sitting at the Joiners bar night after night, being served the finest ales by Smiley Mike's buxom wench of a wife, it was sadly inevitable that Stu developed a crush on her. One night, after far too many pints, Stu declared his undying love for her and insisted that she run away with him and start a new life. I don't know what happened exactly, but evidently Smiley Mike was within earshot and for once the smile vanished. Stuart (who sadly died in 2001) was banned from the Joiners for the rest of their tenancy."

100 BIG ONES!
26/1/88 - 15/2/90

NEXT BIG THING

1988....
1 STITCH
2 BLURT
3 FLIK SPATULA
4 SALAD FROM ATLANTIS
5 SCUM
6 THE SHRUBS
7 ROTE KAPELLE
8 FSK
9 S E ROGIE
10 THE McALLISTERS
11 ROUGH,RUFF & READY
12 THE TRUDY
13 THE HOOK & PULL GANG
14 DAEVID ALLEN
15 PIG BROS
16 STITCH
17 BAM BAM & THE CALLING
18 FIRST MEN IN SPACE
19 DEE U U
20 SCUM "ABBA-RATION"
21 THE LEVELLERS
22 JAB
23 THE JUWON TRIO
24 WHO'S IN THE KITCHEN
25 M.D.M.A.
26 ATTACO DECENTE
27 THE WISHING STONES
28 THE RHYTHM SISTERS
29 THE FLATVILLE ACES
30 THE ELECTRIC SOFA

31 STITCH
32 BLURT
33 THE TRUDY
34 THE CRANES
35 SCUM DO IN THE SOUND OF MUSIC
1989....
36 THE WOLFHOUNDS
37 WAZZ
38 SCUM
39 BLYTH POWER
40 ATTACO DECENTE
41 CLEA & McCLEOD
42 WAZZ
43 WHO'S IN THE KITCHEN
44 ROUGH,RUFF & READY
45 THE MAYFIELDS
46 RORY McLEOD
47 THE FLATVILLE ACES
48 MARSHALL LAW
49 THE WALTONES
50 FLIK SPATULA
51 SCUM.BALL
52 UNDER NEATH WHAT
53 PRESS GANG
54 BIG DIPPER
55 CLEA & McLEOD
56 THE POPGUNS
57 BASTI
58 UNDER NEATH WHAT
59 ANGEL GANG
60 THE BUTTONS
61 DAEVID ALLEN
62 THE PERFECT DISASTER
63 THE LEVELLERS
64 THE HOOK & PULL GANG
65 WHO'S IN THE KITCHEN

66 THE FLATVILLE ACES
67 THE FAMILY CAT
68 THE SPOONS
69 STITCH
70 UNDER NEATH WHAT
71 PRIMAL SCREAM

72 THE CLAYTOWN TROUPE
73 FLIK SPATULA
74 THE SNAPDRAGONS
75 THE LURKERS
76 THE LEVELLERS
77 THE JAZZ BUTCHER
78 THE PARACHUTE MEN

79 THE WOODCHILDREN
80 BLTYTH POWER
81 THE FAMILY CAT
82 THE POPGUNS
83 THE BOMB PARTY
84 COLORBLIND JAMES EXPERIENCE

85 A.C.TEMPLE
86 THE TELESCOPES
87 LUSH
88 THE WOLFHOUNDS
89 BADGEMAN
90 THE DRISCOLLS
91 FLIK SPATULA
92 JANE POW

1990....
93 THE MILD MANNERED JANITORS
94 AUTOMATIC DLAMINI
95 RIDE

96 EAT
97 THE JUSTICE LEAGUE OF AMERICA
98 GOD'S LITTLE MONKEYS
99 THE CHARLATANS
100 1 GIANT SAND

NEXT BIG THING
& SOUND INFO
DARKLEAD Ltd.

• LISTINGS 1990 - 1991 •

6 December: Jane Pow
8 December: Looking Glass
13 December: Mild Mannered Janitors (NBT)
15 December: Judacutters
18 December: Chaos UK
19 December: The Membranes (NBT)
22 December: White Lies
23 December: Bruce Roberts
29 December: Baelrath
31 December: Looking Glass

1991

3 January: Evol
4 January: New St George
8 January: Ten Point Five
10 January: Outback (NBT)
11 January: Jerry's Beaver Hat
12 January: White Lies
15 January: The Reapers
16 January: Bruce Roberts
18 January: Tom Paley
23 January: Kingmaker (NBT)
24 January: Strange The Butcher (NBT)
25 January: Jez Cowe
29 January: Jane Pow
30 January: The Love Buttons
31 January: The Darkside (NBT)
5 February: Palookaville
6 February: Basti (NBT)
7 February: Into Paradise (NBT)
9 February: White Lies
13 February: Ben Gunn
14 February: Trip
15 February: Flatville Aces
19 February: Quicksand
20 February: Sarajevo

21 February: Pogrom (NBT)
27 February: The Firekites (NBT)
28 February: The Honey Smugglers (NBT)
1 March: Show Of Hands
2 March: Looking Glass
6 March: Late Again
7 March: God's Little Monkeys (NBT)
9 March: White Lies
14 March: Sofahead (NBT)
16 March: Jail Cell Recipes
20 March: Spin (NBT)
21 March: Manic Street Preachers (NBT)*
23 March: Drive
26 March: Bitter and Twisted
27 March: Milk (NBT)
28 March: Love's Young Nightmare (NBT)
1 April: Press To Play
3 April: Bleach (NBT)
4 April: RDF (NBT)
10 April: Dodgy (NBT)
11 April: Outback (NBT)
13 April: White Lies
18 April: The Morrigan
20 April: Evol (NBT)
23 April: Accrington Stanley
24 April: Dreamspeed
25 April: Foreheads In A Fishtank (NBT)
29 April: Majority of One
30 April: Rednecks
1 May: The Heat
2 May: Blyth Power (NBT)
3 May: Martin Carthy
7 May: The Deserters
9 May: Catherine Wheel (NBT)
15 May: Bruce Roberts

• LISTINGS 1991 •

16 May: Kingmaker (NBT)
18 May: Older Than Dirt
21 May: Knucklehead
22 May: Daevid Allen (NBT)
23 May: Into Paradise (NBT)
24 May: The Morrigan
28 May: Evol
29 May: Bruce Roberts
30 May: Mass (NBT)
4 June: Go
5 June: No FX
6 June: Bob (NBT)
7 June: John Renbourne
11 June: Studio 68
12 June: Bruce Roberts Band
13 June: Daisy Chainsaw (NBT)
18 June: All In The Mind
19 June: The Deserters
20 June: Thousand Yard Stare (NBT)
25 June: Morrison Hotel
26 June: The Primitives (NBT)
27 June: Inside Out (NBT)
28 June: Dr Brown
2 July: Easy Weather
3 July: Bruce Roberts
4 July: The Prime Movers (NBT)
6 July: Older Than Dirt
9 July: The Green Egg
10 July: Malcolm Tent and the Void
11 July: 35 Summers (NBT)
12 July: Stone Cold
13 July: Evol (NBT)
15 July: Jane Pow
17 July: Econochrist
18 July: Five Thirty (NBT)
19 July: Bloom
23 July: Older Than Dirt
24 July: John Otway

25 July: See See Rider (NBT)
26 July: Doris and the Dots
27 July: Strange The Butcher
30 July: The Rhythmites (NBT)
31 July: Bruce Roberts
1 August: Foreheads In A Fishtank / Pram (NBT)
2 August: Press To Play
7 August: Danielle Dax (NBT)
8 August: The Steamkings (NBT)
10 August: White Lies
15 August: Spitfire (NBT)
17 August: Older Than Dirt
21 August: Kingmaker (NBT)
22 August: Bruce Roberts
28 August: The Honeythieves
29 August: Thin White Rope (NBT)
This was a legendary night, remembered by Mint as one of the best ever.
30 August: Decadence Within
4 September: Crash Marie
5 September: The Rockingbirds (NBT)
7 September: Jail Cell Recipes
11 September: One Dead Hunter
12 September: Top (NBT)
14 September: Stone Cold
16 September: Dodgy (NBT)
18 September: Wreckless Eric
19 September: God's Little Monkeys (NBT)
24 September: The Venus Beads (NBT)
26 September: Therapy? (NBT)
Keep your eyes peeled for further examples of early appearances by big bands.

Tony Eccles,
manager 1991 – 1993

"The Joiners, what a magical word. Sweaty, smoky and packed to the rafters, full of music-crazed fans. I first went to the Joiners when I was at the college next door. I used to pop in at lunch time and usually stayed far too long. Three years later, I left the college with qualifications but far more knowledge of the inside of the Joiners. There was occasional live music back then, but you couldn't call it a venue.

When Sam and Julia Costa ran the pub, they would have lock-ins at weekends with blues artists who would play until the drink ran out. I started my band Doris and the Dots in 1980, and Sam and Julia put us on as often as they could. The band came from High Wycombe and we would travel down and do mini-tours of Southampton: the Joiners, the Park Hotel and the Onlsow.

Sam and Julia eventually moved to the Bournemouth area to run a B and B. Alarm bells began to ring about the future of the Joiners, but along came Mike and Jan Gulliver, who continued to promote bands, including Doris and the Dots. In the early Eighties, I continued to prop up the bar and arrange Doris tours of Holland from the phone box next door and from a stool in the public bar. After a few years of gigs, Jan and Mike told me they were going to leave the Joiners to run a newsagents shop in New Milton. From late nights and too much alcohol to early mornings and newspaper deliveries – what a change! God bless them, they both passed away within a few years. My advice would have been to stick to the alcohol and music! Mandi, my girlfriend, and I thought, 'Shit, who's going to take over?' Mandi, ex of the Park Hotel, had sworn never to run a pub again, but after an hour, I said 'Hey, I know, I'll run it'. Mandi wondered why it had taken so long for me to realize the bleeding obvious, and Mike's reaction was the same.

I then approached Eldridge Pope, who wanted a business plan, so they could be sure I knew what I was doing. I had many meetings with them, and at last a date was set for the completion of the deal. On the day of completion, and with my deposit in my hand, I received a phone call from E.P., saying they had changed their policy and now only wanted me to manage it.

91

They wanted to make all the money without any effort, so I told them to Fuck Off, put all my money into another venue and lost every penny. Two years later, I heard that the current Joiners landlord had been sacked for (*reason deleted, but see page 108! – Ed*). I phoned E.P. and asked if they remembered me, and was told they could never forget someone who told them to Fuck Off, and when would I like to take over?

I ran the Joiners from 1991 through to March 1993. Having played there so many times, I was determined to keep it as it should be, with no place for tribute bands or safe and boring music.

To my mind, there are many people who made the Joiners the great venue it is, and the king of them all must be a wonderful human being called Mint. Without him, lots of fans, bands and artists would have been lost for years, just wandering around with nowhere to belong. I also loved the S.T.E. collective, who would always come up with excellent hardcore bands from anywhere in the world. Sadly, the Fo'c'sle Folk Club and the Joiners just grew apart, so they found another venue. Quiet, relaxed evenings, in my opinion, just didn't fit the Joiners.

It was good that punk bands enjoyed playing the Joiners. When bands like Sham 69, 999 and the UK Subs appeared, all the grown-up punks would squeeze themselves back into their 70s gear and re-live what they needed in their lives (pure bliss).

Reggae never really had a good shout at the Joiners, but my band Doris and the Dots could provide the goods when needed. Having played there before for previous landlords, it was natural for us to play there while I was managing the joint. We've played since as well, and it's still the best gig in the world!

John Otway and Wild Willy Barrett would come and entertain, and the best thing Otway did was give me John Cooper Clarke's home phone number. I was therefore able to talk to God and yes, he actually did play a few gigs. Same suit, same carrier bag, same John Cooper Clarke – brilliant!

What a night it was when The Selecter came to do a gig, so many fans came that it was dangerous. Pauline Black then booked another sell-out show but cancelled the night before because she wanted to rehearse a play. I had to stand at the front door with copies of a fax from her agent blaming her and not me. There were lots of pissed-off punters and I never called her for another date.

The blues nights continued on Sundays, but I was always

burnt out, due to high octane levels from Monday through to Saturday. On Sunday nights, I just died. Bruce Roberts has played the Joiners forever. He could play anything, with anyone, in any condition. Mick Taylor from the Stones was scheduled to play at the Joiners with the Bruce Roberts Band backing him, but leaves from Columbia prevented him from performing. We also promoted a gig with Wreckless Eric from Stiff Records, but only four people turned up to see him. 'Alas', said Eric, 'this has been happening rather a lot lately'.

My son Charlie was born in the Joiners in October 1992, and we decided (my daughter Faye mainly) to relocate and run a fishing hotel in the Highlands of Scotland. Charlie asks why we ever left a venue that has had all these amazing bands, and the answer is, I don't know!"

Doris and the Dots with Tony Eccles (centre).

• LISTINGS 1991 - 1992 •

28 September: Doris and the Dots

3 October: The Prunes (formerly Virgin Prunes) (NBT)

5 October: Thrilled Skinny

7 October: Thousand Yard Stare

8 October: D-Void

9 October: Dave Sharp and the Barnstormers (ex-Alarm) (NBT)

10 October: The Rhythmites (NBT)

17 October: Faith Over Reason

24 October: Milk (NBT)

26 October: Evol (NBT)

30 October: The Family Cat / PJ Harvey (NBT)

31 October: St Christopher

6 November: Amazing Windmills

7 November: Outback (NBT)

9 November: Leatherface (NBT)

14 November: Daisy Chainsaw (NBT)

16 November: The Brilliant Corners (NBT)

20 November: Gary Lucas (Magic Band) (NBT)

21 December: PJ Harvey / Moonshake (NBT)

23 November: Stitch

26 November: Smashing Orange (NBT)

27 November: Flux of Pink Indians (NBT)

28 November: Bob (NBT)

30 November: UK Subs

3 December: The Cropdusters

4 December: John Otway

5 December: Accrington Stanley (NBT)

7 December: Dr Brown

9 December: GBH

10 December: Midway Still (NBT)

11 December: Bruce Roberts

12 December: Fabulous (NBT) *See Joiners Madness section.*

14 December: Doris and the Dots

16 December: Cropdusters

18 December: Thousand Yard Stare (NBT)

19 December: Dodgy (NBT)

21 December: Judacutters

24 December: The Deserters

27 December: Older Than Dirt

28 December: Mad Cow Disease

30 December: Grown Up Wrong

1992

Blue Sunday continued throughout the year, as did the Fo'c'sle Folk Club every Friday.

1 January: Quicksand

2 January: Evol

9 January: Edward II

11 January: Flaming Katies

15 January: Accrington Stanley

16 January: Even As We Speak

18 January: Bruce Roberts

23 January: Chunk / Trip

25 January: One Dead Hunter

27 January: Prairie Oysters

29 January: Flaming Katies

• LISTINGS 1992 •

30 January: Resque
1 February: Freedom Fighters
5 February: Bruce Roberts
6 February: Sunshot (NBT)
8 February: Pele (NBT)
12 February: Chelsea
13 February: Rev Hammer
(NBT)
15 February: The Cropdusters
19 February: Bruce Roberts
20 February: Giant Sand (NBT)
21 February: Mick Taylor
22 February: The Venus Beads
24 February: Bedazzled
26 February: The Morrigan
27 February: Sultans Of Ping
(NBT)
29 February: The Vibrators
2 March: Sealab Sisters
3 March: The Globe Show
*This was a Tuesday
residency.*
4 March: Flatville Aces
5 March: Gallon Drunk /
Asphalt Ribbons
*The support band is
mentioned because they later
became Tindersticks.*
7 March: Creaming Jesus
9 March: Looking For Adam
10 March: The Globe Show
11 March: The Hamsters
14 March: Dr Brown
15 March: Sarajevo
16 March: Green Egg
18 March: Rev Up
19 March: Accrington Stanley
21 March: The Rhythmites
22 March: Tarresque
23 March: One
25 March: Citizen Fish

26 March: Outback
28 March: Kandy Love Satellite
29 March: Jacknife
1 April: Born Against
2 April: Miracle Legion
3 April: Mad Cow Disease
4 April: The Lurkers
5 April: Metropolis
7 April: Globe Show
8 April: John Otway
9 April: Stare
10 April: Sofahead (NBT)
11 April: The Revs
12 April: Lore
13 April: 29 Palms
15 April: The Morrigan
16 April: The Hinnies (NBT)
17 April: Blurt (NBT)
18 April: Rev Up
19 April: Durin's Bane
20 April: Candy Love Satellite
22 April: Stormed
23 April: The Prime Movers
(NBT)
24 April: The Spacehoppers
25 April: UK Subs
29 April: The Cropdusters
30 April: Stare (NBT)
1 May: Sham 69
2 May: John Cooper Clarke
3 May: Tabitha Zu
4 May: Adorable (NBT)
6 May: Strange The Butcher
7 May: Captain America (NBT)
8 May: Jadis
9 May: Bruce Roberts
10 May: Atom God
11 May: The End
14 May: Edward II (NBT)
15 May: The Popinjays (NBT)
16 May: Loonie Tunes

Dear Mint

Find enclosed a tape by P.J.Harvey who has her first single out in October on Two Pure Records home of the Faithealers. I am at this time looking for dates in October to coinside with the single and I would appreciate a date at the Next Big Thing.

ALL THE BEST

N. Osborne

Nick Osborne

PJ Harvey

Whilst some of this year's "Best Gigs at the NBT" have been under-attended (Into Paradise, Inside Out) some of them have been packed out sweat-a-thons (Manic Street Preachers, Five Thirty, Thin White Rope), this, the Family Cat's fifth visit to the Joiners was one of the latter, with many a punter being turned away (Book yer tickets early!).

Support band PJ Harvey were to my mind, the main attraction. Polly J Harvey is a short demure woman from Cornwall. She is an intelligent songwriter and ferocious-but-feminine singer and guitarist in what is decidely her band, hence the name. The rhythm section, two males, were not chosen for their haircuts or sartorial elegance but for their imaginative proficiency on fluid, growling bass and lolloping, jazzy drums. Like the wonderful A House or Kingmaker, PJ Harvey don't really fit into any convenient category or 'Scene' (Thank God!) so can only be described as New Cool Rock with that Something Special. PJ's songs or more specifically lyrics are a lot to do with what makes them Great. Songs like *You Leave Me Dry* and *Oh My Lover* deal with the female side of sexual politics and are emotionally charged (and perhaps scarred) works of genius. The music is mid-paced but songs tend to build, if you know what I mean. Some songs are jagged, but polished. Lopsided but immediate. All have a contained sense of anger or frustration which never quite explodes.

PJ Harvey are destined for Big Things, if that's what they want. The only thing that worries me is that at times, Polly's voice sounds ever so slightly like Sinead O'Connor's ...Not a good sign.

UPDATE

The first time PJH played the Joiners was the week after their first Peel session was first broadcast. Grown men cried. They were THAT good. Can't wait for the new LP can you?

Review by Ged Babey.

P J HARVEY

21 years old from Dorset, began song-writing four
years ago.

In 1990 she formed her own three-piece band, (Rob
Ellis; drums, Olly Oliver; bass), and favouring
a live approach in the recording studio, recorded
three tracks; the results are hard, raw primitive
and seductive.

More recently, as well as writing new material,
P J has been playing live to enthusiastic audiences
(including sell-out gigs) in and around her native
West-Country, leading her to being described by the
press as 'an interesting new talent'.

Following a recent union with the record company
'Too Pure', there will be a debut single realeased in
September, and extensive live performances, possibly
accompanying fellow Label-mates, 'The Faith Healers'
and 'Silverfish'.

In her spare time P J plays guitar with Bristol
based band 'Automatic Dlamini', with whom she has
toured East and West Germany, Poland and Spain.

**Rob Ellis, PJ Harvey's drummer: "Playing the Joiners with PJH
came at a time when the virtual 'overnight success' of PJH
made most experiences of the time a little unreal and hazy. If I
remember rightly, it was the venue for a particularly important
PJH gig where we debuted a lot of the songs for 'Rid of Me'
for the first time, and I remember them sounding very good
(better than the album, by which time we'd played them too
much!). It was very helpful for us inexperienced types to play
these songs in intimate venues like The Joiners, where we
were able to ignore any stage fright type worries or large PA
system detachment from the music, and just concentrate on
performing the songs as well as possible, at least that was my
point of view, I won't speak for Polly or Steve, certainly I don't
think stage fright has ever been much of an issue for Polly! This
particular gig was special because the lighting consisted of
one knackered old light with no gel, which cast a strong white
wash from the side of the stage and made great shadows on
the walls, which neatly summed up the simplicity of means that
was our philosophy at the time, and this idea has been present
as a lighting design factor at PJH gigs ever since."**

• LISTINGS 1992 •

17 May: Tokyo Blade
18 May: Corporate Grave
19 May: Globe Show
20 May: Extreme Noise Terror (NBT)
21 May: Moonshake (NBT)
22 May: The Judacutters
24 May: Fudge Tunnel
25 May: The Selecter
27 May: Airstream (NBT)
29 May: This Ragged Jack
30 May: Jane Pow
31 May: Broken Bones
1 June: Green Egg
2 June: Globe Show
3 June: No FX
5 June: Press To Play
6 June: Charlie Massiah
7 June: Sunshot (NBT)
8 June: Whisky Priests
10 June: 29 Palms
11 June: Suede / The Auteurs
12 June: Rock Doctors
13 June: Edgar Broughton Band (NBT)
17 June: Sealab Sisters
18 June: Evol (NBT)
20 June: Bruce Roberts Band
22 June: Pridenjoys
24 June: Attilla The Stockbroker / John Otway
25 June: The Rockingbirds (NBT)
26 June: Man
1 July: Tabitha Zu
2 July: Heavenly (NBT)
4 July: Jadis
7 July: Globe Show
8 July: Mr T Experience
9 July: Mexico 70 (NBT)
10 July: Verve (NBT)

11 July: Charlie Massiah
12 July: Finitribe
13 July: Pridenjoys
14 July: Globe Show
15 July: Jackdaws
16 July: The Jennifers (NBT) *This was an early version of Supergrass.*
17 July: DF 118 (NBT)
18 July: Anna Palm (NBT)
22 July: Older Than Dirt
23 July: Ludicrous Lollipops (NBT)
24 July: Pressgang
29 July: Adorable (NBT)
30 July: Blaggers ITA (NBT)
31 July: Perfect Alibi
1 August: Kandy Love Satellite
2 August: Adorable
4 August: Globe Show
6 August: Back To The Planet (NBT)
7 August: Space Hopper
9 August: Popinjays (NBT)
12 August: Traitor
13 August: Buttermountain Boys
14 August: S.U.N. (NBT)
15 August: The Family Cat (NBT)
17 August: Family Go Town (NBT)
18 August: Globe Show
19 August: Onward
20 August: Eugene Chadbourne (NBT)
21 August: Press To Play
22 August: Loonie Tunes
24 August: Corporate Grave
26 August: Lunachicks (NBT)
27 August: Eat (NBT)

99

• LISTINGS 1992 •

28 August: Bruce Roberts Band

1 September: Globe Show

3 September: Daevid Allen's Magick Brothers (NBT)

4 September: Junk

5 September: John Cooper Clarke

6 September: Anti Vera

8 September: Globe Show

9 September: Scumpups (NBT)

10 September: Sunshot / Puressence (NBT)

11 September: Three Men and a Nightie

12 September: Harbour Kings

15 September: Globe Show

16 September: Hair

17 September: The Bardots (NBT)

18 September: John Otway and Wild Willy Barratt

19 September: Mad Cow Disease

20 September: The High (NBT)

22 September: Globe Show

23 September: Goober Patrol

24 September: Eugenius / Urge Overkill
How odd that this cool American support would soon have a cheesy hit with "Girl You'll Be A Woman Soon", before disappearing.

25 September: Watch You Drown

27 September: Skaw (NBT)

30 September: Five Thirty

1 October: Big Truth (NBT)

2 October: Wax Climax

3 October: Necropolis

4 October: Whipped Cream (NBT)

7 October: Th'Faith Healers (NBT)

8 October: Pitchshifter (NBT)

9 October: Stereolab (NBT)

10 October: Dr Brown

11 October: Patricia Morrison

12 October: Dan I and the Freedom Fighters

13 October: Dave Vanian
Yes, him from the Damned.

14 October: Green Egg

15 October: The Popinjays (NBT)

16 October: Moonshake (NBT)

17 October: Brainfork

21 October: Cosmic Love Wave

22 October: Headcleaner (NBT)

23 October: Dumpy's Rusty Nuts
Well, obviously they had to turn up sooner or later!

24 October: One By One

26 October: Brighter (NBT)

28 October: The Cranberries
See Mint's reminiscences for details of the debacle.

29 October: Rev Hammer (NBT)

31 October: Blade (NBT)

2 November: Accrington Stanley

1 November: Jackdaws

4 November: Bang Bang Machine

5 November: Airstream

6 November: Steamkings

7 November: Kandy Love Satellite

8 November: Decomposed

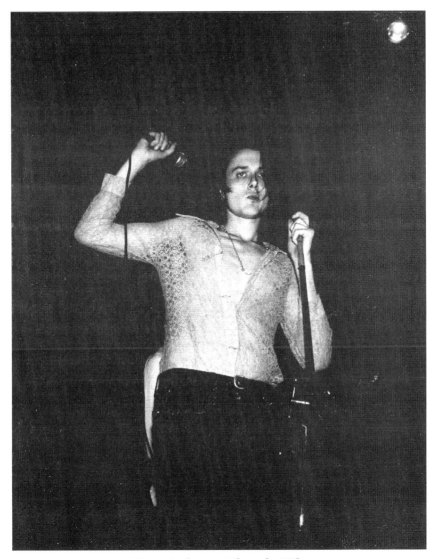

Brett Anderson. Photo by Dik.

GRAB THE HAND OF SUEDE, AND BE TEASED ALONG A WARM AND TWISTED PATH OF
POP MUSIC, WHERE ELEMENTS OF BOWIE AND BOLAN SEEP ALONGSIDE THE FLAMBOYANCE
OF THE 70'S , BUT BRING YOU BACK INTO VOGUE WITH FIGHTING, CRASHING
GUITARS AND SEDUCTIVE DELIVERIES.

THEY GOT HIP SWINGIN' POP TUNES THAT'LL DRIP ALL OVER YOU
WITH THE SINGER AND SONG IN THE FOREFRONT AND ATTITUDE THAT STINGS
FROM THE HIP.

UNLESS YOU WANT TO LOOK REALY STUPID , CHECK'EM OUT BEFORE YOUR FRIENDS
DO.

FOR MORE INFORMATION CALL JON AND ONLY JON

Richard Ashcroft. Photo by Dik.

LIKE SUEDE, ANOTHER SENSATIONAL NEW INDIE CHART TOPPING ACT...

VERVE

"THE FUTURE STARTS HERE!" M.M.

FRI 10 JULY £4 IN ADVANCE

THE JOINERS

ST MARYS ST SOUTHAMPTON 225612 ACCESS 1 STEP DOORS OPEN 8.00
ADVANCE TICKETS TO ALL NBT GIGS AVAILABLE FROM BEHIND THE BAR

• LISTINGS 1992 - 1993 •

9 November: Downcast
11 November: Blyth Power (NBT)
12 November: The Aquinitas (NBT)
13 November: Chumbawumba (NBT)
15 November: The New Cranes
16 November: Shonen Knife (NBT)
Photo overleaf.
18 November: Lovecraft (NBT)
19 November: Eden Burning (NBT)
20 November: Passing Clouds
21 November: Wizards of Twiddly (NBT)
22 November: Bleach (NBT)
23 November: Pat Temple
25 November: Airstream (NBT)
26 November: Wonky Alice (NBT)
27 November: The Rhythmites
28 November: 999
29 November: Bang Bang Machine (NBT)
30 November: New England
1 December: Crane (NBT)
3 December: Ludicrous Lollipops (NBT)
4 December: Dodgy (NBT)
5 December: Gomorrah
6 December: Dance of Kings
7 December: Flue Man Flue
9 December: Perfect Ending
10 December: Jad Fair (NBT)
11 December: Mad Cow Disease
12 December: DF 118
15 December: Phantom Chords

17 December: The Sea (NBT)
18 December: La Cucina
19 December: The Vibrators
20 December: Edward II (NBT)
21 December: Flying Alexanders
23 December: Blade
27 December: Totally Brasic – *"Ex-Motorhead", it says here.*

1993
Globe Show residency continues every Tuesday.

8 January: The Cropdusters
9 January: Alloy
13 January: Orange Deluxe (NBT)
14 January: Cornershop (NBT)
15 January: John Otway *See Joiners Madness page.*
16 January: Big Five *"Ex-Selecter, Bad Manners, Rico."*
21 January: Foreheads In A Fishtank (NBT)
22 January: The Buttermountain Boys (NBT)
28 January: Terrorvision (NBT)
30 January: 999
31 January: Dead Flowers
3 February: Atom Heart Mother (NBT)
4 February: Blaggers ITA (NBT)
5 February: Wax Climax
6 February: Kandy Love Satellite
9 February: Radical Dance Faction (NBT)

• LISTINGS 1993 •

10 February: Perfect Ending
11 February: DF 118 (NBT)
12 February: Rev Hammer /
  David Gray (NBT)
  Yes, you did read that
  correctly.
13 February: Dr Brown
14 February: Kinky Machine
  (NBT)
15 February: Big Stack
17 February: Circus Lupus
18 February: Radiohead (NBT)
19 February: Altogether
  Elsewhere (NBT)
20 February: Pressgang
25 February: The Sea (NBT)
26 February: Tarresque
28 February: Terminal
  Cheesecake
 3 March: The Auteurs (NBT)*
 4 March: Here And Now
  (NBT)
 5 March: Lovecraft (NBT)
 6 March: US Creek
 9 March: Birdland (NBT)
  See Joiners Madness page.
11 March: God Machine (NBT)
12 March: Citizen Fish (NBT)
13 March: Burial Garden
14 March: Life … But How To
  Live It?
  "From Norway" – it says
  here.
18 March: The Ukranians
  (NBT)
19 March: Road Kill
20 March: Black Couch
22 March: Chumbawamba
  (NBT)
25 March: Orange Deluxe
  (NBT)

29 March: Gallon Drunk /
  Cornershop (NBT)
31 March: KMC
 1 April: Dr Phibes
 2 April: Chelsea
 3 April: The Astronauts
 7 April: Big Stack
 8 April: The Magic Mushroom
  Band (NBT)
 9 April: Brilliant Corners
  (NBT)
11 April: Jadis
14 April: Zuzu's Petals (NBT)
15 April: Crazy Alice (NBT)
16 April: Transglobal
  Underground (NBT)
17 April: The Zimmerframes
19 April: Green Day
20 April: Jellyfish Kiss
21 April: SMC Big Band
22 April: The Heart Throbs
  (NBT)*
23 April: Flying Alexanders
24 April: The Rye (NBT)
27 April: Nightlord
28 April: The Lurkers
29 April: Mandragora (NBT)
 1 May: Emperor Sly
 2 May: World Gone Crazy
 3 May: Death By Crimpers
 4 May: Down By Law
 6 May: La Cucina
 7 May: Watch You Drown
 8 May: The Bardots (NBT)
 9 May: Press To Play
10 May: The Hinnies
11 May: DF 118
12 May: The Marionettes
13 May: Anathema
14 May: Evol

Radiohead, 18 February 1993:

Christian Francis: "'Bollocks' was the cry, as a skinny git barged past, knocking my pint all over me. He pushed past me with much vigour and dismissal of the devastation he had caused. I stood aghast, staring at the empty glass.

'Where's the support band?' my mate Rob asked, as he sidled up beside me, looking at the stage. 'And where's your beer?' he added, smirking as he looked at my now empty glass and my sodden clothes. So I went to refill, and the bar being what it is, I had to stand for fifteen minutes, being ignored by a barmaid who obviously hated the world. I refuse to admit that it could have been because I was stinking of beer and probably looking like a kitten molester.

With with new pint in hand, I eventually rejoined Rob in the back room. Feet firmly stuck to floor (which is the norm in the Joiners), we stared at the people getting on the stage. And now I could see the 'git' strapping on a guitar. Great, so the evil man was in the band!

In all truth, I wasn't impressed at first. I don't know why, but they seemed too earnest. I had never heard of this band in my life. What the hell did Radiohead mean? Then again, I remember about twenty minutes in, hearing a song which turned it all for me. This was the song 'Ripcord', from the album 'Pablo Honey'.

Then started some amazing songs and I felt that this was a band that was going to be big. It was indie rock with amazing hooks; I was actually excited by this band and wanted to see what they could do but had to wai t a few months until the first album appeared. And I had to wait two years to hear the album 'The Bends', of which they played the title track that night in The Joiners.

The performance was exactly how I see Radiohead now, too much emotion and heartfelt angst for simple pop rock. They seemed to over-blow the songs. They were something great that night, it was excellent, but marred by their pretension, which later in life would – in my opinion – kill the music that they showed such talent at playing.

After they played, they disappeared quickly. So quickly, in fact, that I could not ask the 'git' if he wanted to get me a new pint.

So we headed to the kebab shop, where we remembered a few of the songs played that night and discussed them. Rob and I both knew they were going to be big, but we disagreed on one thing. Rob said, 'That song, 'I'm Creepy' or whatever, is going to be huge'. I said, 'Nah, no one would buy that, it's shit!'"

NEXT BIG THING

RADIOHEAD

+ BLAB HAPPY

£3
IN
ADVANCE

THURS 18 FEB
THE JOINERS

ST MARYS ST SOUTHAMPTON 225612 ACCESS I STEP DOORS OPEN 8.00
ADVANCE TICKETS TO ALL NBT GIGS AVAILABLE FROM BAR

Radiohead. Photos by Dik.

SUEDE
& SUPERGRASS
AT THE JOINERS..

DETAILS INSIDE..

Mint Burston, who had been music editor at Due South, came up with the idea of a house music magazine for the Joiners, adding character and depth to the gig listings. The first edition appeared in February 1993 and the magazine continued until November 1996, by which time it had morphed into "Son Of Sound Info" as times grew fiscally harder and it had to reduce itself from A4 size to A5. It continued Due South's tradition of fostering good journalism, with regular contributions from Southampton music enthusiast Ged Babey and also future Melody Maker editor and BBC 6 Music presenter Mark Sutherland. The latter contributed exclusive interviews with Throwing Muses, Carter, The Levellers, The Orb and Suede, among others.

Great live photographs of Joiners shows by "Dik" featured in every issue. After lengthy attempts to contact Dik to ask whether he'd mind us using his photos in this book, we had to give up, as he seems to have disappeared without trace. We are confident he would be happy, as he contributed his photos free and framed versions adorned the Joiners front bar for many years. Sadly, the majority of them disappeared during one of the many clear-outs. We hope this book will find its way into the hands of Dik.

THAT'S RIGHT! BUT IT WAS IN 1992 & EARLIER THIS YEAR RESPECTIVELY!

YOU MAY HAVE MISSED OUT ON THOSE & MANY MORE, SEE BELOW, BUT THERE'S MORE TO COME, JUST SEE OUR LISTINGS OPPOSITE!

Next Big Thing started promoting gigs at The Joiners in January '88 bands that made appearances during that year included **CRANES** and **THE LEVELLERS**.

The following year.. 1989 I promoted shows by **PRIMAL SCREAM, RIDE** (they supported **THE TELESCOPES**), **THE LEVELLERS** played several more gigs, **CARTER USM** did three supported gigs during the year, and there were also shows by - **LUSH, THE FAMILY CAT, PERFECT DISASTER,** and from America, **COLORBLIND JAMES EXPERIENCE,** and **BIG DIPPER**.

1990 saw gigs by **THE CHARLATANS, THE BOO RADLEYS, RIDE** (headlining this time - with **CARTER USM** supporting!!) and gigs by.. **SWERVEDRIVER, CHAPTERHOUSE, SILVERFISH, FINITRIBE, EAT** and **GIANT SAND**.

In 1991 we played host to.. **MANIC STREET PREACHERS, THERAPY?, DODGY, PJ HARVEY** (3 gigs), **KINGMAKER, DAISY CHAINSAW, THE LEVELLERS, and THIN WHITE ROPE**.

SUEDE are currently the most successful band to have played The Joiners during 1992 but we also had gigs by **VERVE, SULTANS OF PING, STEREOLAB, URGE OVERKILL, BACK TO THE PLANET, GALLON DRUNK,** and from Japan **SHONEN KNIFE**.

1993 was a good year too. It included shows by..

RADIOHEAD, SHAMPOO, TERRORVISION, CHUMBAWAMBA, SALAD, SLEEPER (a free gig!), **GUNSHOT, GOD MACHINE, THE AUTEURS, COMPULSION,** and **CREDIT TO THE NATION**.

Last year, 1994.. **OASIS, SHED 7, ECHOBELLY, GENE, ASH, WEDDING PRESENT, SMASH, DEUS, DRUGSTORE** and **TRIBAL DRIFT,** all did gigs here at The Joiners.

And this year 1995 so far has seen appearances by.. **SUPERGRASS, REEF, DRUGSTORE, EUSEBE, SKUNK ANANSIE, THE BLUETONES, GORKY'S ZYGOTIC MYNCI, HEAVY STEREO, WE KNOW WHERE YOU LIVE, TIMESHARD, PORCUPINE TREE, DUFFY, THE SELECTER,** and **OUT OF MY HAIR**.

So, as you can see, about once a month there's gonna be a gig by some future stars happening at our venue. The above list doesn't include other bands that have since split up with one or more members going on to bigger things, plus we have also seen shows by brilliant acts perhaps too leftfield to ever get into the charts, including - **PETER PERRETT, DAVID THOMAS, DAEVID ALLEN, ATTILA THE STOCKBROKER, ROBYN HITCHCOCK, GARY LUCAS** ('BEEFHEART'S guitarist), **JAD FAIR, KEVIN COYNE, JOOLZ, EUGENE CHADBOURNE & JIMMY CARL BLACK** (ZAPPA'S drummer), **RORY McLEOD, KRAMER & DOGBOWL, JOHN COOPER CLARKE, MIKE HERON,** , and a few ex chart toppers - **DR & THE MEDICS, JOHN OTWAY** and **ARTHUR BROWN**.

Also the STE collective have put on over fifty hardcore punk gigs on at The Joiners over the last several years including **GREEN DAY, NOFX, JAWBREAKER, SAMIAM, HUGGY BEAR** and **QUICKSAND**.

So if you are into your music you'll want to check us out, if you don't know of us already. Our phone number is 01703 225612. We can put you on our mailing list, ask for details. There's a map and further details (left) to help you find us..

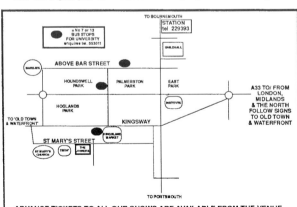

ADVANCE TICKETS TO ALL OUR SHOWS ARE AVAILABLE FROM THE VENUE - OUR PHONE IS 01703 225612. IF YOU ARE CONECTED TO THE INTERNET ETC FURTHER INFORMATION CAN BE OBTAINED VIA OUR ADDRESS THERE.
http:/www. soton. ac.uk/ `ckw/sound info/ intro. htm/
Southampton University muscians coop also sell our tickets contactable via their pigeon hole ASK FOR MARK OR MAT or call at 49 GRANBY GROVE - OR E MAIL @ mcm92sq @ soton. ac.uk

YES! THE JOINERS NOW HAS A LATE LICENCE
UNTIL 1.30 AM ON A FRIDAY AND SATURDAY NIGHT
HOW WILL THIS AFFECT YOU?

THIS MEANS EVERY FRIDAY - DJ HAMMY'S NIGHT - IT WILL BE FREE TO GET INTO THE PUB BEFORE 9.30 PM. £1 UP UNTIL 10.30 PM. £2 UP UNTIL 11.30PM. STRICTLY NO ADMISSION AFTER 11.30PM. HAPPY HOUR WILL NOW BE FROM 7- 9 PM (2 HOURS!!)
HAMMY'S NIGHTS WILL BE MEMBERS ONLY - IF YOU ARE NOT A MEMBER YOU WON'T GET IN! IF YOU ARE NOT ALREADY A MEMBER YOU CAN JOIN ON THE DOOR - IF YOU BRING ALONG SUITABLE I.D. E.G. DRIVING LICENCE, NUS CARD - MEMBERSHIP IS CURRENTLY FREE!!

SATURDAY NIGHTS
IF THERE ARE JUST BANDS ON IT WILL BE FREE TO GET INTO THE FRONT BAR BUT YOU PAY TO SEE THE BANDS IN THE BACK ROOM. MOST SHOWS WILL START AROUND 8.30PM AND FINISH AROUND 11.30PM YOU DO NOT NEED TO BE A MEMBER TO SEE BANDS. THERE IS NO ADMISSION TO THE PUB OR GIG AFTER 11PM.

FOR THE '3 FUNKI NINJA' CLUB NIGHT ON THE 23RD YOU DO NEED TO BE A MEMBER TO GET IN TO THE PUB. IT WILL BE FREE BEFORE 9.30 PM. £1 UNTIL 10.30. PM. £2 UP UNTIL 11.30 PM. NO ADMISSION AFTER 11.30 PM AS THESE WILL BE MEMBERS ONLY NIGHTS IF YOU ARE NOT A MEMBER YOU WON'T GET IN! AGAIN IF YOU ARE NOT ALREADY A MEMBER YOU CAN JOIN ON THE DOOR IF YOU BRING ALONG SUITABLE I.D. E.G. DRIVING LICENCE, NUS CARD - MEMBERSHIP IS CURRENTLY FREE!!

FOR NEUROLOGY NIGHTS THE FRONT BAR IS FREE TO GET IN TO BUT YOU PAY TO GET INTO THE BACK BAR. THE LIVE ACT WILL BE ON AROUND 9.30PM UNTIL 10.30PM FOLLOWED BY DJS UNTIL 1.30 AM. THERE IS NO ADMISSION TO THE PUB OR CLUB AFTER 11 PM. YOU DO NOT NEED TO BE A MEMBER TO GET INTO THE PUB ON THESE NIGHTS.

FOR CHEMICAL BEATS NIGHTS. YOU DO NEED TO BE A MEMBER TO GET IN TO THE PUB . THE ADMISSION CHARGES ARE YET TO BE CONFIRMED (THE NEXT ONE MIGHT STILL BE FREE). NO ADMISSION AFTER 11.30 PM - AS THESE WILL BE MEMBERS ONLY NIGHTS IF YOU ARE NOT A MEMBER YOU WON'T GET IN! APPLY AS ABOVE.- MEMBERSHIP IS CURRENTLY FREE!!

ALL OF YOU OUT THERE WHO'S MEMBERSHIP HAS CURRENTLY EXPIRED PLEASE JUST SWAP YOUR OLD CARD FOR A NEW CARD NEXT TIME YOU ARE DOWN - IT'S STILL FREE!

THE JOINERS
IS NOW OPENING
WED & THURS LUNCHTIMES
12.00 - 3PM WITH VEGETARIAN
FOOD AVAILABLE
& FREE POOL GAMES!

& ON FRIDAY NIGHTS WE HAVE
A 'HAPPY HOUR' 8- 9PM
WITH PINTS OF KRONENBOURG,
CASTLEMAINE, DORCHESTER
AND CIDER ALL AT ONLY £1.10!

SOUND ENGINEER
REQUIRED FOR THE JOINERS
SOME EXPERIENCE REQUIRED
TEL 01703 225612 BETWEEN MIDDAY & 5PM

• LISTINGS 1993 •

15 May: Samiam
16 May: Terrorvision
17 May: Darling Heart
18 May: Tindersticks / Pram (NBT)
19 May: No Man
20 May: The Sea
21 May: The Undead
22 May: Older Than Dirt
23 May: Duballup
24 May: L Kage
25 May: Kevin Coyne (NBT)
26 May: Midway Still
27 May: The Enid
28 May: Transcendental
29 May: S Church
31 May: Compulsion (NBT)
1 June: State of Grace
2 June: Jacob's Mouse
3 June: Credit To The Nation (NBT)
4 June: Heavy Duty
5 June: UK Subs
6 June: Eugene Chadbourne + Jimmy Carl Black (NBT)
Dave Misselbrook's musical dream come true.
7 June: Alloy
9 June: Edward II (NBT)
10 June: Bang Bang Machine (NBT)
11 June: Dub Warriors (NBT)
13 June: The Coal Porters (NBT)
14 June: Gutless (NBT)
15 June: Mike Heron's Incredible Acoustic Band
16 June: Tiberius Minnows
17 June: Blyth Power (NBT)
18 June: Gilli Smyth / Kangaroo Moon (NBT)

19 June: Wat Tyler
20 June: Duballup
21 June: Green Egg
22 June: Dumpy's Rusty Nuts
23 June: Dodgy (NBT)
24 June: Arthur Brown (NBT)
25 June: Misconstrued
26 June: The Mavericks
It seems unlikely that this could have been THE Mavericks, but it's the Joiners, so who knows?
27 June: Paradox
28 June: The Candyskins (NBT)
29 June: Perfect Ending
30 June: Older Than Dirt
1 July: The Bhundu Boys (NBT)
2 July: Real
3 July: Econochrist
4 July: Burial Garden
5 July: Robinson
6 July: Voodoo Queens
7 July: Mad Cow Disease
8 July: The Revs
9 July: Mambo Taxi (NBT)
10 July: Flying Alexanders
11 July: Older Than Dirt
12 July: Orange Deluxe (NBT)
13 July: Die Cheerleader (NBT)
14 July: Sunshot (NBT)
15 July: Heavenly
16 July: Wordbug
17 July: X-Axis
18 July: US Creek
19 July: Goober Patrol
20. July: Underground Lovers / ILA
21 July: Pain or Pleasure
22 July: FMB
23 July: Pressgang

This is the answer to the question posed at the beginning of this book: Green Day did indeed play at the Joiners, in a gig organised by the S.T.E. punk collective. According to Ben Myers' Green Day biography, the unofficial "Kerplunk" release party occurred at the gig, because they happened to first receive finished copies of their second "Lookout!" LP while they were in Southampton. The band stayed with the S.T.E guys and, according to DJ Hammy, nicked all the food from their fridge. More details in the Punk section starting on page 115.

Publicans face forgery charges

TWO Southampton publicans have been sent for trial at the city's Crown Court on a total 16 allegations of false accounting and forgery.

Allen Harris, 48, of Kingsclere Avenue, Weston and Shelagh Harris, 38, whose address was given as the Joiners Arms, St Mary Street, were each given bail by Southampton Magistrates.

Each is charged with eight offences alleged to have happened between June and September.

Echo, 24 May 1991.

THE JOINERS

141 ST MARY ST, SOUTHAMPTON
(0703) 225612

APRIL'S GIGS

THU 1. DR PHIBES
+ SWEET JESUS
FRI 2. CHELSEA
SAT 3. THE ASTRONAUTS
+2000 DS
WED 7. BIG STACK
THU 8. THE MAGIC
MUSHROOM BAND
FRI 9. BRILLIANT CORNERS
SAT 10. T.B.C.
SUN 11. JADIS
TUE 13. SHELTER BENEFIT
WED 14. ZUZU'S PETALS
THU 15. CRAZY ALICE
FRI 16. TRANSGLOBAL
UNDERGROUND
+ PROGRESSION
SAT 17. THE ZIMMERFRAMES
+ NECROPOLIS
+ SPECIAL GUESTS
MON 19. GREEN DAY
TUE 20. JELLYFISH KISS
WED 21. SMC BIG BAND
THU 22. THE HEART THROBS
FRI 23. FLYING ALEXANDERS
SAT 24. THE RYE
TUE 27. NIGHTLORD
WED 28. THE LURKERS
THU 29. MANDRAGORA
FRI 30. DANCE NIGHT
phone to confirm
IF YOU WANT TO BE ON OUR FREE MAILING
LIST LEAVE YOUR NAME AT THE BAR

Punk at the Joiners

Pete Harvey, musician and journalist:

"In 1977, as punk swept through the UK, the Joiners, like all the other pub venues in the country, dealt in rock and blues. Southampton's home-grown punk bands, Stratejacket and Catch 22 soon annexed it with a couple of historic gigs.

'I used to hang about the Joiners when I was a kid, 77-81. It was the punk scene then and we thought we were pretty legendary', says Catch 22 (and latterly The Men They Couldn't Hang) guitarist Paul Simmonds. 'Bands had really fluid line ups, so we all ended up playing in each other's groups sooner or later. It was like a home from home, except the living room had a pool table, a bar and live bands. So it was better than home. It wasn't so much about the bands as the audience, to be honest. It had real punk democracy.'

The Untalented Mob supported Stratejacket at the Joiners in 1978. 'I didn't know where the Joiners was', says singer Ray Missons, 'so I cycled down St. Mary Street looking at all the buildings until I found the Joiners. I was excited to be looking at the place where we were going to play our first gig. I went in and there was no stage, just this one guy playing guitar on his own out the back. I kept thinking 'this is going to be a bit weird'.'

Before the gig, Ray and his guitarist brother Andy visited London to pick up some stage clothes. 'We went down the Kings Road and bought day-glo tops in a bondage shop, we thought, 'We'd better have some kind of image, 'cos our music's crap'.'

Punk, new wave, post-punk, indie, the Joiners embraced every genre as we turned up in St. Mary Street with our out-of-tune guitars. As Stratejacket's Terry O'Brien said: 'The legacy of Southampton's punk scene was that place, the Joiners.'

Tony Keall from UX Diver remembers: 'By the time I was going to pubs (about '81) the Joiners was the place, full of punks, post punks, rockabillies and a fantastic juke box. The juke box had Spizz Energi, Link Wray, Roxy Music and Joy Division. UX Diver played the Joiners on many (mostly forgettable) occasions. We were very proud of the fact that we were VERY LOUD. It wasn't until I saw Silverfish there, who were so loud I had to leave, that I realized what a painful experience being subjected to that was. I saw a lot of the first wave of punk bands' nostalgia gigs. We played with the UK Subs, I loved the Vibrators, lost a tooth dancing to the Lurkers, got chatted up by Gene October and shit myself working security at the Sham 69 gig. We were convinced the skins were coming.'"

115

The S.T.E. Collective

You can't talk about Punk at the Joiners without mentioning the S.T.E. They kept D.I.Y spirit of punk alive in the venue and put on some incredible gigs. Here is their story, as told by Rich Levene:

"I was a teenage provincial punk from Eastleigh and my first concerts were the big punk bands at the Gaumont (now The Mayflower), from 1980 onwards. It wasn't until Christmas 1984 that I went to my first 'self-organised' punk gig in Southampton, when Suicide Pact played a benefit at the Joiners to pay 'Stop The City' (anarchist day of action in the City of London) fines, and it was great. I met several people there who would become the crux of the DIY punk scene in Southampton for years to come. PJ from Suicide Pact (who evolved into Nox Mortis) was later a cohort of mine in the S.T.E., whilst Chris London from The Mad Thatchers would become the Joiners' soundman for years to come.

In Spring 1988, frustrated by the fact that there hadn't been any touring punk bands in Southampton for a while, and inspired by what some of us had experienced of the hardcore scene in mainland Europe, and above all determined to do something positive after the tragic death of Nox Mortis' Simon Gregory at Easter 1988, the S.T.E. was born.

A group of ten people from bands, fanzines and local scenesters attended a meeting at The Joiners (we all drank there anyway) and put a tenner each into a starting kitty. PJ came up with the S.T.E. (Southampton, Totton and Eastleigh) Collective name, simply from the places where the bulk of us lived at the time. The first gig we did at the Joiners was Joyce McKinney Experience with Wat Tyler and Pompey's Watch You Drown, in October 1989. It was a cracking gig and for the next 10 years,

The Joiners became the spiritual home of the S.T.E. & the local punk/hardcore scene in general.

From the word go, the S.T.E. operated on a set of guiding principles and I'm proud to say that, although some mistakes were made, these remained in place for our duration. We wanted to avoid big business practices, so there were no contracts, guarantees or major label bands (early on, we declined gigs by Manic Street Preachers and Therapy?, who both later did Next Big Thing gigs). Things operated on mutual trust; the gigs were set up directly through the bands, or by friends of ours who were booking tours simply because they were into the music. The S.T.E. was strictly non-profit making. Gig admission was as cheap as possible (with concessions for those who were unwaged) and we endeavoured to promote an environment that was friendly, fun and free from violence, racism, sexism or homophobia. After a while, the core of the active S.T.E. participants slimmed down to myself, PJ & Rob Callen and, after all our work, Southampton and the Joiners became established as one of the best and friendliest places to play in the U.K.

In terms of the calibre of bands we put on, probably the 1991-93 period was the heyday of the S.T.E. in most people's eyes. During this time we put on gigs for several bands that would later become huge. In December 1991, Green Day played The Joiners with Jail Cell Recipes and Older Than Dirt (singer Mike put them up afterwards at his flat!). Green Day were on their first UK tour and played to around 75 people. As it was near my birthday, they got me onstage and sang 'Happy Birthday' to me. They were due to play for us again in 1993, but the tour got cancelled and by the time they returned, they were on a major label and massive. Later, they were to tell journalists from the music press that the Joiners was one of their best ever gigs, whilst Kerrang! reproduced the poster from our gig in a feature and mocked the fact that the door admission was the 'princely sum of £3/2.50'!

NOFX played two S.T.E. gigs in the summers of 1991 and 1992. The gigs were fantastic but at the second one, Rob ended up arguing with Fat Mike from the band over £20. We paid them the remaining door money of £180, but Fat Mike insisted on £200. Suffice to say, we didn't pay them the extra (we didn't have it!) and didn't put them on again. The next night in London, our friend Selina drunkenly heckled them with '£200 you green-haired bastard!' to bemused looks from people in the crowd!

We always felt that local bands were vital to the strength of any local scene, and above all, the members of these bands were often our friends. The two Southampton bands most associated with the S.T.E. were Older Than Dirt and Minute Manifesto, who coincidentally both played 17 gigs for us! Honourable mentions are also deserved by Corporate Grave, Hate That Smile, Watch You Drown, Fusion, Smog (UK), Haywire, Thirst, Pogrom, Portiswood, the Zimmerframes and many others. As well as the overseas visitors, we built up relationships with some wonderful bands and people from across the U.K. Two bands I have particular fondness for are Harlow's Travis Cut and Shutdown from the West Country, who played ten and seven S.T.E. gigs respectively. I named my cat 'Travis Cat', as he turned up as a stray just as Travis Cut left, the morning after played their first gig for us in 1994. They even credited him on the sleeve of one of their singles, how punk is that? Twelve years on, Travis is still going strong! Shutdown's gigs here were amazing and I will always remember the memorial gig they did at the Joiners for no money after the tragic death of my best friend (S.T.E. co-founder and Thirst guitarist) Steve Burgess in 1994.

People always ask what were my favourite S.T.E. nights at the Joiners, and I always pin it down to three. In joint second would be Norway's Life … But How To Live It? in 1993. The D.I.Y. punk scene on mainland Europe was always an inspiration to us, so to see one of the greatest ever bands from the continent here was pure joy. Level pegging with Life... would be the second Joyce McKinney Experience gig in 1990, with my Austrian friends Target Of Demand and Brighton's Sleep (bassist Danny Leigh is now a renowned author). As well as being exhilarating musically, it was notable for the textbook way the packed crowd dealt with a troublemaker without ruining the atmosphere of the gig.

My top S.T.E. gig, though, would be Richmond, Virginia's Avail, in 1995. We knew the records but had no idea how incendiary they were going to be live. Almost from the start, the place exploded. It was their first gig outside North America and afterwards they told us that initially they were apprehensive of the amount of people dancing, as in the States gigs could be very violent. However, when they noticed that there were women stage-diving and that people had huge grins on their pig-piling faces they relaxed! They came back for two more S.T.E. gigs but that first one was the stuff of legends!"

Chris T-T:

"I first got into gigging in 1990. Back then, in Winchester, the nearest real gig – the one that meant you were actually doing it – was in Southampton at the Joiners Arms. It was a kind of mystical interface between being a local unknown nobody and being part of a legitimate touring circuit. It was also the only place to see the cool touring indie bands you could hear on Peel. For visceral stuff, the sound of actual amps, the language of touring life and the smell of musicians, there was only the Joiners.

Then, the following Saturday, you'd head back down St Mary's Street, into one of the little record shops, to buy a bootleg cassette of the gig you'd seen the week before. Every Hampshire-based band-loving thirty-something must remember the Southampton bootlegger who wrote all his tracklistings with deliberately wobbly acid-freak handwriting, photocopied onto brightly coloured paper, so the cassettes looked psychedelic but you couldn't read what any of the songs were.

I still have his jaw-droppingly good recording from 1993 of Radiohead's Joiners headline show. I hadn't been that excited about a new band since Carter but sadly I didn't manage to persuade a single friend to come with me to the gig. So I was pathetically alone in a two-thirds full Joiners, while they were already playing tracks from *The Bends* live and the inventiveness was revelatory. There's a fine moment on the tape where Thom Yorke moans about *Pablo Honey* being slagged off in *NME* and a voice shouts, 'They gave you seven! That's not so bad!' whereupon Thom agrees and berates himself for complaining. That was me. Awesome.

Girl (top of her lungs): 'Where's my letter?'

Thom: 'What?'

Girl: 'Where's my fucking letter? I sent a stamped addressed envelope!'

Thom: 'Er, well, when did you send it?'

Girl: 'Last week!'

Thom: 'We're *on tour* for fuck's sake!'

So anyway, playing The Joiners was vital, a rite of passage, after which you'd obviously get the big record deal and be rock stars in a bus with roadies and groupies by next spring. Fuck the GCSEs, stardom awaits. After gigging around Winchester to the same fifty school friends way too many times, my school band I.L.A. (don't ask... influences: Marillion and The Cult) scored a Joiners support slot with a 'proper' female-fronted alt-rock quartet called The Heartthrobs, courtesy, if I remember rightly, of the editor of this book. They were a damn good Peel-ish touring band who'd released stuff on Rough Trade and, though most of us didn't know who they were, we were stoked. It was The Beginning.

Arriving, as we unloaded from the alley into the big black box of the Joiners back-room, we were told there was a third band added to the line-up, to go on first. They'd been blagged onto the bill by Bob Stanley out of St Etienne and – terrifyingly – this meant he'd actually be present at our gig, along with the less impressive Lawrence from Denim. To us, if I'm honest, what most mattered was the tiny possibility that Sarah Cracknell might show up.

The opening band in question was called Shampoo and consisted of two squealing blonde sisters from out of London's crusty fanzine circuit, backed by a grumpy ageing blues-rock session trio. History says the 'Poo went on to have that hit single "Trouble", plus a big-selling album, invented "girl power" and even achieved near mega-stardom in Japan, where they may still be the biggest selling act of all time. Our gig was long before all the chart bothering action and must have been one of their first ever shows, a kind of warm-up to a career. And by the gods, they were bad! I can clearly remember everyone who was in the room for their opening set – including the clique who'd brought them down from London – leaning against the back wall of the room to get as far away as possible from the horrendous noise flooding off the stage like a toxic spillage. Nowadays at the Joiners, you pay to enter the pub. Back then, when the stage was 90 degrees to the left of where it is now and the sound equipment considerably more basic, you could drink in the pub for nowt and only had to pay to get into the back room itself. Tragically, this meant there was nowhere to go to escape Shampoo, without the kerfuffle of getting back in afterwards.

Obviously, the St Etienne scenesters were long gone before

I.L.A. played a note, leaving our tiny bemused fan base and a few Heartthrobs followers to pick up the pieces of the evening. Volume being everything when you're 16, we still had an awesome night, rocking out through the big PA system. But it wasn't ever going to make wobbly-written bootleg tape status.

It has to be said, over the following three or four years, witnessing Shampoo's brief but undeniably sizeable pop success, having got so physically close to them and discovering at first hand how genuinely execrable they were on every level, was the single biggest lesson I ever learned about the music business. Thank God the bubble burst so early, is all I can say.

I played the Joiners many times over the next decade-and-a-bit: great ones and shit ones, support and headline, half-empty and rammed – but that's the one I always remember."

• LISTINGS 1993 •

24 July: Rufus Stone
25 July: Jadis
27 July: The Epiphany
28 July: Poisoned Elektrik Head (NBT)
29 July: Mother Carey's Chickens
30 July: Press To Play
 1 August: Real
 2. August: Robyn Hitchcock and the Egyptians / Heather Nova (NBT)
 3 August: Banana Fish
 4 August: Shampoo (NBT)
 5 August: Wild Orchids
 6 August: Crazy Gods of Endless Noise (NBT)
 7 August: Progression
 9 August: Big Stack
10 August: Hair and Skin Trading Co.
11 August: Mint 400 (NBT)
12 August: Blade
13 August: James Ray's Gang War
14 August: Oi Polloi
15 August: Chapterhouse (NBT)
17 August: Bewley Brothers (NBT)
18 August: Sayonara
19 August: Dr and the Medics (NBT)
 Not unlike Urge Overkill, they too would shortly have a one-off No. 1 hit.
20 August: Scorpio Rising
21 August: Rufus Stone
23 August: Big Stack
24 August: Mock
25 August: Eat (NBT)

26 August: Buttermountain Boys
27 August: Bruce Roberts
28 August: Burial Garden
30 August: Ween (NBT)
 1 September: Red Letter Day
 3 September: The Steamkings
 4 September: Flying Alexanders
 6 September: Orange Deluxe
 7 September: New Cranes
 8 September: Green Egg
 9 September: Anathema
10 September: Frantic Spiders
11 September: Dezerter
13 September: Sarah Sarah
14 September: Stereolab (NBT) (SI gig review available)
15 September: Collapsed Lung
16 September: Pan
17 September: Terminal Cheesecake
18 September: Zimmerframes
19 September: Catherine Wheel (NBT)
20 September: Valley Of The Dolls
22 September: Wizards of Twiddly (NBT)
24 September: Nova Coma (NBT)
25 September: AOS 3
27 September: Gutless (NBT)
28 September: Kong
29 September: Critical Mass
30 September: Well Oiled Sisters
 1 October: Methadreame
 2 October: Bruce Roberts
 3 October: Duballup
 4 October: Lovecraft

123

• LISTINGS 1993 •

5 October: Neverland
6 October: Nuns on Napalm
7 October: Oil Seed Rape
9 October: Daevid Allen (NBT)
10 October: Atari Teenage Riot (NBT)
12 October: Jimmy Cooper
11 October: Various Vegetables
13 October: The Ukranians (NBT)
14 October: Revolutionary Dub Warriors (NBT)
15 October: Dr Brown
16 October: Ringo
18 October: Beatnik Filmstars (NBT)
20 October: Stretch Armstrong
21 October: Spacemaid
22 October: John Otway Big Band
23 October: Herb Garden
24 October: Hair and Skin Trading Co. (NBT)
26 October: Salad (NBT)
28. October: The Wedding Present (NBT)
29 October: Flying Alexanders
30 October: Rufus Stone
31 October: Transcendental
1 November: Nilon Bombers
2 November: Nova Coma
3 November: Crazy Gods Of Endless Noise
4 November: The Cropdusters
5 November: La Cucina
6 November: Real
7 November: Blurt (NBT)
9 November: Co-Creators / Atari Teenage Riot (NBT)
10 November: BMX Bandits / 18 Wheeler (NBT)

11 November: Attaco Decente (NBT)
12 November: Stan Webb's Chicken Shack
13 November: Joyce McKinney Experience
14 November: Instant Karma
15 November: Bowlfish
17 November: FMB
18 November: Straitjacket Fits
Legend has it that American Music Club's Mark Eitzel attended this gig.
19 November: Invisible Opera Company of Tibet
20 November: Nosferatu
22 November: The Revs
23 November: Sloppy Seconds
24 November: Loonee Tunes
25 November: Tony McPhee's Groundhogs
26 November: Shutdown
27 November: Burial Garden
28 November: Gunshot
29 November: Sleeper (NBT)
An experiment with free gigs.
30 November: Eternal
1 December: The Buttons
2 December: Orange Deluxe / S*M*A*S*H* (NBT)
3 December: Duballup
5 December: The Sea
7 December: Skyscraper
8 December: Citizen Fish
9 December: James Ray's Gangwar
10 December: Shine
11 December: One By One
12 December: Jacob's Mouse
13 December: Beautiful Life
14 December: Goodchilde

NEXT BIG THING

£0.00 £0.00 £0.00 £0.00 £0.00

FREE GIG!

"YOU REALLY, REALLY MUST SEE THIS BAND"
(MELODY MAKER)

SLEEPER

'IMAGINE A DEMONIC DUSTY SPRINGFIELD FRONTING THE PIXIES'

+

FROG'S LIFE

IMAGINE A DUSTY PIXIE FRONTING THE DEMONIC SPRINGFIELDS - ERR...

MON 29 NOV.

THE JOINERS

ST MARYS ST SOUTHAMPTON. TEL. 225612
ACCESS I STEP. DOORS OPEN 8.30. R.O.A.R.

• LISTINGS 1993 - 1994 •

15 December: Zimmerframes
16 December: Mandragora
17 December: Transcendental
18 December: Chicken Bone Choked
19 December: Edward II (NBT)
22 December: Green Egg
23 December: Pressgang
24 December: Nova Coma

1994

6 January: Nova Coma
7 January: Flaming Katie
8 January: Burial Garden
10 January: Annie Hates Cordial
12 January: Pooka (NBT)
13 January: Blessed Ethel (NBT)
14 January: Attilla The Stockbroker
15 January: Fabric
17 January: Strange The Butcher
19 January: S*M*A*S*H* (NBT)
21 January: Son Of Noise
22 January: The Wishplants (NBT)
23 January: Neverland
24 January: Various Vegetables
25 January: Mad Cow Disease
28 January: Wasteful Cross
29 January: Rufus Stone
31 January: Tony Head Experience (NBT)
2 February: Fifteen
3 February: Sharkboy / Drugstore (NBT)
4 February: Flaming Katie
5 February: Revolutionary Dub Warriors (NBT)

9 February: Perfect Ending
10 February: Skyscraper
11 February: Dr and the Medics (NBT)
12 February: Up Balloon Up
15 February: Sleeper (NBT)
16 February: Jay 9
17 February: Passion Fruit
18 February: Papa Brittle
19 February: Voodoo Queens
22 February: Gunshot
23 February: K Passa
24 February: Bandit Queens
25 February: Orange Deluxe
26 February: Nessun Dorma
2 March: Bob Pearce
3 March: Edgar Broughton Band (NBT)
4 March: The Producers
5 March: Chicken Bone Choked
10 March: Tiny Monroe (NBT)
11 March: Dr Brown
12 March: Rufus Stone
15 March: Emperor Of Ice Cream
16 March: Moose
17 March: Spacemaid (NBT)
18 March: Transcendental
22 March: Done Lying Down
23 March: Pooka (NBT)
24 March: The Flamingoes
25 March: Oasis/Whiteout (NBT)*
26 March: Wizards Of Twiddly (NBT)
27 March: Jackdaws
30 March: Shed Seven / Compulsion (NBT)
31 March: Incubus Succubus
1 April: Freedom AKA (NBT)
2 April: Rufus Stone

• LISTINGS 1994 •

5 April: Mike Peters (Alarm)
5 April: Blessed Ethel /Ash (NBT)*
6 April: Looney Tunes
7 April: Rev Hammer (NBT)
9 April: Green Egg
13 April: Far Canals
14 April: La Cucina
15 April: Poisoned Elektrik Head (NBT)
16 April: Shutdown
20 April: Daevid Allen (NBT)
21 April: Pressgang
22 April: Fundamental
23 April: Black Couch
25 April: Mock
26 April: Salad (NBT)
28 April: Daisy Chainsaw (NBT)
29 April: Bob Pearce
30 April: S*M*A*S*H* (NBT)
3 May: Accrington Stanley
4 May: Jesus Jones (NBT)
5 May: Funkabubble
11 May: Weddings, Parties, Anything (NBT)
Not many Australian bands have graced the Joiners' stage, but this was one.
12 May: C Charge
13 May: Orange Deluxe
14 May: Burial Garden
18 May: Rhythm Collision
19 May: Dr Didg
21 May: Rufus Stone
24 May: Rise
25 May: Foreheads In A Fishtank
26 May: Revolutionary Dub Warriors (NBT)
27 May: The Tansads
31 May: Shed Seven (NBT)

1 June: Jacob's Mouse
2 June: K Passa
3 June: Herb Garden
4 June: Haynes Boys
7 June: The Nubiles
8 June: Peter Perrett and the One (NBT)
9 June: Land of Barbara
10 June: Beautiful Life
14 June: Ran
15 June: The Bundhu Boys (NBT)
16 June: Merry Go Round
17 June: Black Couch
18 June: Kandy Love Satellite
20 June: Green Egg
21 June: Echobelly (NBT)
22 June: Children On Stun
23 June: Arthur Brown (NBT)
24 June: The Producers
25 June: Rufus Stone
29 June: Vertigo
30 June: Pussy Cat Trash
^1 July: John Otway
^2 July: Orange Deluxe
^4 July: Gorky's Zygotic Mynci (NBT)
^5 July: Shed Seven (NBT)
^6 July: Looney Tunes
^7 July: Telstar Ponies (NBT)
^8 July: Transcendental
^9 July: Oi Polloi
11 July: 60 Ft Dolls (NBT)
13 July: Dodgy (NBT)
14 July: Press To Play
15 July: The Alexanders
16 July: Burial Garden
19 July: Fatima Mansions (NBT)
20 July: Ash (NBT)
21 July: Well Oiled Sisters

[NEXT BIG THING]

WHITEOUT
+ OASIS

TUE 29 MARCH £3 IN ADVANCE

THE JOINERS

ST MARYS ST SOUTHAMPTON 225612 ACCESS I STEP DOORS OPEN 8.00
ADVANCE TICKETS TO NBT GIGS AVAILABLE FROM THE BAR, WEASELS,
& HMV RECORDS - THOUGH SOME WILL BE AVAILABLE ON THE NIGHT

Andrew Napier, Daily Echo reporter:

"A mate of mine saw Oasis at the Joiners in 1994. He asked me if I wanted to see this 'new band being hyped by the NME.' He told me who they were and I replied, 'They sound shit' and went back to pruning the roses. I was sort of right."

OASIS

OASIS

C/- IGNITION 8A WYNDHAM PLACE LONDON W1H 1PP
TEL 071 706 2234 FAX 071 723 4676
VAT NO: 628 1555 34

INVOICE TO: NEXT BIG THING
C/- THE JOINERS
141 ST MARY'S STREET
SOUTHAMPTON

ATTN: MINT BURSTON

INVOICE NO: OA/32

DATE: 22.3.94

RE

Performance fee re OASIS as follows:

NO.	ITEM	VAT CODE	AMOUNT
	Joiners, 29.3.94		
1	Guarantee	1	£ 100.00
2	Plus 35% after £485 Gross Receipts		

VAT SUMMARY				
VAT CODE	0	1	**NET**	
NET AMOUNT	£ 0.00			
VAT %	0.00	17.5	**VAT**	
TOTAL VAT	£0.00			
			TOTAL	£ 150.—

Received with Thanks

Partners: L. Gallagher, N. Gallagher, P. Arthurs, T. McCarroll, P. McGuigan

Oasis

Martin McNeely: "I went to the Joiners fairly regularly around the mid 1990s. Although I was a student in my native Northern Ireland, I indulged in a bit of journalism for various papers and fanzines, both in NI and England. My family lived near Winchester, thus the Joiners became the local music haunt when I was out of Ulster. The thing about the Joiners was that, despite its limited size, it just seemed to be the most important venue for an up and coming act to play in. Of course, because the Joiners only held about 150 to 200 punters at an absolute push, it precludes people from claiming that 'they were there' on the night Oasis played. I mention this because at a certain students union in Belfast, hundreds claimed to have seen the Stone Roses early on in their career. The truth is, only 150 people saw the Roses. But because the Students Union held 500, there were a lot more claimants! But I was there the night Oasis played at the Joiners and, indeed, so were maybe 200 others absolutely stuffed into the joint.

Oasis rolled into Southampton as part of a big Creation records push. I had got friendly with a girl in the record company and she let me hear a demo of theirs which sounded pretty amazing at the time. There was a real sense in the Creation office that this band was going to be massive. It says something about the Joiners that the band had to be seen there on their way to the top.

Oasis arrived looking conspicuous in this massive tour bus, which they shared with labelmates Whiteout from Glasgow. Whiteout were first on stage and sounded fantastic – a kind of typical Glasgow-meets-LA laid back rock. The boys had a sense of humour and jollied the crowd, a complete contrast to what came next. Who knows where Whiteout ended up?

For anyone who can remember all the early Oasis gigs, the one at the Joiners was typical. For a start it was brief, maybe 40 minutes at most. None of the band moved a muscle, least of all Noel and Liam. If memory serves, they started with Supersonic. The reaction was split three ways. Undeniably, a minority thought the band were a joke. A handful of punters, bless them, down at the front were going mad. Liam liked this. I could tell, because he didn't abuse them. He did abuse quite a few other people though, lots of staring, muttering the odd verbal insult. The rest of us, watching this from the back, were bemused by the whole thing. Was this band for real?

They sounded like every band that I ever loved all rolled into one: The Jam, Clash, Who, Beatles with a bit of the Pistols about them too. They played Shakermaker and Columbia, which sounded sublime. But could anyone take all the posing seriously? It was a laugh. When they walked off after 40 minutes, a few punters wanted their money back. The rest of us thought it was a break before an encore. We were waiting for a long time. I met Noel afterwards and did an interview for a couple of publications. I spent an hour alone with him in his hotel. He kept up the whole rock star thing fairly well, until we talked about Paul Weller and the pair of us were lost in a dream world reminiscing. We had a chat about the troubles in Ireland and about his family. He was a nice bloke. Liam, on the other hand, bounded in and came across aggressively. He would swing to an upbeat mood when talking about Man City.

Everything the media have subsequently reported about the moods and the scrapping would strike me as being about right. If you can imagine all that rock and roll anger squeezed onto the tiny stage at the Joiners, just think how mesmerizing it was to be there."

Ash/Blessed Ethel, 5 April 1994

This gig maybe explains the inaccurate urban myth that Nirvana played at the Joiners. Martin McNeely explains:

"Ash weren't even old enough at the time to buy a drink. In fact, when they were drinking beforehand, it was strictly shandy, which I paid for. They came to the Joiners with a bizarre outfit called Blessed Ethel. Other bands around at the time were the likes of Elastica, who were part of the so-called riot grrrl scene. Blessed Ethel were lumped in with this and right enough, the lead singer did have an attitude about her.

It was the night that news reached our shores about Kurt Cobain's death. The girl from Blessed Ethel announced on stage something like 'By the way, I've just heard that Kurt Cobain has shot himself', or words to that effect. The weird thing was that one of the Ash entourage was connected to Courtney Love through the PR machine and that person took a mobile call which confirmed the news we'd just heard from Blessed Ethel.

It was a spooky thing from then on, as the young Ash trio, so patently influenced by Nirvana, tore into their set. Tim Wheeler never had a great voice, but they could really play hard onstage. It was so strange watching them rock out, while coming to terms with the news from the States."

• LISTINGS 1994 •

22 July: The Producers
23 July: Rufus Stone
24 July: Byetail
25 July: Gene (NBT)
26 July: Messy
27 July: Huge Baby
28 July: La Cucina
29 July: Dr Brown
30 July: Haynes Boys
1 August: Edward II (NBT)
4 August: Rugrat
5 August: Beautiful Life
6 August: Creaming Jesus
10 August: Bandit Queen
11 August: Sloppy Seconds
12 August: Transcendental Love Machine
13 August: Huggy Bear (NBT)
19 August: Burial Garden
20 August: Rufus Stone
26 August: Jadis
27 August: Press To Play
31 August: Blaggers ITA
1 September: Blyth Power (NBT)
2 September: Sam Saturn and the Stardust Sensations
3 September: Chimpanzees
7 September: Huge Baby
9 September: Smog
10 September: Black Couch
15 September: Shed Seven (NBT)
16 September: The Steamkings
21 September: Blink
23 September: K Passa
24 September: Jadis
27 September: Tailor Made
28 September: Nash
29 September: Bewley Brothers (NBT)

1 October: Jess Roden Band
Back after all these years.
4 October: Lashout
5 October: Hookers For Jesus
6 October: The Enid
7 October: Dr Brown
8 October: Flaming Katie
10 October: Looney Tunes
11 October: Nova Coma
12 October: Unwound
13 October: Revolutionary Dub Warriors (NBT)
14 October: Eden Burning
18 October: dEUS (NBT) 19 October: Mutiny
20 October: The Ukrainians
21 October: Incubus Succubus
22 October: Black Couch
25 October: The Informers
26 October: Sunset Heights
27 October: Freedom AKA
29 October: Rufus Stone
1 November: Jawbreaker
3 November: Animals That Swim (NBT)
4 November: Courage Of Lassie
5 November: Nosferatu
8 November: Thud Gullet
9 November: Perfect Ending
10 November: Mandragora
11 November: Nova Coma
12 November: Travis Cut
15 November: Rub Ultra
16 November: Luminous
19 November: Citizen Fish
22 November: The Nubiles
23 November: Kinky Machine (NBT)
24 November: The Dharmas
25 November: Press To Play

• LISTINGS 1994 – 1995 •

26 November: Rufus Stone
29 November: The Sea
30 November: Blame The
  Weather
1 December: AOS 3
2 December: Goya Dress
  (NBT)
3 December: Voorhees
5 December: Done Lying
  Down
6 December: Laika / Gorky's
  Zygotic Mynci (NBT)
7 December: Pressgang
8 December: Tribal Drift
9 December: John Otway
10 December: Wirehead
12 December: Magnesium OK
14 December: Blubber
15 December: One Planet
16 December: Press To Play
17 December: Shutdown
18 December: Edward II (NBT)
20 December: The Horatti
21 December: Resonate
22 December: Sid James
  Experience
23 December: Decline
31 December: Rufus Stone

1995

*Every Friday starred DJ
Hammy plus local bands.*

18 January: Dub War
20 January: Fin
26 January: Thrum
27 January: Smog UK
28 January: Firework Party
1 February: AC Acoustics
  (NBT)
2 February: Beautiful People

4 February: Code
6 February: The Popguns
9 February: Supergrass /
  Bluetones (NBT)
11 February: Goober Patrol
14 February: Whiteout (NBT)
15 February: Mazey Fade
16 February: Bettie Serveert
  (NBT)
18 February: Black Couch
21 February: Flinch
22 February: Drugstore (NBT)
23 February: Skunk Anansie
  (NBT)
  *Shortly to be big – and then
  not so big. They loved the
  Joiners.*
25 February: Grateful Dub
26 February: Atilla The
  Stockbroker
6 March: Sleeper (NBT)
19 March: David Thomas and
  Two Pale Boys (NBT)
2 April: Eusebe (NBT)
4 April: The Ukrainians (NBT)
5 April: Wierd's War
11 April: Winter of Torment
12 April: Rosa Mota (NBT)
  *Officially the loudest band
  ever to have played the
  Joiners.*
13 April: Fits of Depression
15 April: The Moonflowers
  (NBT)
17 April: Tatlin
18 April: Joolz (NBT)
19 April: Blameless
20 April: Rosetta Stone
22 April: Reverse
23 April: Attila The Stockbroker
25 April: Mary Springs

DJ Hammy

"I was born in Swaythling, in the house I live in now, in the very bedroom I sleep in now! I started going to the Joiners from '77 on, just to odd local gigs. In general, we didn't go there for punk gigs, other than Stratejacket. The landlord was Sam Costa, the James Bond lookalike. I actually bought my first mobile disco from him. Sam had a 'film night' every Monday in the back bar. It started off with 'proper' films, but soon went downhill. Very few people had a video recorder in those days, so it was always packed. Remember that the back bar was half the size it is now. We used the Joiners as a 'pre-club' pub before going on to Manhattans night club.

Round about 1980, we started to go more regularly. Mike Gulliver, the landlord from '83, had worked for me in a Cash and Carry in Eastleigh. What I loved about it was that it was a pub. You could just drink in the front bar, and I started DJing straight away, mainly parties at first. I once DJ'd there with The Men They Couldn't Hang, when they were called Catch 22.

In Replays Records in St Denys, I met Dave Misselbrook, who it turned out had been a mod in the sixties, along with my brother. A few years later, he told me he was going to take over the Joiners, so lo and behold, I became the Friday night DJ and had the time of my life there for three years.

The policy of bringing in live bands was to bring in the crowds, to be frank. It was a shithole, that's all I can say. Dave bought a carpet off the back of a lorry. After the first night it was full of fag burns. We had no dance floor, and when the carpet had had a few pints of lager spilt on it, it was like dancing in a swamp! And don't even mention the toilets, no seat, no bog roll, dripping pipes leaking effluent into the dressing room in the cellar. But Dave and Mint put everything into the place to make it a success.

Stan and Dicky, the dance night bouncers, with Hammy's assistant Matt and landlord Dave Misselbrook.

Thief took DJ's CDs

DRUNKEN Kieran Freebody grabbed compact discs worth £5,000 from the back of a van parked outside a Southampton pub, city magistrates were told.

The records were being loaded into the vehicle after a gig by disc jockey David Hamilton at the Joiners public house.

Mr Hamilton and a friend gave chase and eventually caught Freebody in a nearby industrial estate, said prosecutor Adrian Lower.

Freebody, 22, of Golden Grove, Southampton, pleaded guilty to theft.

He was fined £250 and told to pay £50 costs.

He must also pay Mr Hamilton £120 in loss of earnings for an engagement which he had to cancel.

The trials and tribulations of DJing at the Joiners!

After about a year, it took off big time. People were spilling out onto the streets. My crowd didn't really come to see the bands at all, but I persevered because there was nowhere else for new local bands to play. It was such a mad place, half the people there were under-age and used to mosh around like crazy, knocking things over. Sometimes, my wife would try and sleep outside in our car and would complain that people puked on it, pissed on it and even had sex standing up against it!

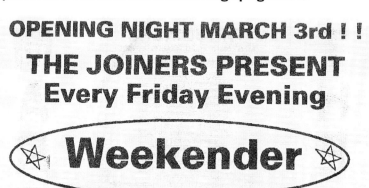

OPENING NIGHT MARCH 3rd ! !
THE JOINERS PRESENT
Every Friday Evening

Weekender

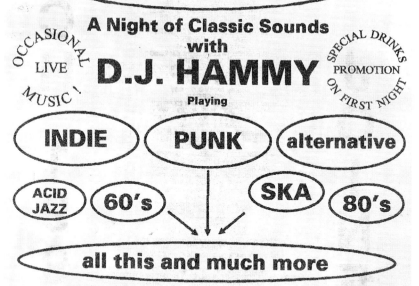

A Night of Classic Sounds
with
D.J. HAMMY

OCCASIONAL LIVE MUSIC!

SPECIAL DRINKS PROMOTION ON FIRST NIGHT

Playing

INDIE   PUNK   alternative

ACID JAZZ   60's   SKA   80's

all this and much more

TIME 8.00PM UNTIL 12.30AM
FREE ADMISSION
(Last Entry 10.30pm)

THE JOINERS,
ST. MARYS STREET, SOUTHAMPTON
Telephone:
01703 225612
01703 552965

☺ *Chill out to Cosmic Vibes in Front Bar*

☺ *Requests Welcome*

☺ *Friendly Atmosphere*

SOUND TRACKS - T.V. THEMES - BRIT POP - GLAM ROCK - MOTOWN

INDIE - ALTERNATIVE

DJ

HAMMY

PRESENTS

SUPERSONIC

EVERY FRIDAY NIGHT AT THE JOINERS ARMS
St Mary Street, Southampton
Tel. 01703 225612

8.30 pm - 1.30 am
(Pub open from 7 pm)
Free Admission!!!

HAPPY HOUR
8.00 - 9.00
ALL PINTS £1.40

No Dress Restrictions
Over 18's only
No Entry after 11.30 pm

ID may be required
R.O.A.R.
Requests Welcome

LIVE BANDS EVERY WEEK
ON STAGE AT 10.00 pm !!!

60'S PSYCHEDELIC - DUB - FUNK - NORTHERN SOUL - DISCO - 80'S

EASY LISTENING - PUNK - HIP HOP - ELECTRONICA - ACID JAZZ - MOD - BAGGY

BIG BEATS - TRANCE - TRIP HOP - SKA - TECHNO

It all came to an abrupt end on Dave's last night, New Year's Eve 1997. The next licensee was called Alison Pennicott, but I did one night which was packed, but the atmosphere wasn't right and neither was the deal. You know when it's time to move on, so I did. I went back for six months in 2001, when it was being run by James Baker, but it fizzled out, although we were still putting on local bands. I have nothing but happy memories of the Joiners and made loads of lifelong friends there."

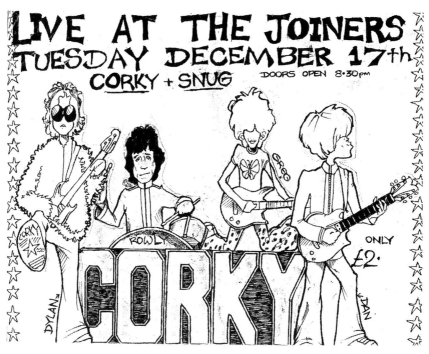

*One of the many bands given their first break by Hammy was Corky,
later to become the Delays.*

Post-gig Corky frolics.

Mint and David's musical shake-up

SOUTHAMPTON'S popular live music venue The Joiners is hitting a different note with a change of management.

Mint Burston and business partner David Misselbrook, who have been running the music gigs at the St Mary Street pub, have now just taken over as managers.

Having put on bands in Birmingham, when Mint moved to Southampton around seven years ago he used his music contacts to put on gigs at city venues including The Joiners. He was later joined by business partner David.

The Joiners' reputation as a venue for up-and-coming bands has grown and many bands return to the pub after they become more well known.

Many bands which started off in the pub's humble surroundings have gone on to bigger things such as Primal Scream who were there in 1989, Shampoo who played there in August 1993 and The Wedding Present and Salad, there early last year.

Other bands have included Oasis, Therapy? Manic Street Preachers and more recently Sleeper and Su-

pergrass. Mint goes for original music from around the world that can range from indie to dub reggae as well as rootsy folk.

"I do take risks with what I put on but I must have a good ear for it because it usually pays off," said Mint.

The Joiners has got a maximum capacity of 150 but is in a higher league than most pubs, as it has a proper permanent stage.

Bands are attracted to the intimate atmosphere of the smallish venue, added Mint. And if only 50 people turn up to a gig, it can still look like a good number to play to.

"From an audience point of view, they are in contact with the bands — some of which are quite big names."

Friday nights is free admission with DJ Hammy presenting classic sounds including indie, punk, acid jazz, 1960s, ska and 1980s.

There's no dress code and live music nights cost around £2.50 to £5, depending on the band.

Daily Echo, 10 / 3 / 95

This fanzine was written by Ged Babey with contributions from Mint, Mark Sutherland, Dave Howell, Gary Revilo, Andrew Matthews and others. Design and all photos by Dik Ng.

• LISTINGS 1995 •

26 April: Reef (NBT)

27 April: Schtum

30 April: Francis Dunnery (PVC)*

This was the first Joiners gig promoted by PVC. From now on, many gigs were promoted either by PVC or by PVC and NBT. For convenience, all gigs involving Ian Binnington are listed as PVC, but Mint had an input on many of those shows.

1 May: ABC Diablo

2 May: Trumans Water (NBT)

4 May: Pet Lamb

6 May: Hair and Skin Trading Company (NBT)

9 May: Edward II (NBT)

10 May: UK Subs

11 May: Porcupine Tree

13 May: The Queers

14 May: 18 Wheeler (NBT)

16 May: Sultans of Ping (NBT)

17 May: Outcast Band

20 May: One Planet

22 May: We Know Where You Live (NBT)

23 May: The Nubiles

24 May: P.A.I.N.

25 May: No Avail

29 May: Skunk Anansie (NBT)

30 May: The Bluetones (NBT)

Mark Morriss: After the gig we played a game of pool with Comfort from Out Of My Hair who was apparently under the effects of mind-altering hallucinigenics, and therefore very easy to hustle. I remember quite clearly the uniqueness of the Joiners. It never really felt like a gig but something more informal than that.

1 June: Velo Deluxe (NBT)

3 June: Green Egg

4 June: Huevos Rancheros / Green Hornets

6 June: Banj Yang

7 June: The Rhythm-Ites

8 June: Mad Cow Disease

10 June: Kinky Machine (NBT)

11 June: Dream Disciples

13 June: Kangaroo Moon

14 June: Michael Chapman

17 June: Black Star Liner (NBT)

19 June: Walls Falling

20 June: Scylla (NBT)

21 June: Outshined

22 June: Rub Ultra

24 June: Smog UK

26 June: Policy of 3

27 June: Boyracer

28 June: Blame The Weather

29 June: J Church

1 July: RDF (NBT)

2 July: All Living Fear

4 July: Blow

5 July: Gorky's Zygotic Mynci (NBT)

6 July: Heavy Stereo (NBT)

9 July: Esoteric

PVC

Many of the coolest shows over the years have been promoted by PVC, often in collaboration with NBT, nowadays on their own. PVC originally stood for Portsmouth Venue Campaign. Anthony Rollinson, in his superb book on the Portsmouth music scene, "Twenty Missed Beats" describes the inception of this organisation:

"Ian Binnington (born Goole, 1960) and Claire Davies (born Derbyshire, 1960) arrived in Portsmouth during 1985. Davies had finished her degree in the summer of 1984, Ian finished his MA in September."

Promoting Portsmouth gigs first at the Hornpipe Arts Centre (they did the La's in front of 28 people, although hundreds claim to have been there), then later at the Wedgewood Rooms and the Pyramids, it was initially a campaigning organisation, running alongside their ground-breaking "Bite Back" label. Ian and Claire still run PVC with businesslike precision, although nowadays its original intention has long since been fulfilled. Despite concentrating on bigger venues, Ian has remained faithful to the Joiners and still promotes several shows a month, often as "try-outs". It's not unusual for a rising band to start out at the Joiners, then progress through the Wedgewood Rooms, the Pyramids, Southampton University and eventually Southampton Guildhall, all shows promoted by PVC. Ian has Mint-like powers of prescience with regard to finding future stars. One extraordinary fact about Ian is that, on a Joiners gig night, he will invariably travel by train, commuting on the shuttle from Southsea. Claire also manages to hold down a full-time teaching job. Talk about troupers!

Ian Binnington: "My first contact with the Joiners was back in the days of running my record label Bite Back, putting on showcase events. We approached Mint for shows for the Cranes and 12-88 Cartel around about '85. As regards promoting, there has been an association with the venue since 1995. This was in the early days of the Wedgewood Rooms, and I asked if Mint had any objections if we put on the odd show. They were acts which had gone well at the Wedgewood Rooms and agents would ask for other venues in the area. There was no 'great plan' at the time. We billed the shows as PVC/NBT, because Mint was totally involved, helping to promote them. Things went well, so the number of shows grew rapidly.

The central attraction of the Joiners was that it was seen as a member of the 'toilet circuit', so there was always the acceptance that it was a bit 'rough and ready'. I liked the way it was, although I wasn't prepared for the first show, when for the first and last time, I drove to St Mary Street. There were fire engines at both ends of the street, putting out fires which had been started in derelict buildings. Then I foolishly wound down my window and engaged in conversation with two charming ladies who I thought could give me directions, not realizing what the street was famous for.

By 1997, the place was being – I can't put it any other way – totally mis-managed. It wasn't really their fault, they had simply bitten off more than they could chew. There had been problems developing, the condition of the venue was deteriorating, and the PA got to the stage where it was packing up in the middle of shows. The catalyst was a gig by the Dust Junkys on the 4th November 1997. They turned up, but it was impossible for them to play. We had some cool shows booked but I pulled the lot, because I no longer had any confidence in the venue. I did go back for a Silver Sun show in mid '98, which I didn't promote but ran on behalf of Metropolis music. I was really shocked at the condition of the building. There was one functioning toilet in the whole place, the carpet was ripped to shreds and the PA and lights were disastrous. It was even worse than I remembered. That was when Alison Pennicott was in charge.

In 1999, the place had been renovated and we met Fred Eynon at the Railway. I liked Jim Sykes and the whole thing was professional again, so we went back in, built it up and we haven't looked back. I would defy anyone to come up with a better venue. It's one of the few which have survived from the early days, it has developed with the times, people have invested in it, and the future looks bright. There's a whole mythology about the Joiners, people always have a good time and now appreciate a better venue which retains the old atmosphere. It's a showcase for new and upcoming acts, shows which people will talk about for years to come. It's also a place for bands to learn their trade and gain experience.

Shows I particularly remember include Feeder. They had already sold out the Wedgewood Rooms and wanted to do a more 'vibey' show. It was in the days before we issued tickets and before the doors opened, there were queues stretching as far as you could see. We closed the doors after fifteen minutes. Hurricane No. 1 had never encored prior to playing the Joiners, but the crowd wouldn't let them back into the dressing room, so they were forced to come back. The shortest gigs I have ever promoted were at the Joiners. Fluffy played for less than twenty minutes. We thought we'd be lynched but we got away with it somehow. The second time we put on the Libertines, they had this thing where they were constantly abusing their tour manager, a really nice guy I had known for years. After getting constant grief from the band, he finally reached the end of his tether and walked out, leaving everyone in total limbo. Luckily, he returned two hours later, Doherty apologized and the show went ahead.

We plan to continue to put shows on at the Joiners for years to come. One thing that it's important to say is that Mint is the defining thing about the venue. He was the Joiners, and he still is."

• LISTINGS 1995 •

11 July: Jadis

12 July: Bivouac

13 July: The Four Brothers (NBT)

18 July: Longpigs (NBT)
An early sighting of Richard Hawley.

19 July: Duffy (NBT)
A late sighting of Steven Tin Tin Duffy, ex-Duran Duran and later involved with Robbie Williams.

20 July: Congregation

23 The Rufus Show

25 July: Thermal

26 July: Elcka (NBT)

27 July: Suffer

1 August: Abdikated

2 August: The Flatville Aces

3 August: Cornershop (NBT)

8 August: Wordbug

9 August: RDF (NBT)

10 August: Sunspeak

14 August: Ban Jwang

15 August: Acrimony

16 August: Bulltaco

19 August: Oi Polloi

22 August: Gouge

23 August: Babylon Zoo (NBT)

24 August: The Caravans

25 August: Heavy Stereo (NBT)

27 August: Horace Pinker

28 August: The Selecter

29 August: Jayne County and the Electric Chairs (NBT)

30 August: Doo The Moog

31 August: Perfume (NBT)

2 September: Scatha

5 September: Blackwater Still

6 September: Peepshow

7 September: Skimmer

14 September: Thurman (NBT)

16 September: Coppertongue

19 September: Gouge

20 September: Thermal

21 September: Headswim (PVC)

23 September: Smog UK

26 September: Nero Circus

27 September: Fluffy (PVC)

28 September: Longpigs (NBT)

1 October: Moonacre Fuzz

2 October: Eusebe (NBT)

3 October: Planet

4 October: Baka Beyond

5 October: Bloated Goat

7 October: Corus Vile

10 October: Blaggers ITA (NBT)

11 October: Nubiles

12 October: Smaller

16 October: Mega City 4 (NBT)

17 October: Defiance

18 October: Out Of My Hair

19 October: Broccoli

22 October: Narcosis

23 October: Coal Porters

24 October: My Drug Hell

25 October: Black Star Liner (NBT)

26 October: Cornershop (NBT)

28 October: Smog UK

29 October: All Living Fear

30 October: The Fuse

31 October: China Drum (NBT)

1 November: Daevid Allen (NBT)

2 November: Loop Guru

4 November: Extinction Of Mankind

5 November: P.A.I.N.

6 November: Peace Sanctuary

7 November: Sid James Experience

• LISTINGS 1995 - 1996 •

8 November: Incubus
  Succubus
9 November: Rub Ultra
13 November: The Real People
14 November: Kevin Ayers
  (NBT)
15 November: Autochre
16 November: Dr Didg
18 November: Voorhees
19 November: Paw (PVC))
20 November: Bear
21 November: Winter of
  Torment
22 November: Mansun (NBT)
23 November: Scum of
  Toytown
26 November: Understand
27 November: Merel
28 November: Soda
29 November: Hugh Reed and
  the Velvet Underpants
30 November: The Bevis Frond
  (NBT)
2 December: Wardance
5 December: Hugh Cornwell
6 December: Scud
7 December: Revolutionary
  Dub Warriors (NBT)
9 December: Drugstore
  (NBT)*
12 December: Jadis
13 December: The Medicine
  Wheel
14 December: Timeshard
16 December: Travis Cut
17 December: Rufus Show
19 December: Babe Rainbow
20 December: Thermal
21 December: Baka Beyond
30 December: Beautiful Life

1996

10 January: Mary Springs
11 January: Freedom AKA
16 January: Coby
17 January: Perfume (NBT)
18 January: Stout
23 January: Gorilla
24 January: Placebo (PVC)
  Keep watching these listings,
  folks!
25 January: Catatonia (NBT)
  See what we mean?
28 January: Coast
31 January: Love Junk
3 February: A.S.E.
4 February: Rufus Show
5 February: Northern Uproar
  (NBT)
6 February: Bang Bang
  Machine
7 February: Skyscraper
8 February: Blyth Power (NBT)
11 February: Number One Cup
  (NBT)
12 February: Sommersault
13 February: Century
14 February: Cecil (NBT)
15 February: War Dance
17 February: Attila The
  Stockbroker
18 February: Loop Guru
19 February: Pusherman
20 February: Involitus
21 February: Battery
22 February: Ex-CNN
25 February: Moloko (PVC)
  See what we mean?
26 February: Christian Death
  (PVC)

Drugstore and the Fake Gold Disc

Craig McEwan: "The wonderful Drugstore played at the Joiners a number of times in 1994-5. Around that time, they also did a free lunchtime gig in the newly opened Virgin Megastore. Ged Babey, Mint's assistant (and my girlfriend) Anja, and myself went along for the show, and also to bag an interview with singer Isabel Monteiro.

Isabel was lovely; as well as regaling us with tales of exploding chickens and her bandmates' underpants, she had a few favourable comments about the Joiners:

'We always get such a good crowd here. I like places where you can create a good rapport with the audience; it's a whole different vibe to festivals'. She also made us guess in which country Drugstore had a number one single. We couldn't, and eventually, laughing like a drain, she told us 'It's Peru! Can you imagine all those baccy-chewing Peruvians in ponchos? The silver disc will be some kinda knitted Aztec thing!'

Which gave me an idea...

The next time Drugstore came to play The Joiners, I took a trip to my local charity shop, where I picked up a raffia table mat and an old picture frame. A quick spray with gold paint, and ten minutes later I had created and mounted my very own Peruvian gold disc!

On the night of the gig, the 'gold disc' was passed on to Ged, who was charged with the task of presenting it to Isabel. At first she was dubious:

'But the label is handwritten!' she protested. Ged's persuasive powers proved irresistible however, to the extent that Isabel asked him to present the disc to her on stage at the climax of the concert. A pale-faced Ged returned to the bar. Realising that this jape was getting a little out of hand, he proceeded to fortify himself in his own inimitable fashion for most of the evening.

Drugstore's show was, as always, superb. They had a knack of making every gig feel like a special event, an intimate gathering that the audience was privileged to attend. The

Isabel Monteiro of Drugstore, photo by Dik.

presentation never happened though; either Ged's nerves, inebriation, or possibly even good sense intervened, and he was still clutching the disc at the end of the set. Probably for the best; following the gig, we owned up to our cruel hoax in the cellar/dressing room. Has Isabel forgiven us yet? Who knows? I hope so. Drugstore never achieved massive success, but to me, and thousands of fans like me, their discs are all gold, and their place in my personal Hall of Fame assured."

147

• LISTINGS 1996 •

27 February: Hugh Reed and the Velvet Underpants
28 February: Dr Didg
29 February: The Kaliphz
3 March: Audioweb / Mansun
4 March: Nero Circus
5 March: Papa Brittle
7 March: Dream Disciples
9 March: Manzarek Doors
10 March: Baby Bird
Soon to be Gorgeous.
12 March: Sullen
13 March: Jocasta
14 March: Killa Instinct
16 March: Doo The Moog
17 March: Tripping Daisy
18 March: Shift
19 March: Sultans of Ping (PVC)
20 March: Sweet Diesel
21 March: Black Star Liner
24 March: All Living Fear
26 March: Carol
28 March: XC-NN
31 March: Midnight Configuration
1 April: We Know Where You Live
2 April: Tiny Monroe / Supernaturals (PVC)
3 April: Drown
4 April: Smaller
9 April: Doughnuts
10 April: Coby
11 April: The Rhythmites
17 April: Mighty Chocolate Gods
18 April: Asian Dub Foundation
20 April: Coaster
21 April: Spite
22 April: Cable

23 April: Spitfire
24 April: Incubus Succubus
25 April: Dave Graney and the Coral Snakes28 April: Baby Chaos (PVC)
29 April: High Llamas
30 April: Super Furry Animals
1 May: Moonhead
2 May: Freedom AKA
4 May: Jesus Jones (PVC)
6 May: Mucky Pup (PVC)
7 May: Scarfo
8 May: Electric Groove Temple
9 May: Kitchens of Distinction (PVC)
12 May: Telstar Ponies
13 May: Send No Flowers (PVC)
14 May: In Aura
16 May: 999
19 May: Animals That Swim
20 May: The Divine Comedy (PVC)
21 May: Whatever
22 May: Portobello Bones
23 May: Porcupine Tree
26 May: Mundy
27 May: Compulsion
28 May: Strychnine
29 May: Cecil
30 May: Citizen Fish
1 June: Manzarek Doors
4 June: Gorilla
5 June: Uresei Yatsura
6 June: Bandulu
9 June: Intastella
10 June: Sneaker Pimps
11 June: Jocasta
12 June: Space
13 June: Hooten 3 Car
16 June: Hiatus

• LISTINGS 1996 •

17 June: Mansun
18 June: Peel
19 June: Aura
22 June: Suffer
24 June: Compulsion
25 June: Done Lying Down
26 June: Cecil
27 June: Timeshard
30 June: Njava
 2 July: The Flaming Stars
 3 July: We Know Where You Live
 4 July: Suffer
 6 July: Thermal
 8 July: The Steamkings
 9 July: Ligament
10 July: Orange Deluxe
11 July: Attila The Stockbroker
15 July: Mary Springs
16 July: Number One Cup
17 July: Tiger / Linoleum
18 July: Gluebound
23 July: Agent Provocateur
24 July: Nosferatu
30 July: The Candyskins
31 July: Honky
 1 August: Heavy Stereo
 3 August: The Mock
 4 August: Abana
 8 August: Spacemaid
12 August: Judith
13 August: The Frank and Walters
14 August: Lodestar
15 August: Embassy
21 August: Snide
22 August: Thermal
24 August: Oi Polloi
26 August: Feeder
 See what we mean?
28 August: Fictional Aardvarks

2 September: Eugene Chadbourne
3 September: Drown
4 September: Sneaker Pimps
5 September: Trash Can Sinatras
9 September: Robyn Hitchcock / Homer
10 September: Cradle
11 September: Elcka
12 September: Baka Beyond
16 September: Kerbdog
17 September: Bennet
18 September: Linoleum
23 September: Cable
24 September: Mansun
26 September: Sullen
30 September: Whisky Priests
 1 October: Thirteen
 2 October: Silver Sun
 6 October: Jolt
 7 October: Smaller
 8 October: Joyrider (PVC)
 9 October: David Thomas and Two Pale Boys (PVC)
10 October: Heavy Stereo
13 October: Fluffy (PVC)
14 October: Nut
15 October: Sub Circus
16 October: Shutdown
20 October: Scarlet
21 October: Feeder
22 October: Asian Dub Foundation
23 October: Los Crudos
24 October: Astralasia (PVC)
27 October: Joolz
28 October: Supernaturals (PVC)
29 October: Drop Dead
30 October: Flaming Stars

149

Joiners Madness

Thieves Like Us, 28 August 1979

Oliver Gray, band manager: "The two-inch high stage was situated at the opposite end of the room to where it is now. Because the neighbours had been complaining, the landlord had invested in one of those evil devices which switched off the PA if the volume got too high. Thieves were the first band to play there since it had been installed, and of course, it wasn't working properly. Every time the volume rose above a whisper, off went the sound. After a song and a half, we had to admit defeat and I sat dejectedly at the door, doling out refunds to the disgruntled audience. To this day, I believe the landlady was throwing the switch because she didn't like the music."

Automatic Dlamini, 11 January 1990

Oliver Gray: "I had persuaded Mint to book this band, as they were the brainchild of John Parish, who was a friend whose earlier bands I had managed. They were mainly percussion driven, but two or three songs were more acoustic and sung by a quiet girl hiding behind a big Gretsch guitar. This was Polly Harvey. I had brought along a video camera, but as I walked backwards to get a wider angle, I leant against the emergency exit, which burst open, so that I fell flat on my back in the alleyway. Mint, worrying about the noise and the neighbours and not realizing my predicament, rushed over and slammed the door shut, leaving me outside. Luckily, I still had the felt-tip mark on my hand, which gained me re-admission."

An Emotional Fish, 11 June 1990

Oliver Gray: "There's always been a tradition of newly-signed bands, eager to show off their wealth, arriving with inappropriate amounts of shiny new gear, crew, etc. Sometimes they have those flight cases full of ten or more guitars, plus a flunky to hand them to them when they swop over after each song. This particular Irish band was on some big label and arrived in St Mary Street with an articulated lorry. Having pronounced the Joiners PA to be inadequate, they proceeded to reverse the artic into the narrow alleyway at the side of the building, where it got stuck and took several hours to remove. During the gig, there was so much gear in there that there was hardly any room for an audience."

Fabulous, 12 December 1991

Martyn Goodacre, now a world-famous rock photographer (he took the iconic picture of Kurt Cobain, known as the most-bootlegged T-shirt image of all time) was a member of Fabulous:

"The Joiners was one of the first places we played out of London. Previously we had played trendy clubs at two in the morning and everybody was out of it on drugs and coolly dressed. The Joiners was a bit of a reality check. It was freezing cold and the crowd were mainly blokes, all dressed in old men's coats with steamy breath and looking miserable, clasping pints of cheap bitter. Our publicity had come before us and the audience were shouting demands of 'shock us', so I did manage to make a leap from one amp to another over the drum kit, a jump that even suprised me, as I thought I would never make it. Apart from that, the performance was very ordinary and I guess we only just about managed to not have the the punters demanding their money back. Our driver at the time was Big Steve, now one half of The Arlenes. He spent the whole of the gig lying in the back of our freezing, clapped-out van with the flu. I thought he might die.

My first visit to the Joiners was my first NME commission in 1989, which was to head down to Southampton and take some shots of a band called The Family Cat. My girlfriend at the time for some reason literally begged me not to go but I had to. I was 28 and had never had a proper job, so I saw this as a big step foward. I met the writer Simon Williams, with whom I had to share a B and B twin room. I remember that night mainly because of the horror of getting my camera lens stuck half on and half off the body of the camera, making it impossible to focus. In desparation, I carried on taking pics, pretending nothing was wrong. I even got the band outside for a few shots outside a butchers shop across the road. Amazingly, I was able to print a couple of shots and therefore saved my career in rock photography."

John Robb of Goldblade

"In the late Eighties, when I was in the Membranes, we did the ridiculous, never-ending drive down to Southampton to play at the Joiners, having been asked down there by Mint. It was dark by the time we got to the Joiners, and raining. We drove into the alley by the side and I jumped out of the van. My foot went straight into a massive pile of dogshit, which I didn't notice at the time. We loaded the gear into the venue and soundchecked. It was only then that I noticed the dogshit footprints round the club, and on my foot. No one else actually noticed, so I guess that everyone who went to the gig went home that night with their own little memento of the show!"

PJ Harvey, 21 December 1991

Oliver Gray: "After the Dlamini show, PJ Harvey, now with her own band, returned to the Joiners. Decorating was going on and a scaffold had been left in the room. As the dancing took hold during 'Sheela-Na-Gig', the floor bounced and one of those heavy scaffolding bolts rolled off, missing my cranium by a millimetre. It would have been a good way to go though."

Birdland, 9 March 1993

Oliver Gray: "This was a band on the way down. Having adorned the front page of the NME and been hyped to no avail, here they were again. They and their crew had lost none of their arrogance, however. The Joiners simply isn't a place for airs and graces, but they insisted that the house lights were dimmed so they could make a spectacular entrance. Mint, obeying their orders to switch off the lights, simply left them off, so that they had to play their first few songs in pitch blackness. 'Oy', they cried in their Brummie twangs, 'switch the bloody lights on, we can't read our set list'. 'Sorry,' replied Mint. 'You asked for them to be switched off, you never said anything about switching them on again.' I often wonder if he did it on purpose, but he ain't telling."

Robyn Hitchcock, 9 September 1996

Maria Croce reports in the Echo: "Mum Joyce Hitchcock recalls that, when she was pregnant with Robyn, her late husband Raymond persuaded a Scottish friend to play the bagpipes to her stomach in the hope that it would give the baby an appreciation of music. 'I often wonder if those bagpipes had anything to do with his chosen career', said Joyce. 'I think his first public performance was on the sands at Weston-Super-Mare when he was two and a half. He suddenly got up on a rock and started singing to everyone. Later, Robyn would entertain old people and rehearse in the billards room at our home in Abbotts Worthy.'"

The Small Print

Dear Mint

RE: AN EMOTIONAL FISH AT SOUTHAMPTON JOINERS' ARMS

Please take this letter as confirmation of the above artiste
appearing at your venue, noting the following details:

TOUR SPONSORSHIP: This tour is the first one ever to be co-
                    promoted by Radio One and it is very
                    important that all ads, tickets, leaflets,
                    etc, carry the exact wording as shown as
                    the billing copy below.

DATE: Tuesday 28 August

TIMES: Doors :   8.30 pm
                    Show Starts : 9.00 pm

TICKET PRICE(S):   £4.00 in advance, £5.00 on door.

---

that the management hereby engages the Artiste and Artiste accepts an

THE CRANBERRIES

present ....

engagement to

appear as ....

(or in his usual entertainment) at the Dance Hall/Theatre or other venue and from the dates
and for the periods and at the salary stated in the Schedule hereto.

Wednesday, 28th October 1992
Joiners, 141 St Marys St, SOUTHAMPTON
Date .... **£150, plus 75% gross takings over £350**
Venue ....
Salary ....

1. The Artiste shall not, without the written consent of the management, appear at any
public place of entertainment within a radius of .... miles of the venue during a
period of .... weeks immediately prior to and .... weeks immediately
following the engagement. **1 x 45 minutes**

2. The Artiste shall play for ... **Cash to artist on night** ....

3. Salary payable by **THE CRANBERRIES** .... to ....
on/within ....

4. .... shall appear personally throughout
6. The Management agrees to pay for and provide a first
class p.a., monitor and lights system (to the Artist's
5. Any rider clauses attached form an integral part of the agreement.
specifications), with operators, for the full, free use
of the Artist.

Mogwai, 12 June 1997

Ian Binnington, promoter: "At the end of the tour, I was chuffed to hear from the agent that Mogwai had cited the Joiners as the best venue of the tour. When I asked why, he explained that they couldn't actually remember the venue, but had particularly loved the chips with curry sauce from the chippy down the road."

Crackout, 14 March 2001

Proving that not all bands love the Joiners.

From crackout.com: "It is drizzling today and the venue is shit because the stage resembles a book shelf, so much so, that the drums have to go at one end of the stage, the bass in the middle, and the guitars and vocals at the other end, which makes playing a gig of any worth impossible. So there. Before the gig, we go and crouch in the extremely low dressing room (which is really a beer cellar). Then we take to the stage and play a really bad gig – I can't hear anything nor can I see anything, and the same goes for Jack and Steven, although www.drownedinsound.com gave the gig a favourable review. After the show, we watch Alex and Graham try to set fire to the ceiling of dressing room.

When we leave the cursed venue, we stop off at a Chinese and order far too much food, which means some of us fall asleep for the journey back. Scot puts some complete wank on the CD player, which leaves Jack and Nigel reaching for their razor blades to gash open their wrists and Jack tells me he is considering jumping out of the bus on the motorway."

John Otway (serial Joiners performer)

Otway: "I must have played at the Joiners getting on for ten times over the years. I had a bit of a reputation as a ceiling destroyer. At one venue in Hemel Hempsted, Richard, my guitarist, decided to copy my attacking of the ceiling tiles, and grabbed hold of one of the aluminium supports. Unfortunately, all these supports were somehow linked together and a domino effect occurred, ending with the entire ceiling coming down. One pub in Richmond insists to this day on a clause in the contract forbidding me to touch the ceiling.

At the Joiners one night, I was able to remove one of the tiles and get right up into the suspended ceiling. My foot went through one of the tiles and for a number of years, the gaping hole remained, together with a plaque saying 'Otway Did This'.

154

The Great Ceiling Destroyer

By the end of the show, the doorman had run off with all the money, but I don't think the two incidents were connected."

The D4, 4 October 2002

Ben Ward, promoter: "This was a band from New Zealand. The singer thought it would be cool to leap onto the sound desk, trampling on it with his Doc Martens. From there, attempting to crowd surf, he hurled himself into the audience but unfortunately, nobody could be bothered to catch him. He fell on to a pint glass, gashing his leg, but dragged himself back onto the stage, covered in blood, and carried on until the end of the set. We then called an ambulance and the next day decided that we would finally have to look into the plastic glasses option. There was actually some talk of the band suing the venue over his injury, but as it was entirely self-inflicted, they decided against it."

Vendetta Red, 12 October 2002

Graham Weaver: "They demolished their equipment on stage. It was only a small crowd but so many of them were stage diving, including the singer! I was so hyped up I wanted to jump off the stage too – and I was in my early forties! The singer raced through to the abandoned bar area at the end of the gig, hollering and bellowing. One band member was collapsed in the archway leading to the stage area while another was unconscious in the alleyway outside!"

Echobelly, 21 June 1994

Paula Hambly: "We had such a great time at Echobelly, with loads of friends, music, beer, all you could want. That's why I loved the Joiners so much, it wasn't just a venue, I would just go down there like it was my local, meet up with other rival record shop workers and we would just be utter music anoraks and geeks!

Towards the end of the evening, one of my friends had been talking to this guy Mark Sutherland. I recall that he had either written or said something to the effect that all bands from Southampton were shit and nobody decent had ever come out of the town, whereupon I got all Southampton defensive and ended up shouting about journos not doing research properly and writing crap, and then reeling off bands to him (I can't remember who now, but they would have been local at the time, Transcendental and Nova Coma spring to mind). I was on a one woman, slighty drunken crusade. All this was happening out at the front of the Joiners. It is allegedly reported that I chased him down the street, waving my fists. There could have been some arse kicking references as well, and I seem to remember he was quite a big bloke! Ironically, I ended up doing some journalism myself, interviewing Louise Wener for Sound Info when none of the guys would do it because they were scared of her!"

Lostprophets, 28 April 2001

James Baker, venue manager: "It was a packed house, the normal chaos, when at the end of the bar arrived a young kid, only 13, with his head covered in blood and a nice big cut in the top of his head. Some idiot at the front of the stage had thrown a pint glass up in the air, landing right on this kid's head and knocking him stupid. We cleaned him up as best we could and tried to get hold of his mum on the phone to take him to hospital. We couldn't get hold of her and all this kid wanted to do was see the show, so we put him up in the sound box and kept an eye on him. I was thinking that the mother was going to turn up, see her bloodstained 13-year old and start calling lawyers. And it was Friday 13th. At the end of the show, I talked to the tour manager and let him know what had happened. The band went to town for him, it was a beautiful sight. 40 minutes earlier he had been oozing blood, in tears, having the worst time ever, and now he had a huge grin, his bloodstained T-shirt was being signed and admired by all the members of Lostprophets and he was having his picture taken with the band. Luckily, this was the moment when his mum arrived. She was expecting the worst but walked in to the sight of her son having the best moment of his life!"

In The Shit

Ben Ward, Promoter: "My favourite (or at least most vivid) Joiners story was when Vic Toms and I were promoting there in the Pandemonium days. We made regular trips there to have a look around and show our faces. One time we went, we found that the sewer outside had blocked up and filled the cellar with sewage, up as far up as the stairs! At certain points it was as deep as your knees. The licensee at the time, Mike 'Mad Dog' Chapman, came down and there was much discussion about the nature of the mysterious water, before he decided to poke some of the mystery mud with a stick. You'd have thought the bog roll, tampons and condoms would have indicated the nature of the water, but he waded in regardless."

At The Drive-In (4 May 2000)

Jamie Summers: "I was lucky enough to go to an ATDI headlining show put on by the local punk collective. I had no idea who they were, and the venue contained about 75 people. Suffice to say, I've never had my expectations (which were zero) blown to bits so easily by a live performance, and it remains one of the greatest things I've ever seen. It's a big shame that they split about a year after."

Ghostly Goings-on

Amy Brown (better known as Scarlet from Scarlet Soho) lived in the flat above the Joiners from 2002 until 2005, whilst working behind the bar:

"Most of the time I was completely hammered, so most of my stories are unprintable, involving lock-ins and my own stupidity. But I am one of the many to have experienced the Joiners Ghost. Lots of different people, members of staff etc, have independently experienced strange feelings of terror at the very back of the cellar, to the extent that they have panicked and had to run for the exit. It's very cold down there and you don't hear the noise from above, so it's a really spooky place."

Taking The Piss

Mike Chapman, licensee: "We were all very excited about the Babyshambles gig in May 2005, because Kate Moss was all over the TV news. Elton John was playing at St Mary's Staduim that Saturday, but all week the local paper was dominated by the imminent arrival of Pete and Kate. In the end, she didn't turn up, but stayed in Winchester prior to the Homelands festival the next day.

Pete arrived with his entourage. His 'driver' appeared to be blasted out of his head. Apparently he hadn't slept for four days. There were five or six paparazzi out front, so they wanted an entrance where Pete could get in unnoticed. I went round to open the cellar door at the back to let him in. Just as I was shutting the door behind him and the NME journalist who was travelling with the band, Pete, realizing there was no loo in the cellar, came rushing back out and had a lengthy piss against the back wall. A photographer appeared round the corner but missed his scoop because Pete had just finished. Afterwards I regretted not getting Pete to piss in a bottle, maybe I could have sold it on eBay."

Temporary doorman

Oliver Gray: "On that same Babyshambles night, I had forgotten about the show and popped over from a gig at the Talking Heads which was starting late. I thought, maybe there might be some band at the Joiners I could pass the time with. Suddenly, all the security disappeared and I found myself in sole charge of the front door for about a quarter of an hour, with all this bedlam going on outside. I tried to give the impression I knew what I was doing, but it was probably the hottest ticket in the UK on that particular day and anyone could have walked straight in and I wouldn't have been able to stop them!"

The cause of all the trouble.
Photo by Mint

• LISTINGS 1996 - 1997 •

2 November: John Otway and Attilla The Stockbroker

4 November: Livingstone (PVC)

5 November: P.A.I.N.

6 November: Real TV

7 November: Sidi Bou Said

9 November: Neurology

10 November: The Cardiacs (PVC)

11 November: J Church

12 November: The Candyskins

13 November: Cecil

14 November: Incubus Succubus

16 November: Dweeb

17 November: All Living Fear

18 November: Scheer

19 November: Peter and the Test Tube Babies

20 November: David Devant and his Spirit Wife

21 November: The Warm Jets

25 November: Speedy (PVC)

26 November: Scatha

27 November: Honky

28 November: Ishen Sound

2 December: Jolt (PVC)

4 December: Spacemaid

5 December: Dr Didg

7 December: Maximum Who

10 December: Revolutionary Dub Warriors

11 December: Pressgang

12 December: Fruit

17 December: Corky

18 December: The Magick Brothers

19 December: Stout

22 December: The Score

23 December: The Poppyheads

1997

DJ Hammy's residency continued throughout 1997. The year's gigs were publicized on pastel-tinted glossy flyers printed (and sponsored) by Indigo Press. One side featured Hammy's nights and the other had full gig listings. Often, punters were lured by brief descriptions of the bands' music, sometimes illuminating, sometimes quaint. Some are reproduced here for your entertain ment.

19 January: Peel

3 February: The Poppyheads

5 February: Candyskins

10 February: Feeder

12 February: Silver Sun (PVC)

18 February: Perfume (PVC)

25 February: Novocaine

26 February: Squat

27 February: Acacia

28 February: Itinerants

4 March: Rhythm Conspiracy

5 March: Hipster

6 March: Rosa Mota

10 March: Kerbdog (PVC)

11 March: Smog UK

12 March: Tribal Drift

13 March: The Driven

17 March: Broccoli

18 March: Waterfall

19 March: Pist.On

20 March: Symposium (PVC)

24 March: Tumblehigh

25 March: Astralasia (PVC)

31 March: Screaming Dead

1 April: A

"The next Kerbdog?"

Ruth-less in front of our mum and dad

RUTH — The Joiners, Southampton.

THEY'RE from Southampton, and they're going to be huge. Ruth are among a growing crop of young local bands hoping to come good and, judging by last Thursday's performance, it is only a matter of time.

Despite a disappointing turnout, Ruth revelled in the fact that they were playing in front of a home crowd and their enthusiasm shone throughout the 50-minute set.

Kicking-off with their current single I Don't Know, Ruth previewed most of the material from their debut album, Harrison, which is out in July.

Highlights included: Biggest Star in Heaven, Valentine's Day, Chickens, and their superb interpretation of the Beatles classic You're Gonna Lose That Girl.

Finishing with the epic Can't Stop Myself, Ruth proved that they will be around for a few years yet.

Singer Matt Hales, from Bitterne, told the Daily Echo afterwards: "We've been looking forward to this gig for some time, it's always nice to play in front of your mum and dad."

Paul Green.

Daily Echo, 13 June 1997. Why's this here?
Because they later became Aqualung.

• LISTINGS 1997 •

2 April: Loop Guru
3 April: Beautiful People
7 April: MU 330
8 April: Ezio
9 April: One Inch Punch
"Justin Warfield hits town."
10 April: Hurricane No 1 (PVC)
"Ride's Andy Bell storms back."
14 April: Senna
"REM meets Radiohead."
15 April: Gold Blade (PVC)
16 April: The Muffin Men
A rare "Tribute Band" – but, as the Muffin Men contained original Mother Of Invention Jimmy Carl Black, it can be overlooked.
17 April: Blue Orange
21 April: Score
22 April: Screeper
23 April: Realise
24 April: Gorse
28 April: Dead Star
"Featuring Crowded House bassist."
29 April: Jocasta
30 April: Kidnapper
14 May: Feil Garvie
19 May: Speedy (PVC)
1 June: Ezio
3 June: Lovers
4 June: Sterling
5 June: Ruth
8 June: Velvet Jones (PVC)
10 June: Unsophisticates
11 June: Northern Uproar (PVC)
12 June: Mogwai (PVC)
15 June: Barnstormer (Attilla The Stockbroker)

17 June: Bug
18 June: Linoleum
24 June: Skyrockets
25 June: Magoo
26 June: Groop Dogrill
1 July: Candystream
2 July: Monkey Island
3 July: Strychnine
8 July: Lig
9 July: Flip Zippo
10 July: Green Hornets
15 July: Dust
16 July: Scarfo (PVC)
17 July: Contrast
21 July: Dystopia
23 July: Sweet Children Trust
24 July: Hitchers
"Irish band set for the big time" – it says here.
25 July: Raindog
28 July: Deptford Beach Babes
29 July: Feeder (PVC)
31 July: Nightnurse
"Mix the Pixies, Shellac, My Bloody Valentine and you have Nightnurse – a tonic for the sensdes (sic)."
6 August: Natural Orange
7 August: Jaguar
14 August: Informer
20 August: Fat Day
21 August: Back To Base
22 August: Pist.on (PVC)
27 August: Verity Suiter
28 August: Stout
1 September: Unsilent Minority
3 September: Superstar (PVC)
4 September: Raindog
6 September: 13
9 September: Tampasm (PVC)

Pat The Doorman

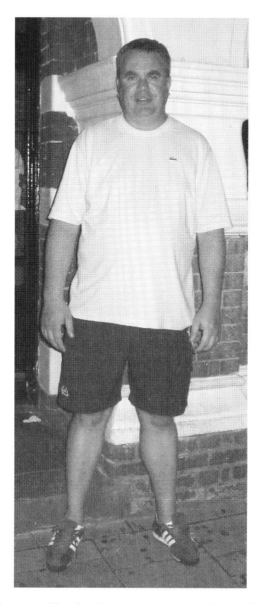

Pat Muldowney: "I'm Southampton born and bred. Most of my family are good musicians. My cousin Dominic Muldowney is Head of the London School of Music and wrote the original score for the film '1984'. I got into my work in an unusual way. I was involved with the left wing group Anti-Fascist Action, combating groups like the BNP. We looked after 'minority groups', specifically the band Blaggers ITA.

In January 1998, someone told me about a job going at the Joiners as a doorman for two days a week. Dave Misselbrook had been replaced by a lady called Alison, who had taken over the Joiners after previously running the Talking Heads. She was a manager, not the licensee. That was a period when not much went on musically at the Joiners, it was mainly a dance venue, which explains how few bands played there at the time. It was the only period when the Joiners' atmosphere was less than welcoming. The sound was crap, the toilets disastrous and it felt like it was on the verge of closing every day. In fact, I was always relieved when I turned up for work and found I still had a job.

December 1999 saw the arrival of Fred Eynon, licensee of the Railway in Winchester, who put in the new PA and installed Jim Sykes as manager. I remained as doorman. Because of my 'dodgy' past, the council threatened not to issue me with a doorman's 'badge', but Fred stood by me to the extent that he said he'd close the place down rather than lose me as doorman. He was putting on good bands and Ian Binnington was back involved by then, but it still wasn't working out financially. Some gigs only had 20 or 30 people, despite the fact that there were several good managers, including Vic Toms, James Baker and Ben Ward.

In 2000, the lease passed to Mike Chapman. Fortunately for the Joiners, but unfortunately for Mike, the night he chose to come down we had Coldplay playing and the place was rammed. If he'd come down the night before, there'd have been four people! In 2002, Eldridge Pope sold the pub to Innhouse Properties. Peter Hilton worked for them and took over the lease from them in 2004. Then, in October 2005, I went into partnership with Glenn Lovell and we now run it together with promoter Kai Harris.

Because I'm always on the door, I've experienced some interesting evenings. Remembering Paul Dominy's description of the Battle Of St Mary's Street, I experienced something similar in October 2003, on a Tuesday when there was a Saints / Pompey grudge match. We stupidly decided to open in the afternoon for Saints supporters, although all the other Southampton pubs were wisely closed. At one stage, 150 Pompey fans decided to visit us. The police said, 'Don't worry, just stand firm'. So we did, and a full-scale riot broke out. It

THE JOINERS

This alternative music venue is small but still a great place to get up close and personal to bands on the rise. Nirvana, The Charlatans, Radiohead, Oasis and the Manic Street Preachers all played here before going on to bigger and better things. It is split into two parts, with a pub at the front and the venue at the back. It has been described as Southampton's answer to CBGB's, the New York club where the Ramones made their name. Also check out DJ Hammy on Fridays – a brilliant Southampton DJ who mixes the likes of Mercury Rev and The Stone Roses with top dance tunes.
Where: 141 St Mary's Street (023 8022 5612).
When: 6 days a week. Check local press for listings.
How much: £3. Phone for details.

The Independent discovers the Joiners. Spot the deliberate mistake.

was only two minutes, but it felt like hours. But, to be fair, anything like that is very, very rare.

The second time Coldplay played, I was at the door as they left and Chris Martin said, 'Thanks for a great night'. I replied that I was sure Coldplay were going to be huge. Chris then said, 'Yes, and when we are huge, I'm going to come back and buy the Joiners'. We're still waiting for the phone to ring.

On the night the Arctic Monkeys played, part of their rider stipulated a case of water, some soft drinks and a cardboard cutout of a local celebrity. I couldn't find one, so instead, I put a cardboard cutout of Paul Weller in the dressing room. They were really happy with that and signed it for us.

The last time Babyshambles played, my daughter Lauren was desperate to meet Pete Doherty. I took her downstairs, to find Pete on his hands and knees on the filthy floor. He said to his manager, 'I can't fucking find it'. He was looking for a rock of crack which had got lost amongst the rubble. I said, 'Any chance of a photo with my daughter?' and he got up and posed like the perfect gentleman he is.

I've always loved meeting the people as they come through the door. I think it's unique in Southampton for the licensee to be the doorman as well. When I started in 1998, it was just a job, but the Joiners gets under your skin and you end up loving the place. In fact, I can't explain it, but the love of the place is just so intense that it comes before everything else. For me, it comes before family, kids, even relationships. I've lost partners in the past because I love the Joiners more than them. My whole life is dedicated to keeping the place alive forever."

• LISTINGS 1997 - 1998 •

10 September: Kangaroo Moon
11 September: Good Grief
13 September: Snoozer
15 September: Michael Chapman
16 September: Hal-Al-Shedad
17 September: Gothic Tarts
18 September: User
This may look like just another forgotten local band with a terrible name, but User's drummer was Andy Burrows (later of Razorlight) and the singer was Pete Hobbs (of The Boy Least Likely To).
22 September: Skin (PVC)
Yes, her out of Skunk Anansie.
23 September: Dweeb (PVC)
24 September: Cuff
25 September: Waterfall
29 September: Groop Dogrill (PVC)
2 October: Lo-Fidelity Allstars (PVC)
4 October: Nightnurse
5 October: J Church
7 October: Contrast
8 October: Broken Brow
9 October: Twisted Pig
11 October: Jaguar (PVC)
14 October: Jell
15 October: Rye Coalition
16 October: Hangovers
21 October: Dream City Film Club
22 October: MU 330
23 October: Orphic Soup
27 October: Arnold
28 October: Cecil (PVC)

29 October: Moke
30 October: Tribute To Nothing (PVC)
3 November: The Van Pelt
4 November: Dust Junkies (PVC)
5 November: Novocaine (PVC)
6 November: Deep
12 November: Natural Orange
13 November: Flaming Stars (PVC)
18 November: The Dandys (PVC)
19 November: Travis Cut
20 November: Incubus Succubus
26 November: China Drum (PVC)
27 November: The O
3 December: Robyn Hitchcock
4 December: Shimmer
5 December: Donkey
9 December: Virgin Soldiers
10 December: All Living Fear
11 December: Mike TV
12 December: The Icons
16 December: Muse
Yes, it's them.
17 December: Seizure
19 December: Fever
30 December: Honey Honey
"From Belgium" – it says here.

1998

The second "Black Hole" in the life of the Joiners.

10 April: Steadman
10 May: Black Couch
23 May: Porcupine Tree

165

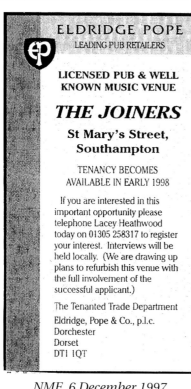

ELDRIDGE POPE
LEADING PUB RETAILERS

LICENSED PUB & WELL KNOWN MUSIC VENUE

THE JOINERS

St Mary's Street, Southampton

TENANCY BECOMES
AVAILABLE IN EARLY 1998

If you are interested in this important opportunity please telephone Lacey Heathwood today on 01305 258317 to register your interest. Interviews will be held locally. (We are drawing up plans to refurbish this venue with the full involvement of the successful applicant.)

The Tenanted Trade Department

Eldridge, Pope & Co., p.l.c.
Dorchester
Dorset
DT1 1QT

NME, 6 December 1997.

The Joiners Revisited

THE JOINERS HAS NEVER LOOKED THIS GOOD!

What's happened? There's a wide, spacious stage with a flown sound system and substantial monitors, a lighting rig that makes the place look like a disco (never mind) and a neat sound booth right in front of the stage for the engineer. There are people flooding in with all kinds and colours of clothing, hair, piercing, political attitudes and pretend ages. Better still, there is a buffet and a press pass with a couple of free drinks on it... excuse me, mmm... gulp. Ahh, that's better.

We've already reviewed the outrageous Rumdum this month (see page 4) but what a great choice of band to kick off the new-look Joiners! Even before their slightly hesitant start they commanded attention just by wearing silly hats. It would be easy to go wrong from there and let yourself be upstaged by your costume department but Rumdum did to the Joiners as God did unto the Sodomites (not that I was there on the previous occasion.) It was a great night, but more importantly the Joiners is once again a great place. Long may they be Joined in Holy Rock'n'Roll. ***GW***

● **THE musical management merry-go-round has swung into action in Southampton as the Joiners and the Talking Heads welcome new bosses for 1998.**

The new team at the Joiners in St Marys Street includes former landlord of the Onslow, Dave Bullpitt, and Alison Pennicott from Talking Heads in Portswood Road.

Dave ran the Onslow when it was a top blues venue, attracting bands from across the UK and the States. But Alison promised the Joiners would not become a dedicated Blues venue, but would try to build on its near-legendary reputation as a rock venue.

She said: "We aim to offer the same style of music and the same choice of exciting new bands, but we've only just arrived and there's a lot of work to do before we build up musical contacts.

"The PA just isn't up to scratch at the moment and the place could also do with a lick of paint, but we'll get there in a couple of months."

Advertiser,
15 January 1998.

The Joiner's Arms, St Mary's Street, Southampton

Everybody's favourite living room, and the place to spot the superstars before even they know who they are.—the Joiner's is in a state of flux after a disastrous year in which there have been tenancy and promotion problems, the sound system has given up the ghost and a host of gigs has been cancelled amidst recriminations and bad feeling. This isn't the place we know and love, so let's hope that the recent *NME* ad which seeks new tenants and promises a renovation programme will bear fruit. If this happens, Mint will doubtless return to the fold and normal service will be resumed.

Favourite moment of 1997: Contracting hypothermia in the company of Robyn Hitchcock.

Hants Chronicle, 2 Jan 1998.

ROCK COLUMN: Oliver Gray

Lights, action and great value

AT last it's back to business as usual at the Joiners. After a clever and sensitive facelift (a lick of paint, a repositioning of the stage, some lights and—yippee!—a new sound system), it's back to great value packages which allow you the privilege of seeing the best new bands before anyone else does.

Take this line-up, for example. Idoru, a guitar trio from Southampton, were young, tuneful and bursting with potential, while Rosita is the new band which has risen from the ashes of Kenickie.

This, wonder of wonders, was their first-ever gig. World debuts we can boast about in years to come, this is what we like!

Kenickie and I parted on very bad terms. As they headed for the end, they over-reached themselves in a big way and fell apart in a most unsightly manner. Now Marie da Santiago and Emmy-Kate Montrose have quickly resurfaced with a

Rosita/Idoru: Joiners Arms, Southampton

style not dissimilar to the original Kenickie, just a bit less frivolous.

Was it chance that the intro tape included *You Only Live Twice*? And will they? On the evidence of this early appearance, it seems doubtful.

Besides the two soberly dressed ex-Kenickies, we have some journeyman musos in the form of a drummer and a guitarist (both excellent at keeping time with their chewing gum but not at much else), plus a charming Scottish keyboard player who unfortunately was completely inaudible.

The all-new set didn't seem to contain any songs that one would be likely to remember, and all the vocals were revealed as being insufficient for the job. When the highlight of your set is a Rubettes' song (*Sugar Baby Love*, thankfully completely over the audience's head), you really ought to worry.

Rosita come across as Blondie without any songs (or, for that matter, any blondes). Still, who cares? We've got our Joiners back.

Hants Chronicle, 16 April 1999.

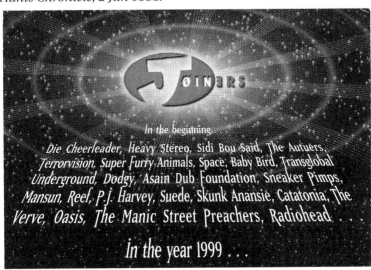

The famous postcard. Note eccentric spelling.

ACE MUSIC VENUE IS GIVEN A $40,000 FACELIFT

Joiners to feel the beat again

Report by
David Schaffer

◆

ONE of the South's most influential live music venues is set to return to its former glory with a major overhaul.

Southampton's legendary Joiners Arms is due to reopen its doors next month after a near-£40,000 facelift.

The Joiners hosted some of the most famous rock names of the Eighties and Nineties; some before they hit the big time. Now it is bidding to re-establish its name. It's two years since the St Mary Street pub was hit by a cash crisis, which made putting on the likes of Oasis, the Manic Street Preachers and Radiohead unviable.

Closed since the end of last year, it will reopen on March 10, under new management, complete with a new sound and lighting system, as well as a new stage. Brewery Eldridge Pope, which owns it, is footing the bill, even though the revamp has gone over budget by £10,000.

New manager Jim Sykes said: "In

Manic Street Preachers

the last two years people have been running this place who don't really know about music, but now all that has changed."

The 22-year-old, who comes to the pub after promoting live music at Winchester's Railway Inn, is undaunted by living up to the past.

He added: "One of the things that we have to live up to is the reputation that the former licensee who booked the bands created.

"He had some great bands down here – but The Joiners is back and it will be as good as it was, if not better."

The man who gave the Joiners its reputation is known only as Mint. He said: "When I left in March 1997, it just wasn't working out financially. The money was coming in but it was also going out just as fast.

"Now with this cash backing, if the management is constantly looking for the breaking bands, The Joiners should come through."

Eldridge Pope business development manager Steve Best said: "We are very pleased to be spending this money. It should return the venue to its former status."

Radiohead's Thom Yorke

Daily Echo, 23 February 1999.

Re-birth of the Joiners

Jim Sykes: "We took over the Joiners in late '98 or early '99. The Joiners was an Eldridge Pope pub and beforehand I had been working for two or three years for Fred Eynon, who runs the Railway Inn in Winchester. The Railway was, and is, a great small music venue. When I worked at the Railway, I did the bar and fairly soon managed most of the band bookings. It was a fantastic place – great local bands, the occasional touring band at the bottom of the ladder, plenty of beer and always a good atmosphere in the back room where the bands played.

I had known about the Joiners for years, although at that stage I think it was in a slump in terms of getting name bands in. Fred had been asking Eldridge Pope for a while to let him take it if the lease ever came up and in 1999 it did. I was 21 at the time and full of unjustified confidence, so it seemed natural to take on the day to day management on Fred's behalf. It never occurred to me that we would be anything other than successful. I pictured name bands every night, queues at the door, NME reviews, groupies etc., etc.

The renovation was a great time. A few of the Railway regulars moved in to help decorate the place. We shifted the stage, got a new PA in, built a sound box, completely redecorated, paid a designer to come up with a logo and had a board created at the front of the venue on which I pictured having band names in foot high letters to advertise the night's gigs.

I moved into the flat above the Joiners, which was pretty spacious. I remember lying in bed on my first night and hearing a heated discussion outside in St Mary's Street between two people arguing over who had paid for some weed. I realised that it would be an interesting place to live. We had CCTV installed a few weeks later, which provided a lot of entertainment in later months. After we had locked up in the early hours we would often see people disappearing down the alley at the side of the pub for sex, drugs or hiding from the police. There was an office attached to the main bedroom and I had a great couple of weeks listening to all the demo tapes and booking the first bands in. Even then, when the reputation had died down, we would receive four or five demos a day. The very first band I booked in was the Jellys, who the week before they were due to play had NME Single of the Week with Lemonade Girl – enough to make me think that we would be successful without having to do any real work. There was a lot of work to begin with though. I had read the NME for years, was fanatical about new music and really believed that for the Joiners to be successful it had to mirror the bands and the customers that we were trying to entice. I wanted it to be cool, brash and arrogant. We did a lot of local press when we opened and I remember there was a guy at the Southampton Echo *(David Schaffer – Ed)* who was great, would always plug the bands playing and did a number of big articles about the place.

If I wanted the Joiners to be arrogant then I absolutely led by example. I immediately offended the previous tenants by doing an interview in which I was quoted as saying (in so many words) that the place had grown stagnant and the only bands that had played in the last couple of years had been punk collectives which were twenty years off from being cutting edge. I also printed a thousand fliers at great expense, which announced that the Joiners 'was back', probably pissing off the previous tenants again, and listing all the famous bands that had played previously. Fred and I really fell out over this, as I ended with the disclaimer 'The Joiners does not host crap bands, tribute bands or covers bands'. The level of arrogance is just what I was trying to achieve but it demonstrated a business sense that clearly showed I wasn't the one who had invested the money. I remember Fred telling me to erase the line on every single flier with a marker pen.

I was at the Joiners for about nine months, and in that time we did have some great bands. We quickly persuaded PVC to start promoting gigs and I guess they were pleased that the place had had a makeover. They continuously came up with the best bands. The Joiners was always one of the best venues on the toilet circuit. Some of the highlights would have been Muse, 'A', Ooberman, Younger Younger 28's, David Gray and many others who were always on the brink of success but never quite made it. Muse were excellent – fantastic songs and lots of rock star swagger. I pissed off the bassist by refusing to give him and his groupies free drinks at the bar afterwards (well, we were hardly raking it in). 'A' put on the best show. The place was full of sixteen year olds who were absolutely into it and having the time of their lives, but must have spent an average of £1 each on cokes, so whilst we were sold out for the first time we made less money than when we were a quarter full. I bought their album afterwards and it didn't live up to the live performance. David Gray played to promote his White Ladder album. I'm ashamed to say that I spent most of the evening in the bar but to be fair the guy did all right out of the album. YY28's were one of my favourites – really cheesy alternative pop and I was convinced that they would make it.

Our biggest problem was that the live music scene was really in decline at that time. Dance music was the biggest puller and the most successful evenings were those where we had a local dance collective in. They would spend all day setting up their PA's and hanging parachutes on the walls and ceilings. They would also spend a fortune on bottled water, which kept the place solvent. We tried a number of things to get the university students back in to the Joiners but none of them really worked. At that time, even the NME lost its way and started putting dance and rap bands on the cover. I honestly feared that live music was on its way out.

There was no choice but to keep to the tried and tested formula of local bands supporting the next big thing. Sometimes it would work well, but often the local bands and supporters would bugger off before the headlining band would perform, which was pretty humiliating for the band, who had travelled all day to get there and negotiated their way through our standard rider of chilli and cheap wine. I still wince at the memory of Monkey Island, who played to some guy who had arrived on his own, me and the two bar staff.

There were some great characters at the Joiners. Stef was the soundman at the Railway and he moved with us to the Joiners when we set up. I knew Stef for years and the closest he came to losing his temper was when people would hover near his mixing desk with pints. He had a permanent grin which amazingly wasn't drug induced and the bands loved him – he could make most of them sound much better than they had before. Pat, the doorman, was an incredible guy. No-one would cross him, he looked hard as nails, but was a bog softie really. Andy, who worked behind the bar, was a Buddhist but I think it's fair to say that he didn't practise his religion for much of that time. He made a good chilli but as that was all he could make, our riders were renowned for their lack of imagination. Quite often, we would have to give the bands a tenner for the kebab shop up the road.

Inevitably, my run at the Joiners came to a close quite quickly. We were barely covering our costs and my attempt to make the place cool again clearly hadn't been an entire success. In the end, I resigned before Fred was forced to sack me and found myself building a career in the unglamorous but more lucrative world of recruitment. I now have two daughters and travel a lot for work, staying in cheap hotels listening to the latest songs from bands that the NME tells me are going to be the big next thing. Maybe not a thousand miles away from the Joiners then."

Saviours of the Joiners:
Fred Eynon and ace barmaid Scarlet (of Scarlet Soho).

Jamie Summers: "The Muse gig was 18th June 1999, four days after their debut single, Uno, came out. I would say there were about 30 people there. They played a 45 minute set, including most of their debut album, plus a few early B-sides. I had already picked up their second EP (self-released before they were signed) and knew the songs from that, and requested one ('Instant Messenger'), which was played straight away after the band had exchanged looks that seemed to mean, 'How the hell does he know that song?'. It was an absolutely incredible gig, as all of their early ones were. At the time Matt Bellamy hadn't become the super confident rock god he now seems to be, and said nothing in between songs other than a few thank yous. They were supported by local band Shimmer."

173

• LISTINGS 1998 - 2000 •

8 October: Hurricane No. 1
31 October: 53rd and 3rd
6 November: The Selecter
15 November: Stampin'
Ground
20 November: Marshall P Nut

1999

9 March: Rumdum
*This was the grand re-
opening of the Joiners after
refurbishment.*
21 March: co.uk
12 April: Rosita (PVC)
Kenickie left-overs.
14 April: Fungus (PVC)
20 April: Formula 1
6 May: Pist.on (PVC)
2 June: Polanski
6 June: A (PVC)
11 June: Fungus (PVC)
17 June: Scott 4 (PVC)
18 June: Muse (PVC)
24 June: Younger Younger 28s
30 June: David Gray (PVC)
Yes, it's him.
20 July: Drunk In Public
*This was a pseudonym for
The Levellers.*
21 July: Toploader
22 July: Smack Daddi
7 August: Amber 9
26 August: Ten Benson (PVC)
9 September: McGonagle
10 September: Llama Farmers
(PVC)
17 September: Fruitbat
23 September: Airbus
24 September: Kill II This (PVC)
28 September: Cyclefly (PVC)

7 October: The View
15 October: Groop Dogrill
(PVC)
17 October: Brassy (PVC)
27 October: Toploader (PVC)
29 October: Countermine
4 November: Earthtone 9
5 November: Tribute To
Nothing (PVC)
9 November: King Prawn
(PVC)
10 November: Janus Stark
(PVC)
15 November: Rico (PVC)
18 November: Jim's Super
Stereoworld (PVC)
13 November: 53rd and 3rd
16 November: Mash
18 November: Bailey
25 November: Paddy Casey
(PVC)
26 November: Abdoujaparov
(PVC)
2 December: Bushbaby
7 December: Ruby Cruiser
10 December: Compound
11 December: Autumn
15 December: Teen Idols
18 December: McGonagle

2000

10 January: Rumdum
13 January: Glueball
23 January: Bellatrix (PVC)
28 January: Rachel Stamp
(PVC)
4 February: Thirst (PVC)
24 February: Ultraviolet
29 February: Inter
15 March: Orange Can

Coldplay at the Joiners

Oliver Gray: *I was there to review Terris for the Hampshire Chronicle.
Little did I know I would be boasting about the evening for years to
come. Here's the review:*

It's the Birdland syndrome. You feel inclined to dislike any band
which has had an NME front page before they've played more
than a handful of gigs. But it was still one of these thrilling
Joiners moments: a stage crammed with expensive equipment
and a promoter biting his fingernails in the realisation that this
package should have been booked into a much larger venue.

It's easy to see why Coldplay are so hotly tipped. They fit
perfectly into what sells today: anguished bloke with acoustic
guitar plus anonymously competent backing band. Not that
that's a criticism, not at all. It means that they stand or fall
on the quality of their songs. Coldplay stand tall, and the
illuminated globe on the bass amp is surely predictive of future
world status. The singer, Chris Martin, is good-looking, friendly
and communicative, with an attractive, falsetto-inclined voice
and warm presence. Years ago, he'd have been a folk singer,
today he fits the zeitgeist like a glove. Songs to listen out for:
"Bigger Stronger" and "Shiver".

Hype or not, Terris were fabulous too. Strangely, I met Paul from
Dogtodogma in the front bar, and Terris have the same Muppet
charm. Studious guitarist, hunched synth player, attention-
seeking singer, all in deeply unflattering flares. Gavin Goodwin
sounds like a drunk trying to do a karaoke impersonation of
Bob Dylan, so you wouldn't want to buy their album, but as a
live attraction, I'd recommend Terris unreservedly.

Promoter Ian Binnington on the 11th June headlining gig:

"I had been in London at a christening and had to hotfoot it
down to Southampton on the train. When I arrived, the Joiners
was full to exploding point. There was nowhere for the band to
go for their pre-show psych-up except the gents' toilet. As we
huddled in there, I said to Chris Martin, 'You won't be putting
up with backstage facilities like this for much longer'. He just
smiled."

16 March: JJ72 (PVC)
19 March: The Jellys (PVC)
20 March: Cay / Crashland
2 April: Terris / Coldplay (PVC)
4 April: At The Drive-In
10 April: Three Way Mirror
11 April: Hefner (PVC)
12 April: Groop Dogrill (PVC)
15 April: King Prawn (PVC)
16 April: Salaco
23 April: Spunge (PVC)
11 May: Clearlake (PVC)
12 May: The Animal House
17 May: Queen Adreena
18 May: Midget
19 May: Capdown
20 May: The Drum (PVC)
24 May: Midget (PVC)
11 May: Clearlake (PVC)
12 May: The Animal House
17 May: Queen Adreena
18 May: Midget
19 May: Capdown
20 May: The Drum (PVC)
24 May: Midget (PVC)
2 June: Crashland (PVC)
5 June: The Crocketts (PVC)
They left stickers in the loo and later became The Crimea.
7 June: Seafood (PVC)
8 June: Citizen Fish
11 June: Coldplay (PVC)
13 June: Whispering Bob
31 May: Crashland
3 July: My Vitriol (PVC)
7 July: Tom Hingley
12 July: Anti-Product (PVC)
16 July: Earthtone 9 (PVC)

24 September: The Crocketts (PVC)
5 October: Elevator Suite (PVC)
21 October: Vigilantes of Love
2 November: Brave Captain (PVC)
4 November: Cousteau (PVC)
9 November: Chris TT
25 November: Sona Fariq (PVC)
29 November: Willard Grant Conspiracy (PVC)
9 December: Thirst (PVC)
15 December: Terris (PVC)

2001

27 January: Bob Pearce
Still strummin' the blues.
30 January: Cosmic Rough Riders
1 February: Jester
2 February: Oberon
3 February: Loonacy
8 February: Omega 3
9 February: The Equidistant Sound
15 February: Peel
16 February: Labman 4
17 February: Cooper Temple Clause
Down from Reading for the day.
20 February: Paul Kinvig
21 February: Roscoe Chenier
22 February: Scarlet Soho
23 February: Llama Farmers (PVC)
24 February: First Degree
27 February: Big D
1 March: Snub

Consolidation, 1991 – 2001

James Baker: "I was 16 when I discovered the Joiners. I was attending St Mary's Technical College and noticed the band posters outside when I walked by and thought I'd pop in and have a look (the front bar was open in the daytime then). I don't know what band I saw there first but one of my favourites was Claytown Troupe. We hung out in the alley, chatted and smoked cigarettes for about an hour after the show, swapping addresses. I got Christmas cards from those guys for about 3 or 4 years after that. Where are they now? Over the next few years, I attended quite a few shows, but missing The Verve has haunted me forever. I had to literally drag one of my friends down to the Oasis show. The brothers just stared at each other menacingly all night. It was a short set, rock and roll, with a punch-up outside, just perfect.

One thing I will always remember about the Joiners then was the framed photos of bands on the walls and one in particular, which is another show I missed and regretted. It was The Charlatans. I have had a chance to meet those guys a couple of times in the last few years and Tim Burgess remembered that show very well, as it was one of their first live shows. I just loved that picture, and I'm very pleased to say that it hangs on the wall in my house nowadays, a wonderful goodbye gift from Mint when I left the Joiners, and something I will treasure forever.

I had a friend called Jerry who worked at the Joiners and got me the bar job. It was fantastic to earn some money, get to see shows, drink free beer and stay for the after-hours parties. It was pretty crazy working there in those days. You would meet lots of people and get quite drunk, but as long as you could still see the numbers on the till you were okay to work. Then Dave Misselbrook and Mint left. The place needed some investment and a bit of love and I guess Dave had had enough. So in stepped Alison Pennicott. Those were dark days, the PA was shot, the Spice Girls were being played in the front bar and there were no good bookings, so I left.

I returned when Jim Sykes arrived as manager. He seemed to have a good idea of what needed to be done, and, most importantly, he knew his music. The next thing I knew, Jim had gone and someone called Andy was manager. Then there was a staff meeting, as Andy was leaving too … 'Who wants to be manager?' One fateful lift of the arm: 'Er … I do'. Only a couple of months before, I had said 'I do' at another life-changing meeting. I had got married to a wonderful girl called Sarah. So being 27 was getting pretty serious. It was October 1999, I think.

In the first year, I learned a lot very quickly, mainly from the great people I had around to work with, particularly sound engineer Stefan Basford (or Stefano Gold, as he was known affectionately), and of course Mint and Ian Binnington, two people without whom it wouldn't have happened. Then there were the OOMF punk shows, always entertaining and frequently boiling hot and very smelly. Jon, Matt, Rooster all that gang were genuine good guys and I think we provided a great venue for their very successful shows.

However, even though the pub was packed, we were not making much money over the bar, as 80 percent of the audience for the pop punk shows were under 18. The only things we sold were peanuts, chocolate and Coca Cola, oh, and lollipops, a top seller! All the kids used to just go outside, hide down the alley or go round the corner and quickly drink whatever they were able to score from the off licence. After that, they would come back in, watch the band, jump up and down a bit too much, overheat and throw up, leaving me, Sarah or one of our fearless employees to clean up. Still, the main thing was that all these kids were having a great time and were really devoted to their music.

My first foray into booking out of town bands myself was the Cooper Temple Clause. This was the first band I ever got excited about upon hearing the demo CD sent to me. Most demos were mediocre and badly recorded. As soon as I heard the first track on their demo, I was on the phone to the agent, and five minutes later, a deal was done. A week before the show, I opened my fresh copy of the NME and lo and behold, my show was Gig of the Week. It was a totally sold out show with an amazing buzz and I even made money. I began to think I might just get on in this business. Maybe.

Sona Fariq were playing one Saturday night. There was a packed crowd for the last date on the tour and all the bands were in the mood for a party. The guys from Boshed, who ran the Friday dance night, had left some of their decor up in the back room. This included a large piece of white netting that hung from the ceiling front to back. This became the focus of the quite inebriated lead singer of the band, who kept jumping up and trying to grab the netting. Eventually, he succeeded. The next thing we knew, the net had come down and was covering the band, who carried on playing, the audience now being covered too. Luckily, I was standing in the sound box, so I grabbed some of the fallen netting and began to go rock/indie kid trawling, gathering up the netting into a big bundle, pulling it from on top of the band, across the crowd and to the back of the room. Disaster was averted (many of the people under this highly inflammable material were smoking).

My Vitriol was another band predicted to be big. This was to be their first headline show on tour and it was sold out, but none of our bar staff showed up. It was time for my wife Sarah to have her first bar shift. She was not amused, but we kept up for a while, until we started running out of glasses. One of us had to collect glasses, leaving just one behind the bar with 200 or so very thirsty concert-goers. We were just about coping when the glass washer broke down. I was now hand-washing glasses, Sarah had got customers as deep as it was possible to go in the front bar, barrels kept running out … It was a very long evening. Still, we survived, although we both still shudder thinking about that night.

It's difficult to expand on so many of the memories, as so much is half-remembered, due to the flow of booze and good times. Queen Adreena redecorated the band room in the basement into a gothic cellar of doom. Then Toploader played their show just before it all went a bit Jamie Oliver in the Sainsburys ads. We had the pleasure of having the lead singer of Toploader build a toploaded spliff for us that night, which he proceded to smoke until it got to the bit with no gear in and then pass it on. What a claim to fame. HIM was the last show I did at the Joiners. There was massive interest, people were phoning from across Europe. The bus driver for the band built a proper Camberwell Carrot at the after party, I was introduced to Jägermeister (nasty but effective) and the band nearly drove off with their bus still attached to the power supply in the front room upstairs in the pub.

There were also endless power supply problems. You would have a huge queue outside, with the doors due to open in five minutes, everybody powered up in the back room and the pub would go black. You just had to learn to rise above it, find your way in the dark to the fuse box and hope you could fix it. Another education was learning all the wonders of bathroom plumbing and how to unblock urinals full of puke, repair toilet bowls which had become detached from the floor somehow and clean up all the wonderful types of body fluid that were distributed around. My memories include getting a formal lecture from Steve Diggle (Buzzcocks) about not wearing a wedding ring, including much finger wagging, not an experience you get every day (I do have a ring now, so it must have worked); having a Carter USM reunion in the front bar after a Jim's Super Stereoworld gig; the Libertines playing a ramshackle gig and having a bit of a session in the basement with all sorts of people, including some guys from the NME, plus assorted weirdos they brought with them in the van. I believe they went on to destroy a room in the hotel they were staying in up the road, costing many times more than they got paid for the show; and having a couple of beers and sitting talking to Chris Martin after Coldplay's second show at the Joiners at a small table in the back room and him telling me if they got big, he would come back and financially support us, because he loved the place. *(He allegedly said the same thing to Pat the Doorman. – Ed)*. He probably said that every night. The next time I saw them, they were playing to 20,000 in an arena in Minneapolis.

When Fred Eynon gave the Joiners up and Mike Chapman came in, I took over the booking. I wanted to build up a good local scene because I figured that if we got a buzz going about a couple of local bands, then other local bands would get out there and go for it, rather than waiting for it to happen. I really tried to create a bit more of a community of bands, rather than have them compete so much. It sounds very hippieish, but music goes in scenes and if Southampton could get one band out there, others might be able to get caught up in it and have a chance at the "big time". Stef was a big part of this, as he spent a lot of his time helping those bands on their sound and giving them a chance to record or rehearse in the back room on our days off. The Delays (apt name really) were a classic example of this, always trying, mainly due to Mike, Greg and Aaron's dad. It was a nice feeling when they got their deal with Geoff Travis of Rough Trade in the back room.

The Joiners has always had a huge place in my heart, from the moment I walked in as an innocent 16-year old, to the day I left at 30 and saw all my belongings leaving the front door of the pub and being loaded onto a Pickfords truck bound for Minneapolis, where I now reside. The place really did shape my life, some of my best and worst experiences happened in that building, I was able find myself a career that I never imagined and I met so many good people, and of course I saw some great bands .

Nowadays, I work for a club called First Avenue, which is located in downtown Minneapolis. It really is a big version of the Joiners, the same sorts of characters frequent it, just with a different accent. I was the operations manager for First Avenue for a year but moved into the production crew, where I now look after the hospitality for the artists we have at the club. In the last couple of years, I have had the pleasure of looking after people such as Moby, Blondie, Ray Davies, Garbage, The Raconteurs, Stereophonics, Gnarls Barkley, Blur, System of a Down, Kings of Leon and The Charlatans. It sort of made up for missing them all those years ago at the Joiners."

Sarah and James Baker with long-time Joiners
sound engineer Stafan Basford.

Home from home: James and Sarah welcome the Delays to Minneapolis.

• LISTINGS 2001 •

6 March: Remote Control
7 March: Budapest
8 March: The Scones
10 March: Good Clean Fun
13 March: Big Joan
14 March: Crackout (PVC)
15 March: Experimental Pop
   Band
17 March: Stout
22 March: Medley
27 March: Belasco
29 March: Powder
30 March: Sounder
31 March: First Degree
2 April: Mo Solid Gold (PVC)
4 April: Steve Diggle
5 April: Oh Susanna
6 April: 3 Way Mirror
7 April: Breeze
10 April: Diesel Boy
11 April: Percy Strother
12 April: Incubus Succubus
16 April: Tom Ovans
17 April: Erskin Oglesby
   New landlord Mike
   Chapman tried out some
   "Americana" nights but with
   little success.
19 April: Bluetip
20 April: Goldrush
21 April: The Peeping Tom
25 April: Horace Pinker
26 April: Idoru
   Later to be Delays.
27 April: Waste Of A Day
28 April: Lostprophets (PVC)
3 May: Witness (PVC)
4 May: Six Way Circus
5 May: The Union
7 May: Hundred Reasons
   (PVC)

10 May: The Lovelies
11 May: Anti-Product (PVC)
15 May: Astrid (PVC)
16 May: Aaron Cray
18 May: Stout
20 May: Link 80
21 May: Clearlake (PVC)
24 May: Harsh
25 May: Kerosene
26 May: Veluria
1 June: One Kick Wonder
7 June: Jim's Super
   Stereoworld (PVC)
11 June: Proud Mary (PVC)
14 June: Sack Trick (PVC)
15 June: Vanilla Pod
16 June: Citizen Fish
23 June: Miss Black America
6 July: South (PVC)
9 July: Black Nielson
14 July: Ed Harcourt (PVC)
16 July: Haven (PVC)
21 July: Terris (PVC)
16 September: Goldrush
18 September: Pernice Brothers
   (PVC)
20 September: Miles Apart
21 September: Haven (PVC)
23 September: Cooper Temple
   Clause (PVC)
25 September: Snow Pony
   (PVC)
26 September: Pez
27 September: Steve James
28 September: Medium 21
29 September: Oh Susanna
30 September: The Music
   (PVC)
4 October: Vigilantes Of Love
6 October: Skuba
9 October: Biffy Clyro (PVC)

Greg Gilbert of the Delays

Photo by Mark Holloway.

Greg Gilbert: "My first experience of the Joiners was during the era known as 'Britpop' (or 'New Wave of New Wave', as it was called at the time). Rowly had won tickets to see Whiteout and so we ventured down to St Mary Street, dressed in our best and not knowing what to expect. After approaching a girl who we wrongly assumed worked there, and proudly announcing that we were the competition winners, we were directed to Mint. He knew nothing about a competition or tickets, but, seeing our malnourished baggy haircuts, took pity on us and graciously let us in. In more philosophical moments, I have wondered just what would have happened if he hadn't. My whole circle of friends, band, music taste, clothes, food, drink etc. has all directly or indirectly been shaped by the place and its people. (Of course, we might just have come down to a later gig, but that's less romantic.)

Walking into its wonderful gloom for the first time feels like the point when I truly woke up, the first signs of what my life would actually be about. I remember seeing so many faces that would go on to become stalwarts of Southampton's alternative scene, orbiting the Joiners and Thursdays for the next few years and following DJ Hammy on to the Academy, Rhino and Dorchester. But, at the time, I knew nothing of that secret world and would let myself be carried away by the sounds of indie Britain c. 1995.

I don't remember much about the gig itself. The support was local band Tatlin, whose name I'd seen scrawled on a St Denys wall near my Grandad's house, which made them celebrities in my eyes. All long legs and scratchy guitars, they summed up the times and would probably fit like a musical glove in 2006, but being Stone Roses devotees, it was the Greenock lads we got down the front for. All bowl cuts and denim, Big Star licks and Jagger poses, Whiteout perectly scored our first real youth moment and the Joiners was suddenly our musical mecca. At this point, we had a band in the very loosest sense of the word; it was Rowly with a snare drum and me with a badly played acoustic guitar. But from then on, getting a gig at the Joiners became the all-encompassing goal. Our gig there wasn't until about six months later.

The day we delivered our first demo tape was quite an occasion. For some reason, we'd decided to pursue a trashy, glam look with eyeliner and leopardskin print, à la early Manics. And it was in this garb that we trooped down on what I remember to be a very cold and grey morning. We were now a BAND: Col was an old school friend, whilst Dan turned up at one of Hammy's Joiners nights. I don't know what we were hoping for, but Mint just took the C90 tape, smiled and left us with an anti-climactic walk home. But the gig itself was everything we could have hoped for, full of new faces, many from the Whiteout gig, loud, sweaty, a bit ropey but the biggest rush any of us had ever had. From then on, we never really left the place. Over the next six or so years, we played there countless times, seeing different people take the helm, Mint and Dave, James and Sarah. Different faces came and went: We miss you Stan! What's Pat up to these days?

But I suppose our main Joiners moment came in 2001. Rough Trade had expressed interest in signing us and wanted to see a gig, but, like countless other bands, we'd been burnt over and over by going to London for A & R people who might or might (definitely) not show. So we played stubborn and said that if they were interested, they'd have to come to us, which they did. We played a private gig at the Joiners, setting up on the floor at the front of the stage, label boss Geoff Travis sitting about 3 yards away, and it remains probably the most nerve-wracking gig we've ever done. But in that situation, we didn't want to be anywhere else; our songs were in a sense written at the Joiners. It felt like home, and it paid off when they offered us a deal at the end of that day.

The more I think about it, the more perfect that seems."

• LISTINGS 2001 - 2002 •

11 October: B-Movie Heroes

12 October: Brezhnev

13 October: Incubus Succubus

14 October: The Elishe

18 October: Orange Can (PVC)

20 October: Pat Buchanan Band

25 October: Miss Black America

26 October: Karmic Jera (PVC)

27 October: Beachbuggy (PVC)

28 October: Trans Am

3 November: Kids Near Water (PVC)

5 November: Crashland (PVC)

6 November: Digger

7 November: David Kitt (PVC)

10 November: Taste

15 November: Goatboy

16 November: Thirst (PVC)

17 November: As Friends Rust

18 November: Number One Son (PVC)

23 November: Cortizone (PVC)

24 November: Six Ray Sun

26 November: Angelica (PVC)

27 November: Black Nielson

28 November: Good Time Charlies

30 November: Clearlake (PVC)

1 December: Chris T-T

2 December: Harsh

5 December: Hardcore Superstar (PVC)

8 December: Buffseeds (PVC)

14 December: Reuben

15 December: Mantoid

17 December: Capdown

18 December: Scarlet Soho

19 December: UK Players

20 December: Dilutral

2002

1 February: The Movielife (PVC)

5 February: Ee-blee

9 February: Equidistant Sound (PVC)

15 February: Goldrush / Buffseeds (PVC)

16 February: Frijid Vinegar (PVC)

17 February: Defenestration (PVC)

19 February: Cyclefly (PVC)

21 February: Biffy Clyro (PVC)

22 February: 45s (PVC)

5 March: Soundtrack Of Our Lives (PVC)

9 March: Halo (PVC)

17 March: Haven (PVC)

21 March: Vacant Stare (PVC)

24 March: Minuteman / Athlete (PVC)

Check out the support band.

29 March: Liberty 37 (PVC)

5 April: Thirst (PVC)

6 April: Beatstakes (PVC)

12 April: Supercoma (PVC)

19 April: The Jeevas (PVC)

20 April: Wilt (PVC)

4 May: Six By Seven (PVC)

6 May: Easyworld (PVC)

8 May: Candiria (PVC)

10 May: Kid Galahad (PVC)

11 May: Sommerset

16 May: Black Nielson

17 May: Actual Size (PVC)

18 May: Number One Son (PVC)

19 May: One Dice (PVC)

20 May: The Libertines (PVC)

• LISTINGS 2002 •

21 May: Boris The Sprinkler
22 May: HIM (PVC)
10 June: Skindred (PVC)
14 June: Ten Benson (PVC)
20 June: The Bees (PVC)
   Over from the Isle of Wight.
 5 July: My Deaf Audio
 6 July: Miss Black America
12 July: Jesse James (PVC)
15 July: X Is Loaded
19 July: Blue Jay Way
20 July: Equidistant Sound
26 July: Barrington
27 July: Reuben (PVC)
 1 August: Spyder Baby
 2 August: The Newtown
   Grunts
 3 August: Aubrey Lemon
10 August: Long Tall Shorty
 5 September: Easyworld (PVC)
12 September: Black Blue Fish
   ... Very Beautiful
13 September: McClusky (PVC)
15 September: The Parkinsons
   (PVC)
18 September: The Libertines
   (PVC)
   First of several Doherty
   visitations.
25 September: Simple Kid
   (PVC)
29 September: Sikh (PVC)
 2 October: Hell Is For Heroes
   (PVC)
 3 October: Rachel Stamp
   (PVC)
 4 October: The D4 (PVC)
 6 October: The Crescent (PVC)
 8 October: Jetplane Landing
   (PVC)

10 October: The Jeevas (PVC)
12 October: Vendetta Red
   (PVC)
13 October: Buffseeds (PVC)
15 October: The Beatings (PVC)
19 October: Martin Grech
   (PVC)
20 October: Goldrush (PVC)
21 October: Hoggboy (PVC)
28 October: British Sea Power
   (PVC)
 2 November: Kids Near Water
   (PVC)
13 November: 80s Matchbox B-
   Line Disaster (PVC)
23 November: This Girl (PVC)
24 November: Delays (PVC)
26 November: X Is Loaded
   (PVC)
 5 December: Five Knuckle
 6 December: Liberty 37
 7 December: Lustria
 8 December: The Henchmen
10 December: Jesse James
   (PVC)
11 December: 3P Sweet
13 December: Douglas (PVC)
14 December: Equidistant
   Sound
15 December: Redhill
17 December: Crackout
18 December: My Deaf Audio
   (PVC)
20 December: One End
21 December: Stu Dent and the
   Wankers
28 December: New Generation
   Of Spacemen

The Kills. Photo by Mint.

Logo

Oliver Gray: The first issue of LOGO magazine was published in July 2002. Alan Downes, who spent every evening hanging about in front of the Joiners chatting to Pat Muldowney, had no background in music publishing but an absolute determination to produce a free quality music magazine. Seemingly undaunted by the existence of the spookily similar Fly magazine (or possibly hoping to vanquish it), he must have ploughed a fortune into this glossy, full-colour A5 booklet, which survived with virtually no advertising for over two years, and built up a formidable reputation. Writers such as myself were delighted to have such an outlet in our own back yard, as LOGO operated from offices above the Joiners.

Alan Downes, LOGO editor: "Okay, so what you *really* want to hear about are tales of rock 'n' roll debauchery – and if not, why not? Certainly, The Joiners has seen its fair share of sex, drugs and, of course, rock 'n' roll. But really, in the majority of cases, you just had to be there. Be there for what? To see LOGO Magazine's deputy editor being given a black eye by a young Pete Doherty for one, a story so long it requires a whole chapter to itself. Suffice to say, it was worn as a badge of (dubious) honour for quite a while afterwards.

I could regale you with tales of walking into the LOGO offices above the venue one night to be confronted with the sight of four naked bodies writhing in a tangled knot, and no, they weren't playing Twister. The real interest though comes not through prurience but through *being there*, being able to observe at close quarters young musicians developing into world beaters. That was why, seeing as LOGO was a magazine dedicated to unearthing new music (new music by our definition being anything from new bands on the way up to bands that had been around for a while but had yet to garner anything but a dedicated cult following), then it was only natural that, when the chance arose to move our offices into a venue dedicated to exactly that kind of music, we grabbed it with both hands.

In the two years we were there, we saw a procession of 'Next Big Things' pass through the venue, in their turn becoming either genuine Big Things (Athlete, The Libertines, Delays), proving their mettle yet staying inexplicably 'cult' (the incomparable Clearlake and I Am Kloot), or sinking without a trace under a mountain of unjustified industry hype (you know who *they* are). The real magic of working in such an environment, though, was the mystery: Was our work today going to be interrupted by a soundcheck that sent chills down the spine, prompting a trip downstairs to get a first look at a new sensation, or was the day going to end in a teeth-clenching grind as we struggled to work through an interminable racket? Happily, for posterity will surely judge the years 2003 and 2004 as a particularly fertile period for music of all colours, much of our time was spent revelling in the excitement of yet another new discovery.

Highlights? There are truly too many to recount, but it's getting under the skin and really getting to know artists that provide the most cherished memories. For one, having a long, heated argument with Ed Harcourt over whether Tom Waits could actually sing or not (I say no, he says yes, but I maintain that Waits has the perfect voice for his material, a point that Ed couldn't register through the red mist). Or the long night spent getting hammered in the company of the fast-rising Cooper Temple Clause, a rock 'n' roll image soon spoiled by the fact that one band member (who will remain nameless lest I destroy his street cred) recognised me as someone he used to play cricket against – cue an unintelligible conversation about silly point and leg gully and much laughter that he still probably hasn't got over.

The real magic of The Joiners (and many other small provincial venues all over the country) isn't the scandal and the high jinks, it isn't even the reflected glory of being able to say 'I saw Coldplay here when they were just a support act', it's the thrill that comes from hearing a particular combination of notes played on a particular combination of instruments at a particular time, having a cheer rise to your throat and a tear to your eye, and the knowledge that one hundred other people in the room are feeling exactly the same thing. It's a feeling I have only ever felt in small venues outside London, venues where people go to have a good time rather than to pose.

That is why small, independent venues like The Joiners matter, and long may they not only survive, but thrive."

• LISTINGS 2003 •

2003

8 January: The Dawn Parade
15 January: Reuben (PVC)
17 January: The Travoltas
21 January: The Thrills (PVC)
29 January: Electric Six
1 February: The Filaments
4 February: Consumed (PVC)
6 February: Olympic Lifts (PVC)
7 February: Brutal Deluxe
8 February: Webbman Jones
9 February: The Warlocks (PVC)
11 February: Dustbyte
14 February: Groovie Ghoulies
19 February: Echoboy (PVC)
21 February: Long Tall Shorty
24 February: Tuuli (PVC)
25 February: Kinesis (PVC)
27 February: Scarlet Soho
28 February: Fake Concept
1 March: Toupe
3 March: The Kills (PVC)
5 March: Mohair
6 March: Cerebra
9 March: Buffseeds (PVC)
13 March: Jump
15 March: Farse (PVC)
16 March: Medium 21 (PVC)
18 March: Clearlake (PVC)
19 March: Stag
Another Andy Burrows / Pete Hobbs band with a terrible name.
21 March: Slaughter Of Souls
27 March: Blue Book Park
29 March: Fleeing New York
1 April: The Star Spangles (PVC)

2 April: The 22-20s (PVC)
5 April: The Fletchers
6 April: 4Ft Fingers (PVC)
7 April: My Deaf Audio
9 April: Burning Brides (PVC)
10 April: Mellaphone
12 April: Amor
See Band Room page.
14 April: The Bandits (PVC)
15 April: Candyheads
16 April: The Basement / The Zutons (PVC)
Anther support band you'd have not wanted to miss.
18 April: Shouting Myke
23 April: Kill Kenada
24 April: Bushbaby
27 April: The Burn (PVC)
28 April: I Am Kloot (PVC)
30 April: Soledad Brothers (PVC)
1 May: Serafin (PVC)
3 May: The Naked Apes
4 May: Tribute To Nothing
7 May: Funeral For A Friend (PVC)
10 May: Snaffler
11 May: Alternative Carpark
12 May: Violent Delight (PVC)
14 May: Pop Vandals
15 May: Leftover Crack
16 May: Rosco
18 May: Longview / Keane (PVC)
Yet another ... oh, shut up.
21 May: Blue Jay Way
22 May: Whitmore (PVC)
24 May: EQD
25 May: Kill II This (PVC)
27 May: Tuuli
28 May: Lapsus Linguae

The Band Room

Jon Amor: "Positioned a few yards behind the mixing desk, there is a small, innocuous-looking door in the wall. Easily missed by the paying public, this little door leads to the "band room", where I have spent many an hour engaged in the traditional, rock and roll pastime of Hanging About. For a man of my height, the descent into the musicians' quarters is awkward and hazardous; I have to practically limbo dance down the narrow staircase to avoid head injuries, and indeed the headroom doesn't improve a great deal when you arrive in the basement area. Feeling like you have stumbled onto the set of a Terry Gilliam movie, you pass through a dimly-lit room made up of wire mesh and blue neon lights, before turning right into the dressing room itself. Here, there is a ragged sofa, a table, and a small fridge full of beer (if you're lucky), but what strikes you more than anything is the anarchic choice of wallpaper. All four walls of the dressing room are completely covered by graffiti. Vandalising dressing rooms with all manner of inane scrawl is, of course, another of Rock And Roll's great traditions, and one that has been practised in The Joiners more than any other venue I have visited in the world. Hours can be whiled away reading these walls – it's better than any novel. Ignore the foot-high self-promoting claims like 'SOULSUCKERS KICK ASS!', and search instead for the smaller, more humble nuggets of wisdom, usually written in pencil in the bottom corner of a wall. For example, 'Nuns Fuck Goats' is one I remember with particular fondness, and who can fail to chuckle at the joyous simplicity of 'Hobbsy Is Gay'?

When you have hours to kill and a big fat Berol marker in your hand, it's hard for a creative musician to resist contributing to this compendium of witticisms and surreal declarations. As for me, I drew a picture of five-times Wimbledon Champion Bjorn Borg just to the left of the light fitting. I'd like to think it's still there, but it may have been obscured by a drawing of a large penis."

• LISTINGS 2003 •

29 May: The Lillettes

1 June: Hope Of The States (PVC)

3 June: Adom
Or it could have been Adem, who knows?

4 June: Delays

6 June: Acid Mothers Temple

7 June: Lovejunk

8 June: Plan B

9 June: Mark Gardener and Goldrush (PVC)

10 June: Sonara

12 June: Harsh

13 June: Dustball

15 June: Skindred

18 June: Engine

19 June: Da Skywalker

22 June: Red 5

23 June: Nylon Pylon (PVC)

25 June: Mos Eisley

26 June: Thirst

28 June: Frog Pocket

30 June: Wrapped In Plastic

2 July: Cosmic Rough Riders (PVC)

3 July: 3 Inches Of Blood

5 July: HFM

6 July: Haven (PVC)

8 July: Not Katies

9 July: Bushbaby

11 July: X-Possibles

12 July: Duff Muffin

13 July: Sounder

16 July: Nizlopi
No, they didn't arrive in a JCB.

17 July: Widescreen

19 July: Stag

21 July: Fallen To (PVC)

23 July: Red Lights Flash

24 July: It's Jo And Danny

25 July: Gilbert French

28 July: Bell XI (PVC)

29 July: Lightside

30 July: Ariel X

31 July: No Comply4 August: Budapest (PVC)

5 August: Harsh

6 August: Spyder Baby

7 August: Midasuno

9 August: Solstis

10 August: Sup

11 August: Rocket Science (PVC)

12 August: Faetal

15 August: Diamanthian

16 August: Stout

17 August: Neil's Children

20 August: Lewd

22 August: Amor

27 August: Adom

28 August: JMU

29 August: Highly Davidson

30 August: Lightyear

31 August: Snub

3 September: Helene

4 September: Black Couch

6 September: 2-Tonic

7 September: The Sights (PVC)

8 September: Oceansize

9 September: The Quireboys

10 September: Harsh

12 September: The Blueprint

13 September: EQD

14 September: Caffeine (PVC)

15 September: The Faith Band

17 September: Gash

19 September: Fleeing New York

20 September: Good Time Charlies

the JOINERS

SPONSORED BY **Vladivar** CLASSIC VODKA & **Veba**

October gig listings

GIG OF THE MONTH

Friday 3rd

six.by seven

"Six By Seven are a near perfect band. They have the mixture of 'originality', 'sensitivity' and 'rock' down perfectly. It's just up to you to discover them before it's too late!"

- NME

Sunday 12th

"Is anyone out there not bored of retro yet? Garage-rock is coiled in a shrivelled heap at our feet, its mangy tail tucked between its crippled legs, dying a wretched, whimpering death. And then Franz Ferdinand get onstage and begin to beat out a new-wave racket that, fuck me, sounds like a skewed, creepy Supertramp. A truely great new band!"

- Drowned In Sound

Franz Ferdinand

SOUTHAMPTON'S LEGENDARY "NEW MUSIC" VENUE!

- www.joinerslive.com - www.joinerslive.com - www.joinerslive.com -

196

• LISTINGS 2003 •

23 September: Simple Kid (PVC)

24 September: The Blueskins (PVC)

25 September: Number One Son

26 September: Samo

27 September: Shootin' Goon (PVC)

28 September: The Boxer Rebellion

29 September: Elviss (PVC)

30 September: The Travoltas

1 October: Chris T-T

3 October: Six By Seven (PVC)

4 October: Jetplane Landing (PVC)

5 October: Frog Pocket

7 October: MASS

8 October: Clear

9 October: Beaker

11 October: Blocko

12 October: Franz Ferdinand (PVC)

Just the right moment to catch them.

13 October: Murder One (PVC)

15 October: Engine

17 October: Headstand

18 October: Schism

19 October: Goatboy

21 October: Whitmore (PVC)

23 October: Toupe

26 October: The Jupiter Few

28 October: Lewd

29 October: Fuck Hate Propaganda

30 October: Ariel X

31 October: Mr E

1 November: Martin Grech

2 November: 22-20's (PVC)

3 November: The Honeymoon Machine

4 November: The Rain Band (PVC)

5 November: Mr Miagi

6 November: Spyder Baby

7 November: Skitz

8 November: Dillusion

9 November: The Glitterati

10 November: Solabeat Alliance (PVC)

11 November: My Friend Flicker 12 November: F-Minus

13 November: Sarah-Jane Smith

14 November: Fony

15 November: Delays

16 November: Tribute To Nothing

17 November: X Is Loaded

18 November: Mower (PVC)

19 November: Aconite Thrill

20 November: Anti-Maniax

21 November: Farse (PVC)

22 November: King Adora

23 November: Million Dead (PVC)

24 November: Apes, Pigs and Spacemen

25 November: B-Movie Heroes

27 November: Stand Aside

30 November: Landmine

1 December: Plastic Hamster

2 December: Black Top Phoenix

3 December: 12 Pound Fine

4 December: The Jupiter Few

5 December: Zounds

7 December: The Dead Lovers

8 December: Sixty Mile Smile

197

• LISTINGS 2003 - 2004 •

10 December: My Deaf Audio

11 December: Solstis

12 December: Dilutral

13 December: Red 5

14 December: Dead Jack

16 December: Cold Light Of Day

17 December: Hijera

18 December: Arthur Brown

19 December: Nizlopi

20 December: Four Letter Word

21 December: Thee Exciters

2004

2 January: The Makes

7 January: Easyworld (PVC)

8 January: Belvedere

12 January: Catch 22 (PVC)

13 January: Fleeing New York

15 January: Home Town Hi Fi

16 January: Stout

17 January: Inhalate

18 January: Sixty Mile Smile

20 January: Razorlight (PVC)
This was the pre-Andy Burrows version.

21 January: Echobeat

22 January: Black Blue Fish … Very Beautiful

23 January: Delays

24 January: Divit

25 January: Phema

27 January: Gonga

28 January: Carina Round (PVC)

29 January: The Morning

30 January: Matchbook Romance (PVC)

31 January: Grifter

1 February: The Ordinary Boys (PVC)

4 February: Gold Cash Gold

5 February: Harsh

7 February: Hydrogen Duke Box

10 February: The Alsakan Pipeline

11 February: Eeblee

12 February: Valen Brosa

13 February: Cherry Atrium

14 February: Die So Fluid

15 February: Span (PVC)

16 February: Headroom

17 February: Winnebago Deal (PVC)

23 February: Not Katies (PVC)

24 February: Helene

25 February: Cayto

26 February: Intentions Of An Asteroid 27 February: Hijera

28 February: The Jupiter Few

29 February: All Livin Fear

1 March: The Vaults (PVC)

3 March: Aconite Thrill

4 March: Sixty Mile Smile

5 March: Entronaught

7 March: Chikinki / Kasabian (PVC)

8 March: Minus Elizabeth

9 March: Fonda 500

11 March: Thirteen Senses (PVC)

12 March: Manifest

13 March: Book Harrison

14 March: John Doe

15 March: Five Knuckle

16 March: 65 Days Of Static

17 March: Denzil

18 March: Rival Joustas

19 March: Mainstream

• LISTINGS 2004 •

22 March: Steve Lawson
23 March: The Boxer Rebellion
24 March: Mystery Jets
25 March: Widescreen
26 March: Planet Smashers
28 March: Pure Reason
   Revolution
29 March: Ricky Warwick (PVC)
1 April: Horror Pops
2 April: Zero Cipher
3 April: Daughters
   Courageous
4 April: The Futureheads
   (PVC)
5 April: South (PVC)
6 April: Eve's Only Son
7 April: Solabeat Alliance
   (PVC)
9 April: Trend Abuse
14 April: Tearjerk
15 April: Scarlet
16 April: Jets vs Sharks
17 April: Ariel X
18 April: Fony 19 April: Rest At
   Nothing
20 April: Zen Baseball Bat
21 April: Mohair
22 April: Cerebra
23 April: Rival Jousters
25 April: Terra Diablo (PVC)
26 April: Intentions Of An
   Asteroid
27 April: Dead Next Door
28 April: Armoured Farmer
29 April: Alistair Goodwin
30 April: Rival Joustas
1 May: Four Letter Word
2 May: Kristtina
3 May: Electric Eel Shock
   (PVC)
5 May: Breed 77

6 May: The Alaskan Pipeline
7 May: Dilutral
8 May: Black Blue Fish ... Very
   Beautiful
10 May: Jets vs Sharks
11 May: Rest At Nothing
13 May: Xavier Floyd Firebird
14 May: Jim Bob Carter (PVC)
16 May: Cherry Atrium
17 May: Trend Abuse
18 May: Reuben (PVC)
20 May: Bushcraft
21 May: Flaming Homer
23 May: Jon Amor
24 May: Halo
25 May: Dlugocecki
26 May: Stamping Ground
27 May: Mark Joseph (PVC)
28 May: Against Me
29 May: Black Box Theory
30 May: Duke Spirit
31 May: My Deaf Audio
1 June: Ikara Colt (PVC)
2 June: Tsunami Bomb
3 June: Six By Seven (PVC)
4 June: Trend Abuse
5 June: Harsh
6 June: 27
7 June: Chikinki
8 June: Chris TT
9 June: Gonga
10 June: Kody
11 June: Alfie (PVC)
12 June: Uncle Brian (PVC)
13 June: Salako
17 June: No Comply
18 June: Plastik
19 June: Inhalate
20 June: The Parkinsons
22 June: Uniting The Elements
23 June: Leech

• LISTINGS 2004 •

25 June: Sounder
26 June: Plastic Toys
27 June: Filaments
29 June: Powerquest
29 June: Number One Son
30 June: Hidden Agenda
1 July: The Servant
2 July: Brutal Deluxe
3 July: Stout
4 July: X Is Loaded (PVC)
5 July: New Rhodes
6 July: Path of Betrayal
7 July: Minus (PVC)
9 July: Hijera
10 July: Fandangle and the
   Perverts
11 July: 209
12 July: John Lester
13 July: The Dead Stars
14 July: X-Possibles
16 July: 65 Days of Static
18 July: Lo*Chine
20 July: Die So Fluid

21 July: Rival Joustas
22 July: Afterglow
23 July: Murmer
24 July: Route 215
25 July: Future Ex-Wife
26 July: Rolling Dog
27 July: Bloc Party
29 July: Babyshambles
30 July: Dead! Dead! Dead!
1 August: Rat Daddy
3 August: Shouting
4 August: Hell Is For Heroes
   (PVC)
5 August: Aconite Thrill
6 August: Moral Low Ground
7 August: Pellumair
8 August: Ariel X

9 August: Youth Movie
   Soundtrack
11 August: The Low Country
12 August: Rhythmic Coughing
13 August: Birdpen
14 August: Total Carnage
16 August: Not Advised
18 August: Harsh
19 August: Coma Kai
20 August: Minus Elizabeth
21 August: The Flying
   Alexanders
22 August: Route 215
24 August: Deadstring Brothers
27 August: Dead! Dead! Dead!
28 August: Webbman
1 September: The Filaments
2 September: Rainstar
3 September: Dilutral
4 September: Bushbaby
5 September: Not Advised
6 September: Ejector Seat
8 September: Midasuno
9 September: Ripchord
10 September: Flaming Homer
11 September: Gutworm16
   September: Black Blue Fish
   … Very Beautiful
17 September: Six Nation State
18 September: The Warm
19 September: The Boxer
   Rebellion (PVC)
21 September: The Littlest Man
   Band
22 September: The Open (PVC)
23 September: Defenestration
24 September: Black Andrew
25 September: Jupiter Few
26 September: Die So Fluid
27 September: Queen Adreena
   (PVC)

The Subways

Oliver Gray: *If you don't mind getting squashed, the Joiners is a good place to get photos of bands you think will end up getting a lot bigger. On this occasion, I had just got a new digital camera and also just started getting live reviews printed in Record Collector. As luck would have it, they were also supported by one of the venue's most respected "stalwart" bands, Thee Exciters. This was one of the Subways' earliest national reviews:*

The elder statesmen of this battle of the generations were local heroes Thee Exciters. While their previous incarnation the Steamkings was a great pop group, their highly physical Iggy-style singer Paul le-Brock makes this the quintessential garage band. Gritty songs with titles like "Mummy's Little Boy" flashed by in a flurry of broken strings, pudding basins, cuban heels and flying microphones.

What is it about girls and bass guitars? From Tina Weymouth, through Stellastarr*'s Amanda Tannen and on to the elfin-like Mary-Charlotte Cooper of The Subways, they bring a charm and elegance to the instrument that your average hairy-arsed rocker doesn't. That's my excuse for watching, anyway.

The Subways are a raucous and entertaining power trio who aren't the future of rock but put on a blast of a show, exploding with tunes. Honours even, then.

• LISTINGS 2004 •

28 September: The Maces
29 September: Neon Vice
30 September: Harsh
^1 October: Cubic Space Division
^2 October: Toupe
^3 October: Viking Skull (PVC)
^4 October: Nizlopi
^5 October: Number One Sun
^6 October: 65 Days Of Static
^7 October: Winnebago Deal (PVC)
^8 October: Howard's Alias
^9 October: This Girl (PVC)
10 October: Cherryfalls
11 October: The Alaskan Pipeline
12 October: Everything For Some
13 October: Rolling Dog
14 October: Leisure Hive
15 October: Seafood (PVC)
16 October: The Equidistant Sound
17 October: Never heard Of It (PVC)
18 October: Bloodshot Dawn
19 October: My Mantra
20 October: 10,000 Things (PVC)
22 October: Second Monday
23 October: 4 Ft Fingers
24 October: Dead Man Skanking
25 October: Oceansize (PVC)
26 October: Engineers (PVC)
27 October: Zero Cipher
28 October: Avoid One Thing (PVC)
29 October: Dive Dive
30 October: The Others (PVC)

31 October: Harsh
1 November: Speaking Of Losers
2 November: The Trend
3 November: The Subways (PVC)
4 November: My Deaf Audio
5 November: Fony
6 November: Deadline
7 November: Esoterica
8 November: Get Amped
9 November: Six Nation State
10 November: Sonic Boom Six
11 November: Rachel Stamp (PVC)
12 November: Neon
13 November: Stout
14 November: The Magnite
15 November: Byzantine
16 November: Caretaker
17 November: G U Medicine
18 November: Goldrush
19 November: Kubrick
21 November: X Is Loaded (PVC)
22 November: Dead! Dead! Dead!
23 November: Dogs
24 November: Scarlet Soho
25 November: Eve's Only Son
26 November: Delays
28 November: 5IVE
29 November: King Adora (PVC)
30 November: The Mooney Suzuki (PVC)
1 December: No Comply
2 December: Entronaut
5 December: Steranko
6 December: Colour Of Fire (PVC)

Willy Mason

Oliver Gray: *Because the stars can't put on any airs and graces, the Joiners is also a good place to get to chat to them and maybe obtain a more informal photo. Not that Willy Mason would put on airs and graces anyway; he likes to do impromptu sets in the streets outside venues. I grabbed the snap as he signed autographs, and the review appeared in a couple of American magazines:*

Who would have thought that the NME would be giving rave reviews to a bloke in a lumberjack shirt strumming an acoustic guitar and and singing songs with choruses like "So long, so long, I must be moving on"? Well who cares, because if Willy Mason proves to be a way in to roots music for a whole new generation, three cheers for him.

For a moment, you think there's no way that a man with a guitar performing a bunch of songs can possibly come up with anything new, but what's special is the sheer quality and the engaging personality. As Willy swops witticisms with the crowd, repeatedly name checks his family and takes endless audience requests, the atmosphere is like a warm enveloping blanket protecting us from the snow outside. With "Where The Humans Eat", he instantly gets all cat-lovers (me) on his side, with "Oxygen", he has written a 40-carat gold classic pop song, and with "In Our Town" he has crafted a charming but chilling tale of urban incident.

And he's only 19. Don't be put off by the hype, Willy is the real deal.

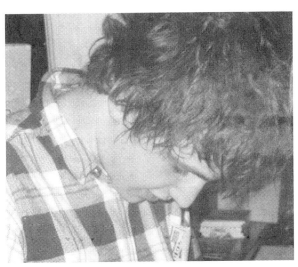

• LISTINGS 2004 - 2005 •

7 December: Selfish Cunt
8 December: Towers Of London
9 December: Phinius Gage
10 December: Red Jetson
11 December: The Flying Alexanders
12 December: Sacred Ace
13 December: The Alaskan Pipeline
14 December: Rival Joustas
15 December: The Fight (PVC)
16 December: EQD
17 December: Dogs D'Amour
18 December: Stu Dent and the Wankers
19 December: Not Advised
20 December: Reserved For Nothing
22 December: Fleeing New York
23 December: The Jupiter Few
31 December: Toupe

2005

3 January: Screwed-Up Faces
4 January: Little Girl Lost
6 January: Bloodshot Dawn
7 January: The Approach
8 January: Jay Et Al
9 January: Working Lunch
10 January: Ghost Of Kings
11 January: Autocircus
13 January: Karalta
14 January: Black Nielson
15 January: Diamanthian
16 January: The Fight
17 January: Sub Rosa
18 January: The Strings
20 January: Parisian Sex Flick

21 January: The Warm
22 January: Captive State
23 January: The Paddingtons (PVC)
24 January: Days In December
26 January: DTX
27 January: Eden Maine
28 January: Vanilla Pod
29 January: Dead! Dead! Dead!
30 January: Plastic Toys
1 February: Holiday Stabbings
3 February: Adam Green (PVC)
4 February: Aerogramme (PVC)
5 February: Hijera
6 February: The Towers Of London (PVC)
Don't believe their arm-wrestling stories.
7 February: The Long Weekend
8 February: Soho
9 February: K.T. Tunstall (PVC)
11 February: Harsh
12 February: Thee Unstrung (PVC)
13 February: The Eldore Parade
14 February: Zero Consent
16 February: 65 Days Of Static
17 February: Steriogram (PVC)
18 February: Fleeing New York
19 February: Fony
20 February: Cherry Hinton
21 February: The Black Velvets (PVC)
22 February: Toupe
23 February: Willy Mason (PVC)

• LISTINGS 2005 •

25 February: My Mantra
26 February: Red 5
27 February: Johnny Panic
28 February: Ariel X
 1 March: Engineers / Mystery
   Jets / The Research (PVC)
   Quite some line-up.
 2 March: Ripchord
 4 March: The Alaskan Pipeline
 6 March: Martini Henry Rifles
 7 March: The Conway Story
 8 March: Blind Summit
 9 March: Whitmore (PVC)
11 March: Tom Hingley
12 March: EQD
13 March: Harsh
14 March: Million Dead (PVC)
15 March: Through These Lies
16 March: A World Asleep
17 March: The Blueprint
18 March: Shorty
19 March: Eve's Only Son
20 March: The Inbreds
21 March: Jango's Loveshack
22 March: The Sound
   Explosion
23 March: Trash Light Vision
24 March: Ben Dlugokecki
25 March: Toupe
26 March: Dead! Dead! Dead!
28 March: Six Nation State
30 March: The Mooney Suzuki
   (PVC)
31 March: No Comply
 1 April: Glitchcentre
 2 April: The Dead 60s
 3 April: Cubic Space Division
 4 April: Working Lunch
 5 April: Happylife
 7 April: Never Heard Of It
   (PVC)

 9 April: 8-Fold
10 April: 65 Days Of Static
11 April: Misty's Big Adventure
12 April: Same Day Service
13 April: May Day Warning
14 April: Harsh
15 April: Sine Star Project
16 April: The Warm
17 April: The Fight (PVC)
19 April: Lydia Lunch
20 April: The Glitterati (PVC)
21 April: The Filaments
22 April: The Rakes
23 April: Zen Baseball Bat
24 April: Streetlight Manifesto
25 April: Stout
26 April: Electric Eel Shock
   (PVC)
27 April: Dead! Dead! Dead!
28 April: Vinny Peculiar
29 April: Unforgiven Kingdom
30 April: Shorty
 1 May: Twin Zero
 2 May: Gutworm
 3 May: Kumiss
 4 May: Silver Sun
 6 May: Tom Vek (PVC)
 8 May: The Splitters
 9 May: Spike and Friends
10 May: Inner Mantra
11 May: MU330
12 May: Art Brut (PVC)
13 May: Syntax Error
14 May: Replenish
15 May: Amsterdam (PVC)
17 May: Byzantine
18 May: Morning Runner (PVC)
19 May: Bearsuit
20 May: Car Crash Television
21 May: Hijera
22 May: Harsh

• LISTINGS 2005 •

23 May: Selfish Cunt

24 May: Nic Armstrong and the Thieves (PVC)

25 May: Babar Luck and the 420s

26 May: Stephen Brodsky (PVC)

27 May: Babyshambles

28 May: Reserved For Nothing

29 May: Love Ends Disaster

30 May: The Caves

31 May: Eden Maine

1 June: International Karate Plus

2 June: Arctic Monkeys
Just days before the chart breakthrough.

4 June: El Presidente (PVC)

6 June: The Rakes (PVC)

7 June: Camera

9 June: DTX

10 June: The Flying Alexanders

11 June: Alfie

12 June: Dollium

13 June: Martin Grech (PVC)

14 June: The Cribs (PVC)

15 June: Captain Everything

16 June: Ambulance Ltd (PVC)

17 June: The Departure

18 June: Sons and Daughters (PVC)

19 June: Planet of Women

20 June: Psyattica

22 June: The Grit

23 June: The Jamm

27 June: Ginger

29 June: I Like Trains

2 July: Green-ish Day

3 July: Second Monday

4 July: Days Of Worth

5 July: MT-TV

6 July: US Bombs

7 July: B-Movie Heroes

9 July: Dive Dive

8 July: Unforgiven Kingdom

10 July: Sound Explosion

11 July: Phinius Gage

12 July: Duels (PVC)

13 July: Howards Alias

15 July: Rico

16 July: Fleeing New York

17 July: The Alaskan Pipeline

18 July: Jarvis Fields

19 July: Parisian Sex Flick

20 July: Psyke Project

22 July: Battle

23 July: The Heights

24 July: Editors (PVC)

25 July: Reserved For Nothing

26 July: Secluded

27 July: Locus Of Control

28 July: Eve's Only Son

29 July: Benny Woo

30 July: Shorty

1 August: Michael Graves

2 August: Brigade

3 August: Mendeed

6 August: The Warm

7 August: Zero Consent

8 August: Yeti

18 August: Honeymoon Machine

20 August: The Alaskan Pipeline

21 August: Phoenix Down

22 August: Mirror Scam

23 August: Schoolboy Error

24 August: No Comply

26 August: Valhalla

28 August: Jarvis Fields

30 August: Daughters Courageous

31 August: Inner Mantra

Front bar, photo by Oliver Gray.

Band room, photo by Mark Holloway.

• LISTINGS 2005 •

2 September: Suffrajets

3 September: The Flying Alexanders

4 September: A World Asleep

5 September: Devil Sold His Soul

5 September: Devil Sold His Soul

6 September: Mystery Jets (PVC)

7 September: Red Jetson

8 September: Aconite Thrill

9 September: Alfie (PVC)

10 September: Get Amped

11 September: Sack Trick

13 September: The Revivals

15 September: Fony

17 September: Dark Craftsmen

18 September: The Fight

20 September: Black Cougar Shock Unit

21 September: Motion City Soundtrack (PVC)

22 September: Flipron

23 September: Million Dead (PVC)

26 September: Telescopes

27 September: Oceansize (PVC)

29 September: King Biscuit Time (PVC)

30 September: Laika Dog

1 October: Dead! Dead! Dead!

2 October: Inept

3 October: Invane

4 October: Desolation

5 October: The Glitterati (PVC)

6 October: Dopamine

7 October: Jupiter Few

8 October: 8-Fold

9 October: The Infadels (PVC)

10 October: Mach Schau

11 October: Second Monday

13 October: Through These Lies

14 October: Kumiss

15 October: We Are Scientists (PVC)

16 October: Laura Veirs and the Tortured Souls (PVC)

17 October: The Eldora Parade

18 October: Turn Down Tomorrow

19 October: Anti-Nowhere League

20 October: 4 Ft Fingers

21 October: The Heights

22 October: Deadline

23 October: Tokyo Dragons (PVC)

24 October: Pure Reason Revolution (PVC)

26 October: Johnathan Rice (PVC)

27 October: Leaves (PVC)

28 October: Dlugocecki

29 October: The Union

30 October: Ephel Duath

31 October: Help She Can't Swim

1 November: Kubb (PVC)

2 November: Test Icicles (PVC)

3 November: Kill Keneda

4 November: Ladyfuzz (PVC)

5 November: Rico

7 November: Army Of Freshman

8 November: Attaku

9 November: Blackbud

10 November: Mendeed

11 November: Sonic Boom Six

13 November: Eve's Only Son

• LISTINGS 2005 - 2006 •

14 November: Thee Unstrung (PVC)
15 November: The Alaskan Pipeline
16 November: The Dude
17 November: Left Side Brain
18 November: My Mantra
20 November: Cry For Silence
21 November: Melt Banana
22 November: Adequate Seven
23 Nove mber: Spike
27 November: Crack Rock Steady Seven
29 November: Johnny Truant (PVC)
1 December: The Littl'ans
2 December: Secluded
3 December: The Alaskan Pipeline
4 December: The Business
5 December: Hi Tech Jet
6 December: No Comply
7 December: The Yo Yos
8 December: The Undertones
9 December: The Warm
10 December: Hijera
11 December: Cubic Space Division
12 December: The Scarlet Letter Union
13 December: Trashlight Vision
14 December: Moral Low Ground
15 December: Babar Luck
16 December: The Fight
18 December: Forward! Russia (PVC)
19 December: Speaking Of Losers
20 December: Eve's Only Son
21 December: The Deads

22 December: Wireless
27 December: Fatal Argument
28 December: Toupe
29 December: Trial and Error
30 December: Chaser
31 December: Rival Joustas

2006
2 January: Sucking Diesel
3 January: Second Skin
4 January: Schoolboy Error
5 January: Arrowshy
6 January: The Reason
7 January: Mendeed
8 January: Preacher Joe
9 January: In Hail
10 January: Bury Tomorrow
11 January: Equilibria
12 January: The Nightingales
13 January: Rage Against The Machine UK Tribute
14 January: Through These Lies
15 January: Psyattica
16 January: Blackbud (PVC)
17 January: Ladyfuzz (PVC)
18 January: Alamos
19 January: My Pet Cow
20 January: Infadels (PVC)
21 January: The Heights
22 January: Vanlustbader
23 January: Four Day Hombre
25 January: Hagakure
26 January: Panic! At The Disco (PVC)
27 January: Sine Star Project
28 January: Shorty
29 January: The Research (PVC)
30 January: Failsafe
31 January: Your Vegas
1 February: In Fiction

• LISTINGS 2006 •

2 February: Interlock
3 February: Toupe
4 February: The Kiks
5 February: The Rock Of Travolta
6 February: The Eldora Parade
7 February: Finger Monster
8 February: Breaking The Girl
9 February: Ed Tudor Pole
10 February: Idiot Pilot (PVC)
11 February: Dead! Dead! Dead!
12 February: Anti Nowhere League
13 February: Zero Cipher
14 February: Zero Consent
15 February: Beyond All Reason
16 February: Dive Dive
17 February: The Pleasant Sounds
18 February: The Boy Least Likely To (PVC)
19 February: Karmakops
20 February: Two Gallants (PVC)
21 February: Morning Runner (PVC)
22 February: Forward! Russia (PVC)
24 February: Get Amped
25 February: My Mantra
26 February: Flipron
27 February: The Fight
28 February: Failsafe
1 March: B-Movie Heroes
2 March: Scars of Tomorrow
3 March: The Alaskan Pipeline
4 March: Hijera
5 March: White Rose Movement (PVC)
6 March: Kat Vipers

7 March: Third Person
8 March: Belasco
10 March: Sultans Of Ping (PVC)
11 March: Dead! Dead! Dead!
12 March: Help She Can't Swim
13 March: The Fight
14 March: The Concept
15 March: Scarlet Soho
16 March: Thomas Truax
17 March: The Flying Alexanders
18 March: Jarvis Fields
19 March: Misty's Big Adventure
21 March: 28 Costumes
22 March: Left Side Brain
23 March: Cosmic Rough Riders
24 March: Plastic Toys
25 March: Breed 77 (PVC)
26 March: Too Much Texas
27 March: Oversol
28 March: Larrikin Love (PVC)
29 March: Mendeed
30 March: Fleeing New York
31 March: Not Katies
1 April: Ivory
2 April: The Hint
3 April: Pure Reason Revolution (PVC)
4 April: Twin Zero
5 April: 65 Days Of Static
6 April: The Business
7 April: Guillemots (PVC)
8 April: Valhalla
9 April: MC Lars (PVC)
10 April: Ladyfuzz (PVC)
11 April: Glen Matlock And The Philistines
12 April: Devil Sold His Soul

Libertines and Razorlight, photos by Mint.

• LISTINGS 2006 •

13 April: Sonic Boom Six
14 April: The Hyperjax
15 April: Dry Kill Logic
16 April: Dopamine
17 April: Bob Catley (of Magnum)
18 April: Subdies
19 April: Archie Bronson Outfit
20 April: Season's End
23 April: The Eighteenth Day Of May (PVC)
24 April: Cult Of Luna
25 April: Brigade (PVC)
26 April: Babar Luck
29 April: Dead! Dead! Dead!
8 May: Duke Special (PVC)
9 May: The Upper Room (PVC)
11 May: Absentee (PVC)
15 May: The Rifles (PVC)
19 May: Kubichek! (PVC)
21 May: Liam Frost And The Slowdown Family (PVC)
28 May: The Wedding Present (PVC)
30 May: This Is Seb Clarke (PVC)
2 June: Roland Shanks (PVC)
9 June: Vincent Vincent And The Villains (PVC)
14 June: Jamie T (PVC)
16 June: Cosmic Rough Riders (PVC)
17 June: Mach Schau
18 June: Solitude
19 June: The Arcades
20 June: The Generators
21 June: Sweet And Tender Hooligans
22 June: Start
23 June: Not advised
24 June: My Mantra

25 June: Murder One
26 June: Chairmen Of The Bored
27 June: Recreation
28 June: Adzuki
30 June: Secluded
1 July: Hijera
2 July: Ginger (of the Wildhearts)
3 July: Rocco Deluca and the Burden
4 July: The Pipettes
5 July: Beyond All Reaso
6 July: Eddie and the Hot Rods
7 July: 01nowon
8 July: Sonic Boom Six
9 July: Saluting Silhouettes
10 July: The Craving
11 July: Finger Monster
12 July: My Ruin
14 July: The Alaskan Pipeline
15 July: Dlugokecki
16 July: Adequate Seveen
17 July: Weapons (Of Mass Belief)
18 July: The Holloways
19 July: The Organ
20 July: Get Amped
21 July: Good Books
22 July: Howling Bells
23 July: Graveltrap
24 July: Twin Zero
25 July: Pinstripe Legacy
26 July: The Fight
27 July: Phinius Gage
28 July: The Reason
29 July: Seafood
30 July: Valhalla
31 July: Forever Never
1 August: October File
2 August: Mike Park

Delays, photo by Mark Holloway.

Getting The Picture

Mark Holloway: "Being the Joiners in-house photographer for the last 5 years has been an amazing experience, and has helped me to develop and build my career as a music and live events photographer.

My role began with taking photos of local bands, before being given the chance to photograph the UK Southern heats of a worldwide Battle of the Bands competition, being run by Glenn Lovell (now co-owner of the Joiners). This gave me both the experience and contacts I needed and I ended up being fortunate enough to phograph artists such as Hard-Fi, KT Tunstall and of course, Southampton band The Delays.

Two gigs that are particularly memorable for me were the Towers of London and Pete Doherty. Knowing the Towers of London's reputation for bad behaviour at gigs, and remembering the last gig they played at the Joiners, when they pulled down part of the ceiling, I was a little apprehensive as to what might happen. It all started well enough, but after a while I started to become aware of some rather odd looks from front man Donny Tourette, until half way through the gig – mic stand in hand – he glared at me as if to say, 'If you don't back off with that camera now, I'm gonna lob this at you!' Needless to say, I beat

213

KT Tunstall, photo by Mark Holloway.

a hasty retreat into the crowd to watch the rest of the gig in relative safety!

Pete Doherty's performance was just as eventful. Not really knowing what time he'd turn up, I decided to get there early to photograph him arriving, so I joined all the other photographers patiently waiting for him outside. By the time the doors opened at 8pm, all the other bands had already sound-checked, but there was still no sign of Pete Doherty. He was due on stage at 9 pm, but knowing his reputation for arriving late and sometimes not turning up at all, I began to feel a bit dubious and made my way inside. The place was completely rammed, but I managed to push my way through and position myself near the front. The man himself finally turned up at 10.30 pm, and as he was escorted to the stage by Pat, I remember there being a huge surge in the crowd as people pushed forward to try and catch a glimpse. As he pushed past me, I lifted my camera in the air, hoping to catch a good shot. He played for about an hour, during which time I couldn't move because it was so packed – but the atmosphere was electric. After the gig he went down into the band room, where I joined him to take some shots that made the papers the following day. It was a memorable night!"

www.hollowayphotography.co.uk

Hard-Fi, photos by Mark Holloway.

Babyshambles, photos by Mark Holloway.

The Future's Bright!

Glenn Lovell (Director, Joiners Southampton Ltd):

"My introduction to the Joiners was in 1995. I had just turned 20 (which is quite late by most people's standards to lose one's Joiners viginity). I went to see a little known band called Skunk Anansie.

The stage was still on the left side at that time, and I remember feeling quite excited with the vibrancy and atmosphere of the place, even if it was dingy and quite smelly! My best memory of the gig was having Skin (Skunk Anansie's singer) lean on my head for most of their set and I have to say it was a great induction to the world of the Joiners!

Throughout the next eleven years, I couldn't get enough of the place. Other than attending as many gigs as I could, I have since been involved with the Joiners in various capacities, from playing in different bands to promoting and putting on gigs myself.

Obviously, the highlights have to be the gigs I have played. My current (and probably best known) band, My Mantra, have shared some great shows at the Joiners over the years, especially with other local bands, the likes of Stout, Rival Joustas and Dead! Dead! Dead!, who, I hasten to add, are without doubt three of the best bands Southampton has to offer.

Although I had been attending gigs and playing at the Joiners for all those years, it wasn't until about the year 2000 that I properly got to know, and become close friends with, Pat Muldowney, affectionately known as 'Pat The Doorman'. We both (separately) attended a book signing of a like-minded favourite author of ours, and it was across the room that our eyes met … Oops! No, strike that!

The next time I was playing a gig at the Joiners, I told Pat that I had seen him at the book signing, we got chatting and the rest, as they say, is history, and we have been very good friends ever since. Over the following years, I made many visits to him on Friday and Saturday nights, mainly to escape my place of work for a few hours. I was the manager of a nightclub called 'The Venue' at the time, and I remember we used to joke about wishing we could take over and own both our respective venues.

Fast forward to October 2005. I had left my job as the manager of The Venue a little while back, and had just started work at the Joiners as the PR Manager. I had only been working there for a couple of weeks when I started to discover how bad a financial state the Joiners was in. There were debts and a looming VAT bill, and a letter of compulsory insolvency was about to be issued. I decided to open up a conversation with Pat about this being the perfect opportunity to step in and take the place over.Without going into detail, we discovered that things were even worse than we realized. The current licensee, Mike Chapman, had commitments with several other projects and that had led to cashflow issues. He had until the next day at 1pm to pay outstanding rent or face closure of the Joiners. Quite simply, the landlord was threatening to close the place down if the rent wasn't paid up to date that very next day.

After careful consideration, Pat and I agreed to go 50/50 on making this payment the day after, just to ensure we keep the Joiners open in the first instance. But we also agreed that we were only going to do this on condition that we were going to take charge of the place. We wanted the Joiners in exchange for paying off the debt. Pat said, 'Leave it with me, I'll call you back in a while'.

The next few hours went by so slowly it was unbelievable. I couldn't concentrate on anything else whilst waiting to hear back from him. I was feeling excited, scared, nervous and concerned all at once. I just wanted the call to be a positive one.

Pat finally did call and told me that he had arranged for Mike to come in and see us both that evening, when he agreed that he would hand the Joiners over to us as soon as we paid the money into the lease. So, on Wednesday 5th October 2005, Pat and I paid across the money and effectively took ownership of the business by doing so.

A few months down the line and with all the legalities of our ownership in place, the position of the Joiners has never looked better. All the outstanding debts were written off in the insolvency of the previous company, and the Joiners got to start from a fresh financial position, free of debt, to live and fight another day.

The Joiners has since gone from strength to strength. By introducing small changes like new working procedures, refurbishing the upstairs offices, making for a more comfortable working environment, to purchasing liability insurance (something the Joiners hadn't had for several years, can you believe!) we have increased the turnover of the barrelage sold, from 60 barrels in the previous year to over 200 barrels in our first year of ownership.

As this book has shown, with every new owner of the Joiners come new ideas and aspirations for the place, and we're certainly no exception to this. We have ideas that include making the venue even more friendly to local and touring bands, whilst maintaining the intimacy and friendliness it has become famous for. We are as committed as ever to the local scene and what it has to offer the Joiners.

At the end of 2005, we introduced on Saturday afternoons the 'Kickstart' project. This project is designed to provide kids of school age a taste of playing live in a bona-fide live music venue. The idea was to introduce the Joiners to our younger generation earlier in their lives, thus nurturing our city's young talent into providing and performing new music at the Joiners for years to come.

Plans are also afoot for the 'behind the scenes' areas of the Joiners. From turning the cellar into an underground bar, to fitting out the back of the cellar with two separate dressing rooms with showers and toilets, bringing the venue up to modern day touring standards. We're also looking to have a stairwell built onto the rear of the building with a doorway knocked through next to the stage, allowing for an immediate entrance onto it. Bands would no longer have to crawl their way through the crowd, as they currently do. These changes are already underway, as we have recently fully upgraded the entire PA system to bring its spec up to current standards.

This is just a snippet of what the future holds for the venue, and I believe it can only be fulfilled with the success and growth of not only the Joiners itself, but with the evolvement of the company as a whole. The team currently behind the Joiners consists of myself (Glenn Lovell), Pat Muldowney, Kai Harris, Tim Hambidge and Simon Fisher. We are all currently active in not only making the Joiners as successful as it can be, but also in promoting shows under the Joiners banner in larger venues throughout Southampton. This also includes plans to open further live venues across different UK locations, all of which are to be modelled on the Joiners. These will be venues which,

I hope, will one day aspire and live up to what the Joiners has achieved throughout its history.

To that end, in February 2006, only five months after we took over the Joiners, we opened the second venue of what will be known as the Joiners Group, which we named 'Joiners Unit 22'. This is a 400 capacity night club which, funnily enough, used to be called 'The Venue.' Oh, how Pat and I joked about the irony. With half of Unit 22 being set up for live music, we use Unit 22 as a breeding ground for new bands, and it now works as a great feeder venue to the Joiners for bands without profile. Thus we can expose bands to a ready-made club audience before they even reach the 'one step' of the Joiners.

Never far from my mind is my awareness that the Joiners is looked upon as an institution by many, many people. This is how I feel about the place myself. Putting aside its successes or failures and our future plans, I know the Joiners means so

Glenn Lovell continues Tony Eccles' tradition of being both a musician and venue owner. With his team, Glenn represents the future of the Joiners.

• LISTINGS 2006 •

3 August: Scarlet Soho
4 August: Secluded
5 August: The Family
6 August: Send More Paramedics
7 August: Ali Fresh
8 August: Exposure
9 August: Tempora
10 August: Inept
11 August: Sex Pistols Experience
12 August: Dead! Dead! Dead!

13 August: Firstborn
14 August: Sworn Enemy
15 August: Electrolyte
16 August: Captain
17 August: Not Advised
18 August: They Don't Sleep
19 August: Pinstripe Legacy
20 August: In Hail
21 August: Enjoy Yesterday
22 August: Fatal Argument
23 August: Carmen Pimps

To be continued ...

much more to people than any of this. Other than just watching bands throw themselves around the stage, this old building has personal meaning to lots of people for much, much more. People have become couples, to likewise becoming single. Friendships have been created, birthdays celebrated, football riots witnessed and lots of money raised for various charities, all within the confines of the Joiners' hallowed walls. This means it is much, much more than, just 'a pub that puts on bands!'As you've discovered throughout this book, the Joiners has played host to many memorable gigs, and, to be fair, many gigs we would like to forget. With the weight of all this firmly on my shoulders, my absolute priority, no matter what happens with the rest of our plans, is never to forget the Joiners' roots and heritage, ensuring that we maintain all that the place has become known for. I'm sure our patrons would expect nothing less.

I want my children and my children's children to grow up and experience what it's like to witness the 'Next Big Thing' first at the Joiners. Rest assured people, your Joiners is in safe hands."

Postscript

Oliver Gray gets sentimental – and then angry:

Researching this book has been not so much a chore as an adventure. Every single person I contacted was exploding with enthusiasm about the project and keen to help and provide material. The love shown towards the Joiners by generations of music lovers is inspirational, and it became clearer and clearer that it has been a crucial factor in the lives of thousands of people. I am one of them. I proposed to my wife Birgit in the Joiners, and after 25 years of marriage, she still didn't mind me spending untold hours finding out about its history and tracking down all the main players. I shed a tear when my daughter Annabel's band eventually graced the hallowed stage. I got to meet people like Hammy and Tony Eccles, and share their undying affection for this enchanted building. I communicated with people like Paula Hambly, Jamie Summers, Martin McNeely and Craig McEwan, who live and breathe rock and roll. And I had the privilege of getting to spend time with Mint, whose spirit runs through the story of the Joiners like a message in a stick of rock.

The people involved in its history also, however, help to point up one of the uncomfortable truths about the music business. Every band starting out on the road to success needs somewhere to play. The people who have run the Joiners over the years have dedicated their lives to providing this opportunity, more often than not operating effectively as a charity. They have suffered lack of comfort, ill health and financial disaster. None of them have benefited even remotely from the untold hours of dedication and commitment they have invested, purely out of their love of music and the buzz they get from the thrill of a great gig. You'd think the industry would be grateful and seek to repay them in some way. But that's not what happens.

I know this because I promote gigs in a small venue myself. Just like the S.T.E. guys, I lose money by putting on shows by bands I love. We put them up in our house so they don't have to sleep in their Transit vans. But as soon as they get their big deals, all of a sudden, we are forgotten. They move on to bigger agents who want nothing to do with little venues. They promise to come back and play secret shows, but (with the very honourable exceptions of Delays and Razorlight), they don't do it. Is it the fault of the bands? I doubt it. What happens is that things are taken out of their hands, they have people to "handle" their affairs.

I wasn't going to talk about this, for fear of ending the book on a sour note. But now I've decided to mention it after all. One notable thing I found out along the way was just how much bands love playing the Joiners. Many (Richard Ashcroft is a particular example) make a point of mentioning how important Joiners gigs have been for their careers.

Yet when I approached industry people to request brief comments and reminiscences from today's stars, all of a sudden, they were "unavailable". I contacted record companies, publicists, booking agents, press agents and management companies. The result: zilch.

I do not believe for one moment that artists such as Coldplay, Radiohead, Primal Scream, KT Tunstall, The Charlatans, Franz Ferdinand and all the others would have responded negatively to such a request. I bet they'd have been delighted, especially as I emphasized that the book is in aid of a particularly relevant charity. No, I believe that the requests were simply not passed on, as the Joiners is, in the eyes of those who run the industry, a convenient stepping stone, to be discarded when no longer needed.

Do we care? Not much. We still have our "favourite front room" and it still has its heart, its soul and its history. And its One Step.